GOVERNANCE AND MINISTRY

GOVERNANCE AND MINISTRY

Rethinking Board Leadership

Second Edition

Dan Hotchkiss

An Alban Institute Book

ROWMAN & LITTLEFIELD
Lanham • Boulder • New York • London

Published by Rowman & Littlefield
A wholly owned subsidary of The Rowman & Littlefield Publishing Group, Inc.
4501 Forbes Boulevard, Suite 200, Lanham, Maryland 20706
www.rowman.com

Unit A, Whitacre Mews, 26-34 Stannary Street, London SE11 4AB, United Kingdom

Portions of this book have appeared in the *Clergy Journal*, published by Logos Productions, Inc. (www.logosproductions.com); *Congregations* and *Alban Weekly* (www.alban.org); and *Perspectives for Church and Synagogue Leaders* (www. congregationalconsulting.org).

This book is designed to provide accurate and authoritative information in regard to the subject matter covered. It is published with the understanding that the publisher is not engaged in rendering legal, accounting, or other professional service. If legal advice or other expert assistance is required, the services of a competent professional person should be sought. (From a Declaration of Principles jointly adopted by a Committee of the American Bar Association and a Committee of Publishers and Associations)

British Library Cataloguing in Publication Information Available

Library of Congress Cataloging-in-Publication Data
Hotchkiss, Dan.
  Governance and ministry : rethinking board leadership / Dan Hotchkiss. — Second Edition.
    pages cm
  Includes bibliographical references and index.
  ISBN 978-1-56699-738-6 (cloth : alk. paper) — ISBN 978-1-56699-739-3 (pbk. : alk. paper) — ISBN 978-1-56699-771-3 (electronic) 1. Church polity. 2. Church committees. 3. Christian leadership. 4. Church management. 5. Church officers. I. Title.
  BV650.3.H68 2016
  254—dc23

2015034705

™ The paper used in this publication meets the minimum requirements of American National Standard for Information Sciences—Permanence of Paper for Printed Library Materials, ANSI/NISO Z39.48-1992.

Printed in the United States of America

CONTENTS

FOREWORD

Not long ago I was meeting with the board of a congregation that found itself wrapped around the axle over the leader of their music ministry. I listened as the fifteen people in the room said why they were for or against the staff person and the kind of music he was doing. People were pretty worked up.

After a while I posed a couple questions: What do your by-laws say about who supervises this person and what authority they have? What are your church policies for staff review and evaluation, and have such evaluations been carried out?

People looked a little uncomfortable as I asked these questions. After some hemming and hawing, one person said, "Well, we don't worry too much about by-laws and that sort of thing. We're pretty informal around here."

While it is possible to become a by-law fanatic and go overboard, often the tendency, as in the congregation I refer to above, runs the other way. There's a serious lack of clarity about who has what job, what authority, and what responsibilities. The appeal to "informality" is a cover for governance or administration that is sloppy and lacks transparency.

There's another thing that happens when congregations aren't reasonably clear about their governance and administration processes and procedures. These congregations end up doing what kids do who are just starting out at soccer—they play bunch ball. All twenty-two players cluster around the ball and hammer away. In the church, bunch ball looks like everybody needing to be in on every issue, conflict, or decision.

On the soccer field the result is sore shins and little ball movement. It's not so different in congregations that default to bunch ball. People get sore and the congregation gets stuck. When this is chronic, many of a congregation's potentially best leaders say, "Thanks, but no thanks," and even leave the church altogether.

There are two reasons for you to get this book, to read it, and to study it with the leaders of your congregation. One is that, without clarity about how we order and conduct our life together as a congregation, things rapidly become a real mess.

The second reason to get and use this book by Dan Hotchkiss is more positive. Here you will find real help in sorting out the appropriate role of a governing board, as well as what is properly on the board's plate and what is not. Clarity about this helps you take the next steps: clarity about the role of staff, of committees, of the congregation.

Beyond that, a really effective governing board is working with pastoral leadership to formulate the big picture of a congregation's mission and priorities. These days congregations that are not focused around a compelling big picture or vision, and are instead lost in the high grass, are at risk. An effective governing board minds the big picture, and in doing so is a good steward of a congregation's resources—human, financial, and spiritual.

One truth in labeling warning: as Dan points out (and I heartily concur), changing a congregation's governance is not year one, or even year two or three, work of a new pastorate. Job one is building trust. No one should take on governance change until trust is firm and the key people know one another and the church they serve.

If trust is established, moving toward a governance system that really works is worth all the time and energy you'll put into it. Governance that is clear, fair, open, and effective goes a long way toward making a congregation healthy and vital.

I commend this book to you. More than that, I urge you to get it, to read it as a leadership team, and to use it. If you have the first edition you will find a lot of new material here. Some of the most valuable elements have to do with the ways different sized congregations operate and what good governance looks like in those different settings. You will also find new help here on leading, and surviving, the change process.

Dan Hotchkiss brings to this work a great combination of seasoned wisdom and field-based experience. I'm grateful for his work.

—Anthony B. Robinson

PREFACE TO THE SECOND EDITION

Since *Governance and Ministry* was published in 2009, it has reached a surprisingly wide audience, including Roman Catholics, Southern Baptists, Ethical Culturists, Mennonites, and Reform and Reconstructionist Jews. The leaders of a number of denominational bodies have used it with their boards and recommended it to local leaders. As a result, my own perspective has broadened, and I have learned a great deal about how to make the book more useful.

I have reorganized this edition to make it easier for readers to find what they are looking for and streamlined the diagrams and terminology. I've written five chapters, 7 through 11, that are almost completely new. Chapter 7 addresses congregation size. Chapter 8 paints a picture of life after governance change. Chapters 9 and 10 walk through the governance change process and the art of making policy, and chapter 11 treats a topic close to my heart: lay-clergy partnership. Finally, in place of a potpourri of policy fragments, appendix A offers a style guide for policy-makers, and appendix B gives a unified example of a board policy book.

The revisions owe a great deal to the curiosity, criticisms, and creative efforts of my readers and consulting clients. I list only a few whose work is reflected here in ways I cannot fully trace:

Isaac M. Wise Temple, Cincinnati
Third Church of Christ, Scientist, Dallas

Edmonton Presbytery, United Church of Canada
First Unitarian Society of Madison, Wisconsin
Newark Presbytery, PCUSA
First Unitarian Church of Omaha
Knox Metropolitan United Church, Regina, Saskatchewan
The Universal Fellowship of Metropolitan Community Churches
And many more, including the participants in many workshops and
    presentations, whose comments and questions helped me sharpen
    language, improve diagrams, and address issues that might not have
    occurred to me

Sarah Stanton, senior acquisition editor for Rowman & Littlefield, delighted me by suggesting this revision and has been delightful ever since.
Beth Gaede, whose editing of the first edition added greatly to its usefulness, has graciously and firmly assisted me in getting this one ready, too,
for which I am most grateful. Niki Guinan, copyeditor at Rowman & Littlefield, raised great questions about my sometimes idiosyncratic usage, for
which I am grateful even when I am not altogether compliant.

This book is dedicated to my consulting colleagues from the Alban Institute. Though Alban ceased to operate in early 2014, we continue to confer
about our work and blog together as the Congregational Consulting Group
(www.congregationalconsulting.org). Their comments and encouragement
have meant a great deal to me while I was writing.

Finally and most of all, I am obliged to my wife, Susan, who waited patiently for me to get around to many other things while I was writing. She
still keeps me happy, and I am so grateful she is in my life.

PREFACE TO THE FIRST EDITION

Once upon a time, Americans joined congregations in the secret hope that one day someone might ask them to serve on a committee. Today that rarely happens. In fact, many of our most vital congregations now lure members by boasting about their lack of tedious "church work" and baroque organizational structure. They recruit, equip, and deploy people into lives of faith and service, not into committees. These new-style churches, synagogues, temples, sanghas, and mosques have discovered something that should have surprised no one: A congregation that invites people to participate in organizational life appeals to only a few, but a congregation that invites people directly into spiritual growth and service appeals to many. The result, among the fastest-growing congregations and their imitators, has been a movement to reduce bureaucracy to make room for ministry.

In such a time, it might seem odd to write or read a book on congregational governance. As an Alban Institute consultant, I have worked with congregations that grew rapidly while streamlining their decision-making processes and with others that tried to maintain scores of committees while their memberships declined from thousands to hundreds to scant dozens. In time, I started to suspect that outdated, overly complex, and inward-focused structures might be one cause of decline in congregations. As I watched more systematically, I came to believe that often-mentioned trends, like the "decline of the Protestant mainline," might have as much to do with governance as with theology. Growing congregations often are the ones that have reformed their structures for governance and ministry, whether they are liberal or conservative in their theology. Even more strikingly, declining congregations across the theological spectrum often share specific organizational patterns. I think those patterns are one factor in their decline—a factor, unlike social and cultural trends, that a congregation can control.

My interest in governance stems from my consulting work with congregations in strategic planning. I work with boards and planning teams to frame critical questions and to engage the congregation and its leaders in a "holy conversation." Planners gather data, pray, and prod boards and congregations to take a fresh look at persistent issues. At last, the team produces its report. Many such reports are timid or routine, but occasionally a planning document expresses a compelling vision of the future seriously different from the past.

Such cases remind me of a question Lyle Schaller, one of the pioneers of church consulting, likes to ask, "What if it works?" When planning works, the congregation has to face what I now call the governance question: What is our process for deciding to make a major change, empowering people to make it happen, and holding them accountable for the results? Too few congregations, I find, have an adequate answer to this question, and the result, sometimes, is a beautiful planning document that makes no difference in the congregation's life.

"OK," I sometimes ask, "when was the last time you decided on and implemented a major change, a significant departure from old patterns in your congregation's life?" Generally, a silence follows, then discussion, with one of the following outcomes:

- No one can remember any major changes.
- The most recent major change happened in 1958 or 1859 or 1598.
- The most recent major change happened because people worked around the congregation's system of decision-making rather than through it. If they had asked permission, the answer would have been no.

At some point, I began to ask the governance question at the beginning of the planning process rather than at the end. When I did, planning teams and governing boards often chose to make their governance structure a central focus of strategic planning. Governance reform became an important part of my consulting practice. Congregations started calling me because they had heard that I knew something about governance. They asked, "Is there a book we can read?" and I had to say, "Not yet."

There is no shortage of resources for boards. Every denomination has books and training guides, each of which has merit. But inevitably such resources, even when they are not literally "written by committee," reflect common practice as it stands more than they try to lead it. Many, many books written for businesspeople have value for religious leaders, but it is not always easy to translate what is of value while screening out what does not fit. Most guides to business leadership focus exclusively on management, all but ignoring the role of stockholders and boards. Some congregational boards—like many corporate boards—gladly hand all power to the clergy leader, intervening only at moments of disaster, scandal, or transition. Most congregations, though, wish as a matter of principle to balance clergy leadership with lay control and find the business-oriented literature only a partial help.

Another family of resources seeks to emphasize and cultivate a sense of the unique character of congregational boards. Charles M. Olsen, in *Transforming Church Boards into Communities of Spiritual Leaders* (Alban Institute, 1995), proposed that boards engage in narrative reflection, scripture study, prayerful discernment, and "visioning" (a word so new in 1995 that it needed to be put between quotation marks!). Olsen's book has had wide influence and has inspired many other resources for helping boards to understand themselves as religious and not simply business leaders. As valuable as these resources have been, most of them neglect key questions: What is the board's exact role? What does it contribute to the organization? How does the board's job relate to the job of clergy, staff, committees, and the congregation? While no one answer will fit every case, a board without a clear sense of its specific role cannot resist the gravitational pull that can drag a community of spiritual leaders back to behaving as a business board. The spiritual emphasis, while essential, needs the protection that only a clear sense of institutional roles and boundaries can provide; otherwise, under pressure, boards revert to more familiar styles of operation.

Sophistication about the role of boards has evolved greatly in the nonprofit world. A wide variety of resources about board governance has become available to help with strategic planning, staff oversight, policymaking, and keeping the focus on top-level governance while staying out of management. But the work of secular thinkers, like John Carver, Richard Chait, and Frances Hesselbein, and resource groups, like BoardSource and the Leader to Leader Institute, have barely begun to penetrate the world of congregations. One of the goals of this book is to translate some of this excellent work and make it more accessible to religious leaders.

An experience from outside my work with congregations prompted me to think about what a helpful book on congregational governance might say. Several years ago, I had an opportunity to volunteer for my son's high school. The principal had heard that I knew something about fund-raising and asked me to help write some grant proposals. I said yes. Soon I got a call inviting me to attend the next meeting of the fund-raising committee. I resisted—in my work I get to go to plenty of committee meetings—but finally relented. The chair assured me, "We'll talk at the meeting about what kinds of grants we want to apply for, and from there on you'll be working on your own."

I drove an hour and a half and sat with the committee. It was a pleasure to meet some of the most committed parents in the school. The doughnuts were particularly tasty. We never did talk about grants, though, because we were too busy stuffing, sealing, and addressing envelopes for the fall fund-raising appeal.

If someone had asked me to stuff envelopes, I like to think I would have done it. But to find myself stuffing envelopes when I had expected to be helping make important policy decisions made me feel that I'd been involved in a game of bait and switch; the experience left me less trustful and less motivated to step forward the next time. I think I would have felt the same way had I showed up to stuff envelopes and found myself dragooned into a meeting about grant proposals.

After a while, I realized that I had just experienced, from below, the kind of volunteer experience I had inflicted on too many others. As a minister and congregational consultant, I had taken it for granted that "committees" should make most of the decisions and also do most of the work in a congregation. It had never occurred to me that people might want to make decisions or do work but not both. The result, I now saw, was to frustrate and repel many of the volunteers who could accomplish the most, whether as workers or as decision-makers.

At about that time I happened to meet Sharon, who told me about a different kind of volunteer experience. Someone had recruited her to work for Habitat for Humanity. Overcoming considerable reluctance, Sharon volunteered for a house-building shift. Her first construction work assignments were straightforward: measuring and marking, laying boards in place, and even—after she had returned to volunteer a few more times—swinging a hammer, Jimmy Carter style. Sharon became a Habitat crew leader and in time even led a team to Romania to build houses there.

Here is what amazed me about Sharon's story: She did all of this without attending a single committee meeting! She attended training workshops and led workshops for her crew, but at no time did she sit around a table to debate and vote on whether to build houses, where to build them, what color to paint them, or how much money they should cost. No doubt someone did these things—Habitat does have a board and no doubt committees, too—but it manages to offer a wide range of opportunities for people who simply want to build a house for somebody who needs a house.

These three experiences—my client congregations' difficulty implementing their strategic plans, my annoyance as a would-be grant writer stuffing envelopes, and Sharon's success as a Habitat house builder building houses—frame the beginnings of my interest in governance for congregations.

This book responds to a strong wish from leaders of congregations for tools and a road map for considering and implementing changes in the way boards and clergy work together to lead congregations. I created this material mostly for and with congregations and their leaders, but other organizations have found the ideas useful, too. Congregations have a lot to learn from progress in the rest of the nonprofit sector and something to teach as well. The particular ideas I present here should be of interest to any organization that has some or all of the following traits in common with most congregations:

- A mission rooted in the founders' deepest values and convictions
- An empowered constituency of people who identify passionately with the organization and its mission
- Stakeholder groups that overlap, making it hard to draw crisp lines between management, staff, clients, donors, members, and the public
- Leaders who think of themselves primarily as members of a profession rather than as managers

A great many nonprofits, businesses, and governmental agencies share some or all of these characteristics and would benefit from some of the lessons congregational leaders are learning about how to govern and manage themselves.

My consulting clients deserve a lot of credit for alerting me to the widespread desire for new ideas about congregational governance, for correcting me when my ideas did not connect with their experiences, and especially for laughing at the good bits so that I would be sure to put them in the book. Here are a few of the congregations that have been especially patient with me:

First Unitarian Universalist Church of Annapolis
Congregation Beth Adam, Cincinnati
St. Peter's Lutheran Church, Hilltown, Pennsylvania

Congregational Church of Needham, Massachusetts
Broadway Presbyterian Church, New York
First Unitarian Church of Philadelphia
First Presbyterian Church, Sandusky, Ohio
Unitarian Universalist Church of Greater Lynn, Swampscott, Massa-
    chusetts
Centenary United Methodist Church, Winston-Salem, North Carolina

I owe a debt of gratitude to these and many other congregations for allowing me to meddle in their business. Each has picked and chosen from the
concepts in this book to shape its own model of governance to fit its mission
and traditions; none bears any responsibility for what I say here.

One client that is not a congregation—the Unitarian Universalist Musicians Network—deserves special mention for the imaginative, artful way its
leaders worked on its reorganization. Who but a group of musicians would
explain a governance restructure using a skit? Under their creative influence, I began to draw the diagrams in chapter 4.

I am grateful to Ann and Fred Stocking, who provided a writer's retreat
along the coast of Maine when I especially needed it, and to all who have
read and criticized the manuscript and encouraged me to finish it. Special
thanks to Alban editor Beth Gaede, who provided her usual close readings
and helpful suggestions. Jean Lyles edited the copy further, giving it a high
gloss marred only by the errors and odd usages with which I absolutely
would not part.

When I began my ministry in 1980, the youngest member of my first
church became the church's first music director. As I began to write this
book, she and I reconnected after more than twenty years apart and married on December 28, 2006. If parts of this book sound happy, you can
thank Susan Land Hotchkiss. Me, too!

This book is dedicated to my colleagues around the Alban Institute consulting table, who have been a rich source of learning and encouragement
for me these nine years. No one could ask for a more stimulating group of
coworkers, nor could any congregation hope for abler navigators in these
chartless and exciting times.

❶

ORGANIZED RELIGION

Religion changes people; no one touches holy ground and stays the same. Religious leaders stir the pot by pointing to the contrast between life as it is and life as it should be and urging us to close the gap. Religious insights provide the handhold that people need to criticize injustice, rise above self-interest, and take risks to achieve healing in a wounded world. Religion at its best is no friend to the status quo.

Organization, on the other hand, conserves. Institutions capture, schematize, and codify persistent patterns of activity. People sometimes say, "Institutions are conservative," and smile as if they had said something clever. But conservation is what institutions do. A well-ordered congregation lays down schedules, puts policies on paper, places people in positions, and generally brings order out of chaos. Organizations can be flexible, creative, and iconoclastic, but only by resisting some of their most basic instincts.

No wonder "organized religion" is so difficult! Congregations create sanctuaries where people can nurture and inspire each other—with results no one can predict. The stability of a religious institution is a necessary precondition to the instability religious transformation brings. The need to balance both sides of this paradox—the transforming power of religion and the stabilizing power of organization—makes leading congregations a unique challenge.

When congregations fail to manage "organized religion" well, they face two special risks. One is the temptation to secure support by pandering to people's fears and prejudices. Finding an enemy to organize against is the easiest and least responsible path of leadership in congregations. The long and bloody history of Christian anti-Semitism; the tragic wars of the Protestant Reformation; and in our own time the deep mutual suspicion among various types of Christians, Jews, and Muslims should alert us that the organizing of religion is a high-stakes game. Preference for one's own group over others is a natural passion that religious zeal can make worse. A primary duty of a congregation is to regulate religious bigotry by teaching the whole scope of its tradition—including the parts about caring for strangers and wayfarers—and by insisting on sound norms of ethical behavior for the congregation and its interactions with the world around it.

A second special risk for leaders is that a congregation can succeed so well at organizing that it loses track of its religious mission. Congregational life becomes so tightly ordered that it squeezes out all inspiration. To historians of religion, the pattern is almost a law of physics: Religious energy diminishes from one generation to the next.

Fortunately, inspiration thwarts our best-laid plans. Just when the institutional routine is polished, someone has a new idea. Religious leaders plan worship, education, and social-outreach projects and define benchmarks, measurable outcomes, and quality assessments. Then somebody says, Why can't we sing exciting hymns like the new church at the edge of town? Or, We say we teach our children Jewish values, but my kids seem to be learning Judaism's just for kids. Or, Thank you, Reverend, for your sermon about Jesus and the rich young man. What do you suppose the Lord would tell our church to do with our endowment? The more soundly you plan to offer people spiritual insights, the more soundly their insights will disrupt your plans.

Organized religion is a paradox, an oxymoron, like *sweet sorrow* or *Hell's Angels*. The challenge of organized religion is to find ways to encourage people to encounter God in potentially soul-shaking ways while also helping them to channel spiritual energy in paths that will be healthy for them, the congregation, and the world beyond. Religious leaders who write bylaws would be well advised to do so, as theologian Karl Barth admonished preachers, with the Bible in one hand and a newspaper in the other, holding realism and idealism in a salutary tension.

TRADITION AND ADVICE

When they organize, many congregations seek help from denominational sources. What they typically receive is a mix of good and bad advice, timeless values, and outdated notions. Most denominations were founded by people who believed strongly in particular ideas about how to organize. The names of the main "polity" families—episcopal, presbyterian, and congregational—mean rule by, respectively, bishops, elders, and congregations. One way of looking at such differences is to picture them along a spectrum, with independent congregations at one end and centralized, "connectional" denominations at the other.

The more connectional denominations publish detailed polity instructions, like the Canons of the Episcopal Church, the United Methodist *Book of Discipline*, and the Presbyterian *Book of Order*. But even congregational denominations favor certain organizational practices and discourage others. "Congregational polity" plays out quite differently depending whether it is practiced by American or Southern Baptists, Unitarian Universalists, Disciples, or the Congregationalists in the United Church of Christ. Groups of independent congregations declare their independence in surprisingly connected ways!

A denomination's polity expresses the beliefs of its founders about who can best discern a congregation's mission and direct its practice. Today's members may or may not share (or even know about) the founders' values. Even when they do, the specific institutional practices and structures recommended in the past may not be the best way to express those values in a changed world or may not reflect the best wisdom currently available about what works in organizations.

In recent years, a number of denominations have worked hard to modernize the advice they give to congregations and to offer local leaders flexibility to organize in new ways. Still, most denominational advice about governance suffers from two flaws. The first is that it works best in average-size congregations. Usually that means that the advice starts working when worship attendance, including children and adults (or, in most synagogues, the number of member families), reaches about 150 and stops working when it exceeds about 400. Many congregations fall within this range, but the number of larger congregations has grown a great deal since 1980, and the percentage of all congregants who belong to them has grown much faster. Larger congregations have long made their own rules, sometimes surreptitiously. Now that more congregations are large—or would like to be—we need fresh thinking about what works in congregations too big to fit the old containers.

The second common flaw in organizational advice from denominations is that it tends to be problem centered. This flaw is most obvious when the advice is published in an official manual. At first, such books attempt to set a standard for the normal operation of a healthy congregation. But as years go by, new regulations mainly address problems, conflicts, and scandals. Soon the book contains more pages about problems than about how a healthy congregation can fulfill its mission. It is important to have rules for how to address problems. When congregations and denominations divide over social or theological issues, for example, it becomes important to know who ultimately owns the property. But vital, healthy congregations need advice, too. It can be a challenge to pick out the ideas that enhance vitality when there is so much emphasis on solving problems.

The most mundane advice, if it comes out of an office at the mother church, takes on a glow of holiness. At points throughout this book, I criticize some practices that have become almost sacred in certain denominations. I make no apology for this, nor do I mean to sneer at the denominational staff who advocate for customary practices. I am an author, but I have been a denominational bureaucrat, so I know how much easier it is to be an author! Denominational leaders are often among the most enthusiastic advocates of fresh approaches because they often see the old ways are failing earlier than others do. When that happens, they can be great allies to congregational leaders who want help to struggle free from habits of behavior (including but not limited to those promoted by denominations) that prevent them from addressing current needs with vigor and originality.

SOME THINGS THAT SEEM CLEAR

In facing this challenge, many clergy and lay leaders have expressed the wish for a clear, up-to-date model of what they should be doing. What clarity they do have generally is patched together from denominational guides, experience in various civic and work settings, and reference books like *Robert's Rules of Order*. All of these have value; none quite fills the bill. Congregations are quite different from other organizations, and the world is different than it was when Robert wrote his rules. Our time is also very different from the years after World War II, when many of our current notions about congregational success were codified. But all is not flux and confusion. Some wisdom about organizations is enduring, especially when considered in the light of recent experience. It seems only fair, in any case, to state some of the assumptions and convictions I bring to this work. Here are some things that seem clear to me about organized religion in America right now:

No One Way

There is no one right way to organize a congregation. I do not believe that an original, correct model of leadership can be found in history or scriptures. History, as I read it, shows that people of faith have chosen a wide variety of organizational forms to meet the challenges of their particular times. Congregations organize in different ways because they spring from different histories, cherish different values, inhabit different places, and inherit different polity traditions.

Religious institutions have always borrowed organizational forms from the society around them: Early Christian churches took on some of the forms of Hellenistic mystery cults, the medieval popes behaved like kings, and the New England Puritans cloned the structure of an English town. Congregations have resembled extended families, noble fiefdoms, parties of reform, cells of resistance, and leagues of mutual protection. Christians speak highly of the "apostolic church," though few have seriously followed its example of communal property or cheerful martyrdom. Jews love to sing the song "Tradition" from *Fiddler on the Roof*, but you could look hard at a Russian shtetl and find little that resembles a Reform temple on Long Island.

I cite this varied history not to be cynical but to free our thinking from a narrow sense of binding precedent. Awareness of the wide range of forms congregations have borrowed from the world around them liberates us to draw wisdom from our own environment. For better or for worse, the main organizational model for contemporary congregations is the corporation, and specifically the nonprofit corporation, which emerged in the late nineteenth century as an all-purpose rubric for benevolent work. The nonprofit garb fits congregations pretty well, though not perfectly. What works for other charities may not be so effective or appropriate for congregations. On the other hand, our culture's vast experience with corporate governance offers us a treasure trove of wisdom to draw on. Our challenge is to draw on corporate experience selectively, with a critical awareness of what makes congregations different.[1]

Some mistakes have been made often enough that it is only fair to warn against them. At the very least, some choices have foreseeable consequences. For example, if a board tries to manage day-to-day operations through a network of committees, it will inevitably spend a great deal of its time on operational decision-making. This outcome follows simply from the fact that, if there is no other place for a buck to stop, it will stop at the board table. Many a board resolves to stop "micromanaging," but until it is willing to delegate real management authority to someone else, the board remains the default chief operating officer.

If this were a *Dummies* book, there would be an icon in the margin every time we came to a cause-and-effect relationship like this. It might show a hand slapping a forehead or a balloon with "Duh!" However, you are not a dummy, so I trust you will recognize these flashes of the obvious yourself.

Good Governance

We can know good governance when we see it. For all the variety of workable ways to organize a congregation, certain traits consistently appear when governance goes well. My own list of criteria for measuring the effectiveness of governance in congregations includes the following signs of health:

- *A unified structure for making governance decisions.* Governance decisions include articulating mission, vision, and strategy; delegating the authority to achieve these things; and ensuring that authority is used responsibly and well. Boards go under various names, including vestry, session, council, consistory, directors, and trustees (in this book, I simply call them boards). Boards are usually accountable to the congregation and sometimes also to a regional or national authority as well. A traditional Quaker meeting acts as its own board, but few other kinds of congregations are willing to require the whole membership to spend the time and energy effective governance requires. In some traditions, governance authority is vested in a single person. But most North American congregations give primary responsibility for governance to an elected board. The clergy leader may chair the board or serve as an active voting or nonvoting member.
- *A unified structure for making operational decisions.* Program leaders (paid and unpaid) work harmoniously to create effective programs with the support of a structure that delegates authority and requires accountability. Anyone who works successfully in a congregation soon learns that multiple accountabilities are unavoidable. Every staff position has a natural constituency whose wishes sometimes conflict with the expectations of the staff leader or the board. Effective congregational systems do not eliminate those tensions but give clear guidance about how to manage them. Full-time senior staff members are expected to manage the politics of their positions, while part-time and lower-level staff members have supervisors to do that for them. Above

all, delegation and accountability are matched. Only after goals are set, responsibility assigned, and sufficient power delegated is it fair to hold the leader accountable for the fulfillment of the stated goals.

- *An open, creative, and accountable atmosphere for ministry.* Members take advantage of many opportunities to share their talents and interests in an atmosphere of trust and creativity in which structure, goals, and purposes are clear. One of the most helpful findings from research on corporate effectiveness is that the command-and-control approach works for only a narrow range of tasks. Even the military, which highly values obedience, has learned that delegating as many decisions as possible to lower-level people while giving clear guidance reduces errors and improves adaptability to changing circumstances.[2] Likewise, no congregation can succeed by relying on its board or staff to come up with all of the ideas. In the most effective congregations, programs and ministries "bubble up" continually from outside the formal leadership.

No list will capture every variation, but where these three criteria are met, I have learned to expect high morale among lay and professional leaders and enthusiastic ownership among the members of the congregation.

In these criteria, I have used the words *power* and *authority*, which make many people uncomfortable. It may be helpful to define them briefly: *Power* is the ability to make things happen. The powers of Congress, the power of positive thinking, and the horsepower of a car are all familiar examples. *Authority* is power that is legitimate. We appeal to authority to justify our power; we do things "by the authority" given to us. When Jesus interpreted the law, he was said to speak "as one with authority." In English, the word *authority* comes from the same root as *author*, suggesting that authority might carry with it some creative license. When a board empowers someone to accomplish something without specifying how it should be done, it delegates authority. The purpose of a governance structure is to deploy the congregation's power in a way that is both effective and legitimate.[3]

Learning from Others

Congregations have a lot to learn from other nonprofits, religious and secular. If religious institutions ever had good reason to look down at secular nonprofits, times have changed. In recent decades, nonprofit boards have become more sophisticated. A wide variety of resources have become available to help boards with strategic planning, staff oversight, policy, keeping focused on top-level governance—and staying out of management. Few congregations take advantage of these resources. In fact, many religious leaders automatically react against them. "Shouldn't the church be different?" "I didn't become a pastor so I could be a CEO!" "Sometimes at these board meetings I feel as though I were at work!"

Congregations are different from other organizations but in ways that may not be immediately apparent. The religious mission of a congregation is important but does not distinguish it from other nonprofits founded from religious motives. The most important special features of a congregation have to do with the overlapping of constituencies and the special role of the clergy leader. In some secular nonprofits, there is little or no overlap between board, staff, and clients. Financial support may come partly from board members but mostly from other government, foundation, and private sources. It is relatively rare for the executive director to counsel the child of a board member or for a major donor to be also a paid member of the staff. In congregations, this kind of multiple role holding is the rule, not the exception. Many maxims of nonprofit management assume a crisp separation of roles and treat "role conflicts" as problems to be solved. Congregations need to manage such role conflicts openly and ethically, but they cannot eliminate them without doing violence to the basic nature of the congregation. Nonprofit wisdom needs to be examined and adjusted to fit congregational realities.

Size Matters

No one fact tells you more about a congregation than its size, and no statistic better captures the size of a Protestant church than its median worship attendance. For synagogues, the most comparable number is usually the number of member families. Size is as important in the field of governance as in any other aspect of organizational behavior. To sustain itself or to grow (or even to decline gracefully), a congregation's structure needs to be appropriate to the size it wants to be. I say a great deal more in chapter 7 about the difference size makes to congregations and the way they organize.

Most of what I have to say in this book relates to congregations that are at least pastoral size (with a median attendance of 100 or more children and adults). I hope to answer a frequent question from congregations in the pastoral-to-program plateau zone (150 to 250 children and adults): How do we need to restructure our governance to grow larger? Congregations stuck at other size transition points (for example, around 400 and 800 in attendance) also need to organize in new ways to break through the barrier.[4] At each larger size, a congregation needs a more clearly articulated structure with an explicitly defined role for each component part. Only by empowering the board, staff, and congregation to play each role to the hilt can a large institution resist the downward pull of habit and rigidity or the centrifugal effect of subgroups digging themselves into private bunkers.

Amid this emphasis on larger congregations, it is important to insert a word about the family-size congregation. About half of North American congregations are family-size, with an attendance of up to fifty children and adults, with a plateau zone stretching up to one hundred or so.[5] Decision-making is informal, and authority is given to those who earn it through longevity, consistent service, and trustworthy personal relationships. The governing board has authority only when its actions reflect the judgment of the organic leaders. The vision of a family-size congregation is the family's vision as spoken by the matriarchs and patriarchs, and any effort at discernment or strategic thinking needs to happen with and through them. This attitude is one reason family-size congregations feel refreshingly informal and unbureaucratic, but it creates a risk that leaders may treat tax-exempt assets as personal or joint property. It comes as a surprise to leaders of small congregations when, occasionally, the IRS or local property assessor takes a nosy interest in family affairs!

Governance and ministry in family-size congregations happen in the same informal way as everything else. Work is done when family leaders assign jobs to people. Susan takes on the annual church fair; John makes sure the lawn is mowed; and Dorothy, who needs help to get out, checks in with people by phone to see that those who need it get the attention and support they need. Once assigned, a task often belongs to the same person until he or she dies or locates a successor. Little real authority is delegated with the job; problems, disagreements, and suggested changes go to the matriarchs and patriarchs for resolution. The small congregation makes decisions as a group. If a lamb strays too far from the flock, there is a shepherd with a crook.

The pastor or rabbi (if there is one in a family-sized group) normally plays the role of lamb, not shepherd. Clergy may be treated with respect in a small congregation, but they can lead only within limits set by those who really are in charge. Many denominations place new clergy—fresh from seminary, full of concepts—into small congregations. Eager to take their place as leaders, these new professionals learn that, unless they stay in place long enough to become matriarchs or patriarchs themselves, they must accept a secondary role. One pastor of a small church said, "I imagined myself sitting at the head of the dinner table, but I'm still a guest. They let me say the prayer; then they talk about a life that I'm not part of." Some family-size congregations put new members into board and other titled leadership positions rather quickly—but then, if the newcomers traverse unspoken boundaries, suddenly pull the plug on their apparent power. Change happens in small congregations but only after consultation and a blessing by the proper elders.

Let this be a caution to readers of this book who serve as clergy in small congregations! Formal structures and small congregations usually do not mix. This is not to say, however, that the underlying concepts don't apply. Governance and ministry are still two different things, even if the same small circle of informal leaders does them both. It helps to separate them, if only into different time slots. Formal titles need to be taken with a grain of salt, but the basic roles of board and staff still need to be played. It is still helpful to take the right group on a retreat (or into the right living room) to talk about the purpose of the congregation, what it does best, and how it will ensure that property and people are kept safe. The results of such a conversation will travel home from the retreat in the heads of matriarchs and patriarchs or not at all. The points to keep in mind are that it takes much longer to become a leader in a small congregation than a large one and that informal leadership trumps what is said aloud or written down.

Other than that, a small congregation is exactly like a large one!

Ministry and Money

Ministry and money should not be separated into departments. Many congregation leaders take it for granted that "spiritual leadership" should belong to clergy and "business affairs" to the laity. This dualistic notion has a long history in our culture. Often it comes with a parental attitude by lay leaders who want to protect clergy from contamination by the rough-and-tumble world of power and money. Some clergy appreciate the protection or have earned the reputation for worldly innocence that justifies it. But separating ministry from money teaches by example that pipe dreams of morality do not apply to the world of money, power, and institutions. This arrangement suited Machiavelli, who advised his prince to "learn how not to be good," but it is a sad day when a religious institution parks its spiritual interests in one pigeonhole and its money in another. Dividing faith and money in this way effectively consigns the sovereignty of God to the Hallmark Channel, leaving CNN, the Nature Channel, and FOX Business to the devil.

In congregations, the practical effect is to divide leaders into two groups: the "money people" serving on the finance, building, and personnel committees, and the "people people" populating worship, education, and outreach committees. Some people belong to both groups, and capable, well-meaning people can make any structure work harmoniously. As a matter of best practice, though, it is important to remember that no goal is so purely spiritual that it requires no money, space, or time and no action is so financial as to lack ethical or spiritual implications. People with differing skills will often differ in their temperaments; visionaries always will come into conflict now and then with bean counters. But there is no need to add force to natural differences by building them into the structure.

"Liberal Theology" and Other Excuses

"Liberal theology" is not the problem, and mimicry is not the answer. Many of the congregations I work with are located on the liberal side of the theological spectrum. They read their scriptures flexibly; claim no corner on salvation; and believe, like the United Church of Christ, that "God is still speaking." The trend for such congregations has been poor in recent decades. Nonetheless, I reject the view that "liberal theology" is the source of liberal congregations' troubles. I think something like the opposite is true: Liberal theology has lost prestige because so many liberal congregations run so poorly. Right-wing churches flourish when they run well, but well-run congregations thrive across the spectrum. Thriving congregations understand that they have something vitally important to share with others. Invigorated by that understanding, they dare to let go of ways of organizing that don't work. Liberal congregations' problem is not liberal theology; it is their doubt that other people need and want a liberal faith. A congregation that lacks confidence in the value of the gift it offers to the world clings to customary ways of doing things and resists the changes that would convey its benefits to a wider public.

I reject also the idea that unsuccessful congregations ought to simply copy modes of governance used by successful ones. Governance in congregations is not the science of achieving optimal results through organizational reengineering. Governance is an expressive art, like preaching—the forms of our organizations must reflect the values at their heart. Are we called to preach our gospel to those who have not heard it yet? Then we should organize for outreach and evangelism. Do we see the congregation as a little commonwealth, a model for the world to be? Then we are justified in following the enlightened polity we want the world to follow, even if that limits our appeal or means that we make decisions slowly. What will not work is to adopt organizational approaches simply because they work for other congregations or in business or nonprofit corporations. We can benefit from the experience of others, but we will not succeed by simply mimicking success.

Governance Can Make a Difference

Effective governance can make a difference to the health not only of the congregation itself but of its community as well. Our society is losing necessary skills for group decision-making. Electoral politics now happen mostly through mass broadcasts from candidates to individuals in front of television sets or other video devices. We have too few conversations about moral and political issues among people who know and trust each other but whose economic interests and political philosophies diverge. An increasing fraction of too many people's time is spent at work, often in large organizations that offer little chance to learn the skills of democracy. Young people spend too much time in closely structured programs—for the affluent this means classes, lessons, sports teams, and tutoring designed to optimize their college applications; for the poor it means, increasingly, reform school, prison, and the military. These environments are a poor substitute for programs like religious youth groups, Boy Scouts or Girl Scouts, Junior Achievement, and school governments that at their best are led by youth and adults in partnership. These old ways of building social capital, for all their faults, have not found adequate replacements.

By governing themselves well, congregations can teach civic skills. Congregations are among the few remaining settings where people of different ages, occupations, and political philosophies have a chance to mix and be in conversation. The religious roof affords just enough in the way of commonality to make serious conversation possible—but only a few congregations take advantage of this opportunity. No wonder that, when congregations can no longer avoid a difficult issue, they so often can respond only by separating the parties. As I write, the most divisive conflicts in North American churches are about sexuality and worship style. I see plenty of division and debate about these issues but too little dialogue. Congregations in our time have an important opportunity for civic education. By daring to keep a few difficult questions on the table at all times and handling the discussion well, a congregation educates its members in the arts and practices of civic life. Society can only benefit.

Leaders of communities of faith are never simply managers of institutions, nor do they have the luxury of being purely spiritual leaders. "A purely spiritual religion," James Luther Adams said, "is a purely spurious religion" because it has no power or purchase in the material world.[6] Congregations are vessels of religious growth and transformation—but to be vessels, they need firmness and stability. A congregation easily becomes an end in its own mind—recruiting people to an empty discipleship of committee service, finance, and building maintenance. Institutional maintenance is a necessary, but ultimately secondary, function of a congregation. If souls are not transformed and the world not healed, the congregation fails no matter what the treasurer reports. Paul of Tarsus put his finger on this tension when he said, "The letter killeth, but the spirit giveth life" (2 Cor. 3:6 KJV).

That's why governance in congregations is not a science but an art. Leaders must continually balance the conserving function of an institution with the expectation of disruptive, change-inducing creativity that comes when individuals peek past the temple veil and catch fresh visions of the Holy.

2

GOVERNANCE AND MINISTRY
IN INTERESTING TIMES

Advice about how to govern faith communities is found in the early literature of most traditions. I am thinking of Paul's letters to the early churches,
the teachings of the Buddha for the leaders of sangha communities, the
Hadith of the Prophet Muhammad, and the debates of rabbis in the Tal-
mud over the emerging shape of Judaism. All of these writings struggle with
the basic paradox of organized religion: how to create a stable institutional
environment in which people's lives will be transformed. These texts were
written in the wake of soul-shuddering spiritual change. It seems that every
transformation of the spirit calls, in turn, for fresh attention to the way communities of faith govern themselves.

Our congregations may or may not face a crisis on the level of the ones just
mentioned, but the world in which they work has changed a great deal in the
last generation or two. However, many congregations organize essentially
the way they did in 1950, with boards and committees dutifully meeting,
taking minutes, passing budgets, and adopting or defeating motions. Each
committee controls all work in its assigned sphere and has to do the work as
well. New ideas require many conversations and approvals; old ideas escape
serious evaluation. It is a system well designed to resist change or—to put it
differently—preserve tradition.

In the boom days after World War II, resisting change was not so bad.
Returning veterans and their families, hungry for stability, flooded into
congregations eager to create the stable peacetime world that meant so

much to them after the profound disruptions of the war. Each kind of congregation could count on its defined market share: Lutherans went to the nearest Lutheran church, Jews to synagogues, and so on. A congregation's mission was simply to be the Presbyterian church at Jefferson and Main, or the Reform temple in Lorain, Ohio. The job of the Lutheran church, then, was to do as good a job as it could do of being Lutheran. Churches and synagogues (at least those of certain accepted types) shared a monopoly on the religious interests of a large fraction of Americans. All they had to do was to be a good example of their type (and perhaps to move when their constituents did).

Congregations in those days—especially middle-class congregations— had another advantage that has since gone away: an abundance of skilled labor done for free by women without jobs outside the home. Top decision-making boards were still mainly or entirely male, but most of the congregation's work was done by women. The world of committees, choirs, altar guilds, and children's programs was a woman's world (with, at most, a man at the head of the table), not to mention women's fellowships and temple sisterhoods, which quietly provided most of the sweat, much of the money, and a great deal of the spiritual heart. Today, only in a few wealthy communities is labor from this source obtainable in such abundance.

It is natural to suppose that the social patterns that prevailed when we, our parents, or our grandparents were young must have been in place for centuries. But "housewives" with time to volunteer were a rare, upper-class phenomenon until the prosperous 1920s. During the Depression of the 1930s, almost everyone was struggling to get by; during World War II, while millions of men were away, millions of women took factory jobs. The mode of congregational life that feels "traditional" to most of us today belongs to 1920–1929 and 1945–1965, periods of general prosperity, domesticity, and (after the war) migration to the suburbs.

The rapid growth of congregations after 1945 sped up a trend that had begun more than a half century earlier, toward what some called the "institutional church." Before 1890, a typical church building was essentially a room for worship plus a few ancillary rooms (not ordinarily including restrooms). The minister or rabbi worked from his home study, writing sermons and making parish calls on a congregation numbering fewer than one hundred active adults. In small towns, clergy often farmed or taught school on the side. Congregations in those days made do with what, to us, looks like a minimum of organizational machinery.

In response to urbanization, industrial development, and the invention of the telephone, that pattern had already begun to change. Around 1890, congregations started to build offices, hire secretaries, install phones, publish newsletters, and canvass for pledges. The minister or rabbi found himself at the head of an increasingly complex institution. Ready or not, congregations coped with budgets, payrolls, fund-raising consultants, and a forest of committees and auxiliary organizations. Each of these things existed in a few, mostly urban, congregations in the 1800s, but by 1920, many congregations had become true organizations, similar in structure to the corporate charities of the burgeoning "benevolent empire."[1]

DR. HUFFER IN SANDUSKY

One minister who lived uncomfortably through those times of transition was my great-grandfather, Charles Emerson Huffer, who served Presbyterian churches in Indiana, Ohio, Michigan, and Wisconsin during the first decades of the twentieth century. My travels as a congregational consultant sometimes give me chances to visit the towns where Charles Huffer lived and to try to picture what it was like for him to be a minister. In 2006, I even had the privilege of consulting with the First Presbyterian Church of Sandusky, Ohio, which he served from 1920 to 1925.

With the cooperation of the Rev. Kimberly Ashley and lay archivists, I read seven years of session and trustees' minutes. The 1920s were turbulent years for Presbyterians, marked by anxiety about the loss of Christian influence over the wider culture; worry that churches had gone soft and needed to be made "muscular" again; and conflict over whether Christians should accommodate or rail against new scientific concepts of sexuality, cosmology, and human origins. In these years, Sandusky gradually accepted women's suffrage and the loss of a major employer, the Cleveland and Sandusky Brewing Company, as a result of Prohibition. (H. L. Pecke of Sandusky found a way to link these issues: At a state convention in Columbus, he attacked suffrage as the cause of women's increased drinking![2]) In society as in theology, the 1920s offered more than enough moral grist for any congregation's mill.

Meanwhile, at "Old First" Presbyterian, the trustees discussed the budget, and the session voted people in and out of membership. The congregation met annually to elect, without dissent, slates of elders and trustees. Possibly the church spoke in some way to the great issues of the city or the world during my great-grandfather's ministry, but if so, I find no record of it in the minutes. One thing is certain: In those years, the governing boards—vested, in Presbyterian polity, with great responsibility for spiritual leadership—stuck to a routine of pro forma votes that today would make the most devoted parliamentarian's eyes bug out with boredom.

One point of mild interest is that toward the end of his Sandusky ministry, Dr. Huffer seems to have gotten into trouble with the board of trustees for failing to raise money energetically enough. In December 1924, the trustees, after voting to pay several bills, including one for $2.01 from Beilstein Laundry, recorded this:

> It was suggested that the Session report the condition of affairs to Dr. Huffer with the view of getting him interested to the extent that he will lend his efforts in raising sufficient money to care for the outstanding indebtedness existing against the church.
>
> There being no further business, the meeting adjourned.

A year and a half later, Charles Huffer had moved on to his next ministry. Apparently, my great-grandfather disappointed the trustees by failing to pay adequate attention to the business aspect of the church. If I needed further evidence for this conclusion, I would find it in a picture of his successor, Dr. Funnell, during whose ministry "Old First" conducted a successful, professionally run capital campaign, renovated the sanctuary, and increased its operating budget—just in time for the Depression. Dr. Funnell chose to be photographed at his desk, leaning manfully into a black candlestick telephone. "Finally," I can almost hear the trustees sigh, "a truly modern minister."

Transported to our time, the modern minister of 1925 would find that telephones have changed shape and that they share the office with a multitude of other ways to stay in touch. Women, formerly sequestered in their circles, lead congregations at all levels, lay and ordained. Downtown congregations, like First Presbyterian, struggle to take hold of a fresh role in ethnically and economically diverse environments. But many governing

It was suggested that the Session report the condition of affairs to Dr. Huffer with the view of getting him interested to the extent that he will lend his efforts in raising sufficient money to care for the out standing indebtedness now existing against the church.

There being no further business, meeting adjourned.

                                                          A. C. Close,
                                                              Secretary.

Figure 2.1.

Charles Emerson Huffer   *Alfred Jennings Funnell*

boards spend time much as they did then: discussing and approving routine matters, authorizing minor spending, and complaining about clergy.

I wonder, Why did these men (they were all men, of course) put up with such a gruel-like diet at their meetings? One likely reason is that, in those days, an invitation to serve on a Presbyterian session, an Episcopal vestry, or the board of a synagogue was a social honor. One sat at a great table in a room not unlike the library of a good men's club. One followed rituals that would not be out of place in a throne room: hearing reports, acting on petitions, and assenting to the actions of one's ministers. Beneath a formal surface of equality among board members, differences of family, seniority, and wealth created subtle rules of deference that the newcomer was obliged to learn and master or be mortified. The priest, minister, or rabbi held a position of respect and sometimes influence, ranking usually just below the heads of a half dozen leading families. One knew that the most important work was done outside formal meetings of the board: in committees, private offices, and parlors. Board meetings proceeded with a sense of dignity and order and adjourned at the appointed hour.

WHAT MAKES GOVERNANCE IN CONGREGATIONS DIFFICULT

If you now serve on a congregation's board, you may have noticed that some things have changed. Most obviously, women have joined most boards; in many, they predominate. Few communities have overt social pecking orders anymore; people who participate in group decision-making expect to do so as equals. Moreover, "group decision-making" is the last thing on many people's minds. Trained from birth to think of themselves primarily as consumers, many people simply find a congregation that feels well matched and get involved—with or without joining. If they become dissatisfied, they vote with their feet rather than their hands or voices. When people with this attitude become members of a governing board, they often have a hard time seeing why they should accept the group's decisions—after all, aren't they customers, and isn't satisfying customers the measure of success for any enterprise? When people join a congregation thinking of themselves primarily as consumers, they can make challenging board members.

Some of what makes governance in congregations difficult is more or less eternal. But our time offers special challenges. I see four trends that seem especially important: the cultural disestablishment of Protestant Christianity; the predominance of paid employment; the growth of a "shopping" attitude; and increasing tensions over clergy, born of both a general distrust of leaders and some special ambiguities belonging to the pastoral office.

A Disestablished Culture

From the 1950s through the early 1970s, when many leaders of today's congregations raised their children or grew up themselves, some 70 percent of Americans belonged to congregations, and nearly half attended on a given weekend.[3] Choosing and attending a church or synagogue was a powerful social expectation. Sociologist Will Herberg heralded a new, broader religious culture in his 1955 book *Protestant Catholic Jew*. By the 1950s, Herberg wrote, Americans' worldview had "lost much of its authentic Christian (or Jewish) content." It did not matter what your religion was; so long as you had one, you were presumed good—as a citizen and as a person. Congregations grew explosively, sales of Bibles boomed while knowledge of the Bible declined sharply, and the distinctive tenets of the various denominations became less important than finding one's social place in the "triple melting pot" of American religious culture.[4] Given the ugly history of religious bigotry and

Protestant privilege in the United States, the three-way détente of Catholics, Protestants, and Jews was undoubtedly a step forward.

Today the scene has shifted. Catholic, Protestant, and Jewish are still options for Americans, but the list has grown. Mormons have achieved a level of acceptance, and millions of Americans practice Asian, African, and pre-Christian European faith traditions. Full acceptance of American Muslims has not yet come, though Muslims now outnumber Jews in the United States. Within Christianity, new sects and innovative styles of congregations multiply. The religious landscape of the United States is far more complex and varied than it was in 1955.

For congregations, the increase in religious diversity means that, for most Americans, affiliation is a choice, not an obligation. Even in a rural southern town, where to be anything but a churchgoing Protestant is still unthinkable, 150-year-old Baptist, Methodist, Episcopal, and Presbyterian churches on Main Street cannot presume a steady stream of new adherents. On the edge of town, new congregations, often started in abandoned warehouses or stores, compete with long-established churches for the loyalty of old and (most especially) young.

In most of the country, the list of religious choices now includes two fast-growing ones that were almost unknown in 1955: "none of the above" and "spiritual, but not religious."[5] More Americans than ever before believe that you can be a good—or even a devout—person without joining a congregation at all. Just as the established churches had to learn to get along without state sponsorship, congregations now are learning to get along without the widespread notion that nice people go to church (or, as Herberg added, synagogue).

For congregations of the types that were the dominant American religious life-forms of two hundred years ago—Presbyterian, Episcopal, Congregational, Unitarian, and such—this new diversity has been especially hard because they bear the burden of a privileged past that did not toughen them for today's challenges. Churches and synagogues that had achieved mainstream respectability by 1955 share part of that same challenge, at least to the extent that they adopted the mentality of privilege of the "mainline" churches.

For Jewish congregations, the clearest sign of the times is the high rate of interfaith marriage. Religiously mixed couples often raise their children as non-Jews (and sometimes as non-anything). Because the central programmatic focus of most synagogues is Jewish education up through bar or bat mitzvah, the attrition of parents who value Jewish education is an existential threat. For many Jewish congregations, the habits of their years of respectability are poorly adapted to a time when, like other Americans, Jews are demanding that congregations make an affirmative case for their participation and support.

Dominance of Paid Employment

A second trend that has crept up on congregations is the growth of work. Since 1950, the productivity of US workers has increased more than fivefold.[6] When productivity grows, a society has three basic options: It can raise pay, work less, or increase taxes. In general, until the recession of 2008, the United States chose the first option: We took the cash and worked even more. The consequences were many: We opted out of the long vacations, social safety net, and high taxes that most Europeans chose. Instead, working-age Americans spend more time at work. The increase in work per person came in part from the increase in women's participation in the workforce. But the hours each worker worked increased as well— professional jobs, which once allowed generous time for golf and lunches, required more hours. Lower-wage workers felt the pressure to take second jobs, and parents took less time to care for children.

The practical effect for most congregations is the loss since 1970 or so of what had been one of their most critical resources: women willing and able to work for little or no pay. A woman who would once have gladly volunteered to fold the church newsletters every month just to get out of the house or would have taught Hebrew school to use her college educa- tion now has more than enough chances to do both. On paper, the amount of volunteer time in society has not measurably declined. But the pattern of volunteerism has changed, and congregations that recruit volunteers the same way they did in the 1950s have felt acutely the loss of younger women's work.[7]

As a result, congregations face a pool of potential volunteers who are much pickier than the volunteers of old. She (or he) requires that the na- ture and scope of the work be defined honestly and clearly, that the benefits be significant and tangible, and that the work itself make good use of the talents of the volunteer. An institution that, in addition, offers volunteers some personal benefits will outcompete the rest.

There have been some countertrends. The number of healthy retired people has increased, and volunteering has become a high priority for many people, thanks in part to schools that require it, employers that support it, and a new breed of nonprofit institutions that market it in new ways. Since 2008, US policy has shifted somewhat. Government efforts to soften the recession and high health-care costs for the poor and middle class—including stimulus spending, jobless benefits, and Obamacare—have lessened, somewhat, the urgent pressure to be employed at all times, especially for young adults and early retirees. But these changes have not come close to restoring the abundance of highly skilled and undemanding volunteers that congregations once enjoyed.

A familiar example of a voluntary institution that has often thrived in the new situation is Habitat for Humanity. Each week, Habitat offers thousands of volunteers finite opportunities for service in which they help create a house that they can see and drive past for the rest of their lives. They can expect to meet the beneficiary—because the family that will live in the house usually works on it with them. They may learn a skill they can use on their own houses. And they become part of a temporary work team in which the likelihood of making friends is high. Congregations that succeed at engaging volunteers follow the example of Habitat and other well-run modern charities. Such congregations talk less about "getting the volunteers we need" and more about "recruiting people into ministry" or "helping members to become disciples." They selectively embrace networking, crowdsourcing, and other new technologies to help people find meaning and purpose through voluntary work. Today's high-expectation volunteers respond enthusiastically when they believe their time will be used well.

Work Cultures

Our work-oriented culture affects congregations in another way. People spend so much time at work that they get a lot of their beliefs and assumptions about organizations from the workplace. If congregations ever were part of a "domestic sphere" with its own values and mores—taught by virtuous women and their friends, the reverend clergy—that time has passed. When people think about how congregations ought to run, their first point of reference in most cases is the way things run at work. The trouble is, everybody works in different places and learns different things.

In my first congregation, for example, we were trying to decide whether to move to a new location. Most of the leaders fell into one of three occupational groups. One group, many of them college professors, formed a study committee. It met frequently, gathered information, and debated the implications of the proposed move for our congregation's purpose and identity, without noticeably moving toward a decision. A second group, comprising mostly middle managers from IBM, was comfortable spending quite a bit of money gathering data and expert opinion while endlessly deferring any action. Meanwhile, a retired entrepreneur, acting on his own, plunked down ten thousand dollars of his own money for an option on a piece of land he thought would be perfect for the church. He said, "You have up to a year to make up your minds. If you don't buy the land, I will—and I'll resell it for a profit!" In the end, we bought the land and were glad we did.

That story ended well despite the lack of insight on all sides. I can't help thinking, though, that we could have made our way more smoothly had we talked about our differing assumptions. Unfortunately, as in many congregations, our culture tacitly discouraged talking about work. In part, this tendency stems from a laudable desire to give every member equal status. What is lost, though, is the chance to take full advantage of the range of gifts among the members.

When the topic under discussion is the governance process itself—how we make decisions, as opposed to what decisions we should make—occupational differences can be quite sharp. Everyone learns important lessons early in life about how to behave in groups, how decisions should be made and justified, and what to do when you do not get your way. In gentler times, those lessons were taught partly at home—and usually in larger families, most of which lived under the guidance of a full-time mother. Today many of us are formed in the artificial "family" of our occupation. Around the board table of a congregation, you can occasionally spot the flabbergasted face of someone learning for the first time that the lessons of his or her workplace are not universally accepted truths. When that happens, pausing to discuss the different occupational cultures board members bring can be worthwhile.

An interesting sidelight to the theme of occupational differences is that people do not always bring the *best* of what they learned at work to church or synagogue with them. Sometimes when someone says, "We should do this because it's what we do at work," I ask, "How does it work at work?" and they say, "Terrible!" It's as though the congregation were a place to make a bad idea good at last or to inflict on others what we can't avoid from nine to five.

The Growth of a "Shopping" Attitude

A third cultural change that makes a difference in what works and doesn't work in congregations is in people's ideas about how to shop for a religion. In the 1950s, people bought religion pretty much the way they bought *Encyclopaedia Britannica*: The customer paid a sacrificial sum for a lifetime supply of correct answers to all of the most important questions she and her children might ask. *Britannica* salesmen made house calls and accepted payment in weekly envelopes. In the early 1990s, this model nearly bankrupted the *Britannica*. Competition from CD-ROM encyclopedias like Microsoft Encarta and the fact that fewer women were at home and willing to receive a salesperson in the daytime were both factors. Still, *Britannica* might well have continued to sell large numbers of printed encyclopedias if not for an underlying shift in mentality: People no longer believed in the one-source theory of right answers. In its heyday, people paid a hefty sum for the *Britannica* because it was *Britannica*. Today, people with questions expect an instantaneous selection of information sources to appear for free, courtesy of Google, Bing, or Wikipedia.

Similarly, visitors to worship once shopped (if they shopped at all) for one source to provide religious answers, a spiritual home, and a social identity. Today, shoppers look for the best buy in each category and are always ready to change brands. Some prefer an undemanding source that delivers standard product at low cost, like Ikea or Walmart. Others look for something more along the lines of Tommy Bahama's $2,500 desk—an affirmation of the buyer's taste, judgment, and discretionary wealth. The few who choose a strenuous religious life will look for congregations offering a religious discipline analogous to hiking gear from REI.

Certain congregations, all across the spectrum and across denominational lines, have learned to thrive in this competitive environment by choosing their niche and strenuously working it, as businesses have had to do. Even *Britannica* eventually budged from its old habits. It released in 1994 a CD-ROM edition with online links—for $1,200. After years of struggle and decline, *Britannica* has ceased publishing bound volumes altogether and updates its online corpus every twenty minutes. For less than one hundred dollars a year, Internet users now sort information wheat from information chaff with help from the *Britannica*.[8]

In religion, a few major players, like the Southern Baptists, Mormons, or Roman Catholics, may hang on to some loyal customers—as *Britannica*, Starbucks, and Apple do—because of the perceived uniqueness of their brand. But for most, the old model does not work because people today believe it's smarter to shop than to be loyal to a brand.

Leaders tempted to complain about "church-shoppers" might consider this point: Churches shop, too. So do synagogues. Once upon a time, most congregations procured most or all of their curriculum materials, worship helps, and outside speakers from one source: the denomination. They relied on regional and national offices to train and supply clergy, organize their missionary work, advise them about governance, and consult with them in times of conflict.

For these services, congregations transferred a high percentage of their local revenues to national denominational and missionary bodies. One of the most striking trends in congregational finance is the decreasing proportion of local revenues that transfer in this way.[9] Congregations prefer to choose their curricula, worship materials, and social ministries themselves. Even clergy, especially those in junior roles, are chosen in a wider-than-denominational marketplace. In short, congregations should not be surprised that people shop: They do it, too.

Tension over Clergy

The fourth and last "new" factor I mention, tension over clergy, is actually anything but new. One of the first recorded church fights, the Donatist controversy of the fourth and fifth centuries, was about whether you could get to heaven by receiving sacraments from a priest who held heretical beliefs or led an immoral life. It was a reasonable question. At that time, with assorted Christianities in circulation and a variety of notions about how priests should behave, a lot of priests had to be wrong one way or another. Did that mean the souls under their care were damned? The church as a whole rejected Donatism, but it has never rid itself entirely of the idea that clergy need to match, in holiness, the One they represent on earth.

Add to that the expectation that the clergy should equal executives in business skills, psychologists in counseling, and TV anchors in mellifluousness, and you can see why congregations often find their clergy falling short. Governing documents frequently express ambivalence about how much power to grant clergy, either treating them as sovereign in their (tiny) sphere or hemming them in as though hierarchy (literally, "rule by priests") were the greatest risk a congregation had to face. At the root of the ambivalence, I think, is the persistent concept that the priest's, minister's, or rabbi's job is to resemble God. On the one hand, that expectation sets impossible performance standards; on the other, it makes some people overreact to clergy leadership because they confuse the power of a clergy leader with the power of God.

Not everyone is so reactive. Mature and older leaders who have seen clergy come and go before can often tamp down congregational anxiety. Such leaders have an opportunity to foster spiritual maturity in others. After all, what could be more important than to learn that finite representatives of God—the clergy or the congregation—are not God? We all know this in our heads, but as life disappoints us and our losses multiply, we have to learn it again and again.

Clergy earn a lot of the criticism they receive. But you only have to be there when one announces his or her resignation to see how inappropriately strong some people's reactions are. Quite simply, people confuse the messenger with the message. If a clergyperson's job is to reflect and exemplify the steadfast love of God, how should congregants take it when theirs says, "I have decided there is something I would rather do than be your minister"? From a human being, such an announcement is understandable; from God's emissary, it can feel like a calamity.

Clergy, and especially clergy who serve congregations, live the paradox of "organized religion" intimately, day after day. Congregations invite people to bring their highest, most idealistic expectations with them when they come; we can hardly be surprised when the best we can offer sometimes comes as a disappointment. One big difference between the role of clergy in congregations and CEOs, curators, and executive directors is the intensity with which people vest them with responsibility for the success not just of the institution but also of their own religious quests.

The combined force of these environmental changes—disestablishment of churches, the predominance of work, the rise of "shopping" as a frame for the religious journey, and increased reactiveness toward clergy—makes this a good time for congregations to consider fresh ways of organizing that will help them meet fresh challenges.

3

HOW CONGREGATIONS ORGANIZE

American religious life, for all of its diversity, has a strong conformist strain. Congregations from a wide range of traditions organize according to a few common templates. The differences between church "polities" (congregational, episcopal, and presbyterian), not to mention the diversity of global cultures, do matter, especially when it comes to choosing clergy or addressing conflict. But even congregations with strong ethnic and sectarian roots eventually bend their traditions in order to adopt some of the organizational forms they see around them: elected boards, paid staff, congregational meetings, and committees. They also adopt some cultural assumptions—for example, that a congregation's purpose is to meet its members' needs; that it should run itself without much meddling from denominational officials; that clergy should defer to laity; and that laity speak their most authoritative word by voting. The resulting way of organizing, which sociologist Stephen Warner calls "*de facto* congregationalism,"[1] helps make American religion democratic, lively, fractious, adaptable, and accessible. It also drains great tempests of ecclesiastical variety into a few well-worn organizational ruts.

As a consultant, I have worked with hundreds of churches and synagogues from more than thirty faith groups across North America and have found them fascinatingly diverse in some ways and numbingly alike in others. Even where a central hierarchy controls important aspects of a congregation's life (as in United Methodist, Christian Science, or Presbyterian congregations), whatever is left to be controlled internally tends to be handled in one of a few ways. I see three broad patterns commonly in use.

THE BOARD-CENTERED CONGREGATION

Congregations usually start with a cadre of highly energetic and committed members. When a congregation grows to the point of wanting anything as formal as a board, it naturally calls on those who have taken charge of pieces of its practical work: music, education, building, finance, publicity, membership, and so on. The resulting structure, which often persists even when the congregation is much larger, is shown in figure 3.1.

Most board seats are filled by leaders of program and administrative areas, who are generally called committee chairs, though an actual committee may or may not exist. A few board seats are filled—depending on the polity—by a lay or clergy chairperson, secretary, and treasurer, plus one or more "at-large" members of the board.

For small congregations, this is a good, workable board structure. With all of the important leaders in the room, questions large and small can be answered on the spot. Board members have earned leadership status by taking responsibility. As leaders of the congregation's daily work, they use

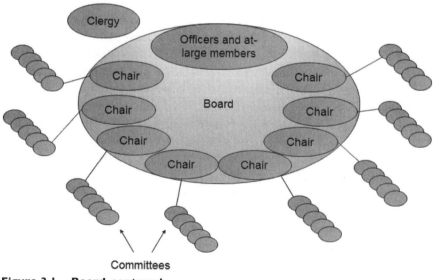

Committees

Figure 3.1. Board-centered.

board meetings to coordinate activities; work out differences; and give each other information, counsel, and support. The board agenda often consists mainly of a round-robin of reports, with the board stopping to discuss anything in a report that interests the members and to authorize spending, resolve differences, or improve on a committee's work. Everybody gets to hear what's happening in everybody else's area. There is little need to publicize the board's decisions because almost everyone who needs to know is already at the meeting or works closely with somebody who is. In small congregations, people find it difficult to see how else a board might be assembled or what else it might do.

The board-centered structure works fine so long as the congregation stays small. But if it grows, programs multiply, and so do the disadvantages of the board-centered structure. On the theory that important programs deserve board representation, the board gets larger and board meetings longer. Each board member spends most of each meeting hearing about areas of interest and responsibility other than his or her own. For committee chairs, the monthly board meeting is just the beginning: Each has (at least in theory) a committee meeting to attend and on top of that an actual program to run. That's three jobs—no wonder it so often becomes difficult to recruit board members! Especially when incumbents wail a righteous noise about their burdens, as too many do, others understandably avoid signing on for a job that requires so many evenings away from home.

The board-centered structure has the virtue of stability. Lyle Schaller used to call family-size congregations "cats"—because nobody owns them and they have nine lives![2] Denominational officials often want to close them down in order to start a larger congregation in the same location, but you can't kill them with a stick. The board-centered structure is one of a small congregation's many bulwarks against change. Standing committees, by their nature, resist new ideas because new ideas require new work and new expenses. Standing committees already have plenty of work piled on their plates and plenty of ideas for their finite budgets. Standing committees resist change naturally; a board made up of chairs of standing committees resists change reflexively.

A board made up of practical program leaders has trouble talking about anything but practical program issues. In a small congregation, the board focuses on program administration because there is no one else to do it. Other functions of a board, like discernment, goal setting, and evaluation, happen, if they happen at all, at an annual retreat. An outside facilitator and a change of venue help to shift the mood. Most of the time, though, a board made up of managers will manage—it can't help it. The larger the congregation, the less satisfactory this structure is and the more the congregation needs a board that rises above day-to-day concerns to think about the bigger picture, not just annually but all the time.

In congregations, each program or administrative area is also a special-interest group. There's nothing wrong with that: We expect musicians to campaign for music, finance people for financial prudence, social activists for social action, and so on. But the board's responsibility is to the mission of the congregation as a whole, so a board member who is there to "represent" a committee must overcome at least a mild conflict of interest.

An example from outside the world of congregations may help illustrate some of these points. In the early 2000s, the American Red Cross had a governance crisis. Since 1905, the members of the Red Cross board of governors had been of two types: a small number of presidential appointees (some of whom were too important to attend meetings) and representatives of the state chapters. The chapters were integral parts of the Red Cross, not separately incorporated. Still, chapters functioned semiautonomously, and "their" board members vied actively to maximize the share of national resources available to their respective chapters. At worst, board meetings looked like logrolling sessions in the US Congress, with the pursuit of common mission overwhelmed by competition to divide the spoils. In the aftermath of serious financial problems in the national body, regulators naturally asked, Where was the board? A special advisory committee of governance experts was called in, which found several structural problems, one of which was that the "representatives" found it difficult to transcend separate chapter interests well enough to pursue the common mission or to watch the common till. The committee recommended that the board be reduced to twenty-five members nominated through a single board-development process. The new board would focus "solely on governance and strategic oversight of the organization," streamline its committee structure, and adopt a "more specific, written delegation of authority" to the chief executive officer. The board's report, *Governance for the 21st Century*, remains an excellent summary of current thinking about common problems and solutions in nonprofit governance.[3]

At budget time in many congregations, you can see problems similar to the ones faced by the Red Cross. A board member selected from (or by) a program group like education, music, or social justice will tend to advocate for the interests of that program area, negotiating or contending for advantage. There is no harm in this, except that it bypasses the "interest" of the board itself, which is to look after the mission of the congregation as a whole. At worst, instead of formulating a common vision of ministry that would attract greater support, the board becomes a venue for competing parts of the community to vie for a bigger slice of a shrinking pie.

If there is a clergy leader, the board-centered structure tends to leave his or her position more or less ambiguous. In a family-size congregation, this ambiguity is a fairly accurate reflection of the truth. But as the congregation grows, the one full-time staff member tends to take de facto charge of many things, simply because he or she is on the scene. Unless the board takes steps to delegate authority more clearly to the clergy leader, the gap between the actual scope of his or her authority and what has been formally authorized can become rather large.

THE COMMITTEE-CENTERED CONGREGATION

The second class of governance structures, and the most common, is the one I call committee centered. The committee-centered model (see figure 3.2) is so widely used that many people assume it is the only proper way to run a church or synagogue. A visitor from Mars might be forgiven for supposing that the chief religious rite of Earth religion, in North America at least, is the committee meeting.

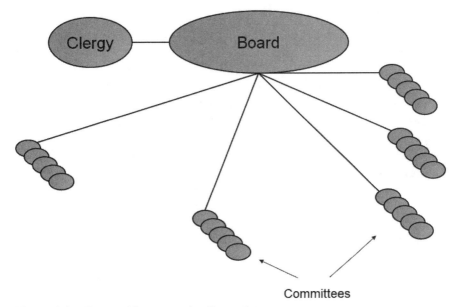

Committees

Figure 3.2. Power Moves to the Committees . . .

The essential trait of the committee-centered model is that both gover-nance (choosing a vision) and ministry (making it happen) are delegated by the board to its committees. Or perhaps *ceded* is a better word than *del-egated* because boards often do not define the scope of their committees' powers or give them much direction.

Sometimes the committee-centered model arises as a solution to the problems of board-centered governance, which increase as congregations grow. The board may wish, for instance, that it could spend more time on planning and oversight. And so the board starts looking for ways to set some distance between itself and its committees. Committee "liaisons" may re-place committee chairs as members of the board. Gradually the action, and the real power, shifts from the board to the committees.

Unfortunately, the committee-centered model rarely enables the board to shift to a true governance role, focused on planning and oversight. Be-cause each committee still (in theory) reports directly to the board, the board still holds the task of supervising them, even if that task becomes unmanageable. In a typical workplace, a full-time supervisor might handle anywhere from three to twelve direct reports, depending on the nature of the work. A board's capacity, meeting two or three hours a month, is real-istically much smaller—and congregations commonly have dozens of com-mittees. Faced with this impossible challenge, a board has several options:

- *The board can abdicate completely*. The controlling motto in some boards is "We Trust Our Committees." Trust is good, but over time, unsupervised committees turn into fiefdoms, operating independently without alignment to a shared unifying vision.
- *The board can leave leadership to others*. Certain committees, like finance and property, control resources others need. As a result, they end up as "supercommittees," making ministry-priority decisions based on their control of resources (see figure 3.3). When the board leaves a power vacuum, these committees fill the gap, and so do pas-tors, staff members, treasurers, and others.
- *The board can become a court of appeals*, deciding questions raised by anyone who doesn't like the answers they got somewhere else. Having given up authority to initiate action, the board reacts to cases, saying yes or no to the actions of others.

None of these alternatives—or any combination of them—feels quite right to most board members. The committee-centered board, in its effort to distribute power, fails to provide the congregation with an authoritative, unifying vision of the future. By fragmenting authority too much, it also

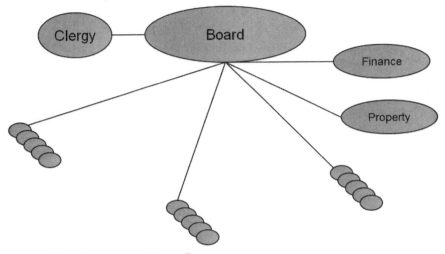

Figure 3.3. Supercommittees Emerge . . .

weakens its ability to ensure that the congregation's human and material resources are cared for and directed properly. Board members wonder, after spending many hours attending and preparing for board meetings, what difference all their work has made.

Triangles

To make things worse, the board, staff, and committees find themselves in multiple triangular relationships. As family therapists are fond of pointing out, triangular relationships tend to create opportunities for problems. Triangles build anxiety, especially when boundaries and responsibilities are not clearly defined. Triangulation starts with the emergence of the supercommittees, to which regular committees go to ask for resources that the board theoretically controls (see figure 3.4). Unless the relationships are clarified with care, issues tend to remain unresolved, leaving disappointments and resentments festering.

As a glance at figure 3.5 shows, new triangles appear as soon as an additional staff member is hired. Every staff position has a natural constituency— and often a committee—with whom the staff member works most closely. At the same time, there is some relationship with the clergy leader and the board. If each of these relationships is not carefully defined to clarify which issues belong to which relationship (If a committee needs its budget changed, should it go to the board or the finance committee?), then triangles become "triangulation," and anxiety begins to build throughout the system.

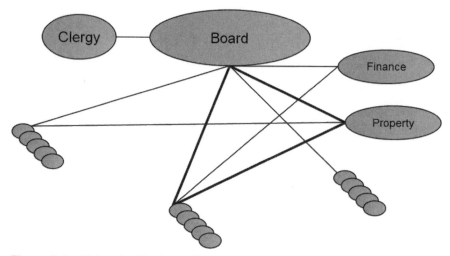

Figure 3.4. Triangles Begin to Form . . .

Program committees, for example, sometimes triangulate "their" staff member into advocating change. A ritual committee might goad an assistant rabbi into championing contemporary worship. When the structure does not clearly say who makes final decisions about ritual, the assistant rabbi might well annoy the senior rabbi by lobbying the board. That is one level of triangulation—among two rabbis and the board.

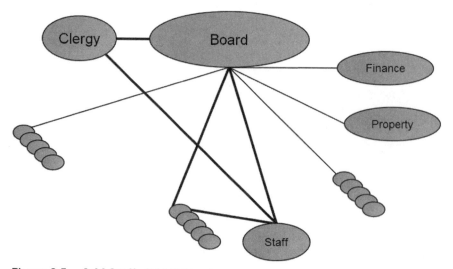

Figure 3.5. Add Staff, Add Triangles . . .

Another level of triangulation in the same scenario is between the ritual committee, the senior rabbi—who no doubt has a history with this issue—and the assistant rabbi. Rather than express themselves directly, congregants often find it more comfortable to pit one staff member against another. By casting the assistant rabbi in the role of "change-agent," the committee may provoke the senior rabbi (or perhaps the cantor) to react by playing the role of "conservative," so staff members play out a conflict that really belongs to groups of congregants. Sometimes a staff member even has to leave—all without direct, open conversation among congregants about their preferences. Because of triangulation, the right people never talk to one another directly (see figure 3.6).

With the addition of a second or third program staff member, a new supercommittee emerges. I call it *personnel*, though it may have another name, like *mutual ministry, staff-parish,* or *ministerial relations*. This committee often tries to play roles normally associated with a supervisor: setting goals, evaluating, and adjusting individual salaries. A personnel committee that invites congregants to complain about staff members practices triangulation of the most troublesome kind. Anyone who tries to "fix" the relationship of two others is likely to fail and certain to increase anxiety, especially for himself.

When the personnel committee's role with the staff team is not clearly defined vis-à-vis the head of staff, especially problematic triangles result.

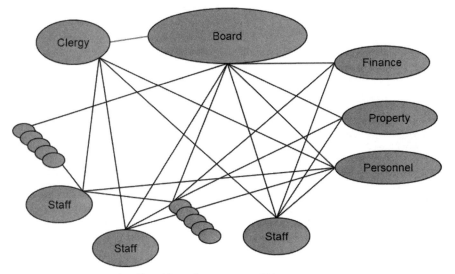

Figure 3.6. More Staff, a New Supercommittee . . .

In many congregations, the personnel committee hangs out its shingle as a problem solver, mediator, or ombudsperson for the staff—in effect, an alternative boss for anyone who does not like the real boss. Triangles multiply. Figure 3.7 shows a full-blown case of the committee-centered structure.

As if the triangles weren't challenging enough, committee-centered congregations often adhere to what I call the map theory of committees, in which every inch of actual and possible programmatic and administrative territory belongs to a standing committee, as though the congregation were a country split up into states, with no frontiers or unincorporated territories open to homesteaders. According to the map theory, if an idea involves music, it has to go before the music committee, and so on. The map theory puts standing committees into a position where they can veto change—which, because they have their hands full, they are too often inclined to do.

As a result of all this unofficial power brokering, triangulation, and tacit boundary drawing, the committee-centered model creates a powerful bias against change. Skilled leaders can make virtually any structure function flexibly and well, but the committee-centered structure does not make innovation easy. What it does best is what it was designed to do: prepare the congregation and its program for next year, provided that next year is 1959. Here are some common, less helpful features of the committee-centered model:

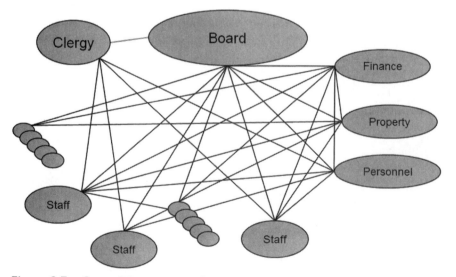

Figure 3.7. Committee-centered.

- *A passive board* that spends most of its time listening to reports, responding to proposals, and arbitrating conflicts rather than envisioning the future, creating long-term goals and policies, and ensuring organizational performance. A committee-centered board has little or no agenda of its own—only the sum of the agendas of its committees. Ironically, this way of spending the board's time often means that the board hardly ever talks about the topics it agrees are most important. As a test of a board's committee-centeredness, try this: Ask board members to list the two or three most important things the congregation does. They may say holding public worship, reforming the city, producing educated Jews, or transforming hearts and lives in Jesus Christ. Then ask when they last had a board conversation about trends in worship music, how the city will look when it is reformed, how educated Jews differ from uneducated ones, or how to tell whether a soul has been transformed. A committee-centered board rarely talks about such concerns except, perhaps, when an outside facilitator prompts them to at a retreat. Instead, it talks about *issues* that *arise out of* the congregation's mission—whether to change building locks or add a staff position—issues that may be connected in some way to the core mission but that do not help the board take hold of the heart, the core, the why of it.
- *A miserly approach to delegation*, in which boards and committees approve projects provisionally and then bring them back repeatedly for criticism, reconsideration, and approval of next steps. This process is frustrating, especially to people who are used to leading major projects from start to finish in their work lives. Unfortunately, such a process attracts people—volunteers and staff alike—who prefer not to be held accountable. In a system that gives no one adequate authority to carry out a project, there are always plenty of excuses for the absence of results.
- *A fragmented staff* whose members connect more strongly with their natural constituencies—educators with parents, musicians with the choir, administrators with the finance committee—than to the staff as a team. Faced with a threatening multiplicity of triangles, many staff members will lay claim to a piece of turf and wall it in. Too often, the result is a collection of disconnected fiefdoms with no accountability for overall results and a strong tendency for staff members to fall into conflict with anyone who trespasses against them.

The net result of all these features is a congregation that strongly resists change. Imagine that you're a newcomer to a congregation and you have a new idea. Suppose your idea is significant enough that it requires money, staff time, and building space to succeed. How many places can you go, in the committee-centered structure, if you want someone to tell you no? Lots of places! You can be rejected by the committee that controls the territory on the map where your idea falls. If that's not enough, the finance, personnel, and property committees all will have good reasons not to try it. Or you might go to the clergy head of staff, who knows how things are done—and therefore knows why your idea can't be done. You can even go to the board, which will, after discussion, refer you to a suitable committee on the grounds that nothing should be voted on by the board until it is first approved by the appropriate committees. Most people never try to run this gauntlet; successful innovators often bypass it entirely.

Why do we use committees as the all-purpose instrument of governance and ministry? Perhaps it's in our national blood. The Continental Congress, our first effort at national governance, operated like a committee-centered congregation. David McCullough reports that Congress had hundreds of committees, most of them "chosen with little or no reference to their expertise or abilities, which meant they were usually incapable of getting much done. . . . General Washington often complained of being bombarded with queries from so many different committees that he wondered if he would have time to fight the war."[4]

From the beginning, the committee has been part of our idea of democracy, used for much too wide a range of purposes. We call people together to make decisions, to gather and reflect on information, to socialize, to serve others, to do work, and to be fed spiritually. But our organizational imagination is so limited that we use one format—the committee—for all these purposes and more. Luckily, not every congregation follows the committee-centered model fully, and most that do have talented leaders who can achieve results even when the system makes that difficult. Many leaders understand that the committee-centered system, while it had its virtues in the past, today is mostly an impediment to needed change.

THE STAFF-CENTERED CONGREGATION

Nothing I have said about the shortcomings of board- and committee-centered governance is particularly new. On the contrary, at least since the late 1960s, an attack on hidebound, plodding, bureaucratic churches and synagogues has been a frequent theme for advocates of congregational reform. The alternative that has received the most attention sometimes goes

under the names *permission giving* or *purpose driven*.[5] To focus on th
organizational aspects, I call this family of governance models staff centered
(see figure 3.8).

The staff-centered model starts with a charismatic clergy leader who articulates the congregation's mission and vision and recruits paid and unpaid
staff to carry it out. The vision is so clear that someone with a new ministry
idea can usually perceive immediately whether it fits or not. In contrast to
the committee-driven congregation, in the staff-centered model, someone
can always say yes to a new idea. In fact, the model mandates the pastor
and staff to say yes, giving permission for an unlimited variety of ministry
activities all under the umbrella of a central, driving purpose.

Where the staff-centered model is followed consistently, the pastor's role
is visionary and entrepreneurial. The staff-centered congregation aims for a
minimum of organizational busywork and a maximum of opportunities for
anyone who wants to get involved in ministry. The "purpose-driven" and
"permission-giving" visions feed a hunger among congregational leaders who
find the old ways lacking. Many leaders long to streamline structures so that
deliberative processes do not get in the way of ministry. One congregation

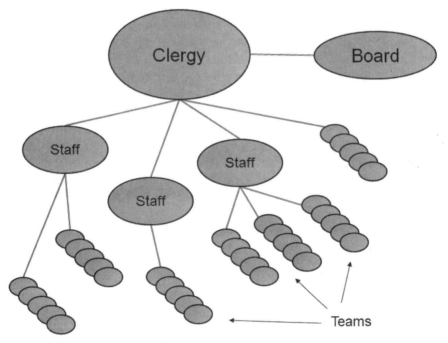

Figure 3.8. Staff-centered.

l in this direction coined a slogan to describe its gover-
ewer meetings, more ministry!" Some of the largest, most
ations in the country operate this way. What's not to like?
ed model, like the others, does have some built-in disadvantages. One is a certain brittleness and vulnerability resulting from its
strong dependence on one leader. If that leader leaves or dies or is dis-
credited, then the institution can take a long time to recover. This problem
can be mitigated by preparing a succession plan, either among the staff or
through the board (yes, even a permission-giving church has a board!). But
depending heavily on a single leader does create a fragile institution, and
this drawback cannot be avoided altogether.

A second disadvantage of staff-centered structures is a disadvantage only
if you believe, as I do, that committed groups are capable of making better
decisions than individuals can. I don't always enjoy group decision-making,
but I have found again and again that a community willing to be patient with
people's differences and indecision will correct and improve the insights of
even the most gifted individuals. If you agree with me that wide participation
adds an essential element to a congregation's search for truth, then a strictly
staff-centered congregation seems wrong. Even if the staff-centered model
were always more effective at producing practical results, it would leave me
dissatisfied because it does not make use of every member's gifts for discerning the congregation's mission. This concern, at bottom, is theological: I
think each of us comes with a built-in antenna tuned to the right frequency
to hear the promptings of the Spirit, and congregations ought to take advantage of it. I also believe what people call the "politics" of congregations has
a good side because a group in conversation can perceive more about what
is good and right than the sum of what its members can perceive alone. For
these reasons, I choose congregational participation with its messiness, even
though I sometimes envy the efficiency of the staff-centered way.

What I want, actually, is both. Occasionally I see a congregation that
manages to balance the efficiency and clarity of the staff-centered model
with other values, like democracy, participative decision-making, and group
discernment. In the coming chapters, I describe how I think this balance
can be struck.

SOME EVEN WORSE IDEAS

First, though, I need to mention several even worse ideas I have run across
in my consulting work. Usually the people who practice them do so under

the impression that denominational polity requires them or that they are widespread. The fact that one or both of these impressions may be correct does not make the ideas any better.

Elected Committees and Committee Chairs

In some churches, the congregation elects every committee chair and sometimes every committee member as well. I find it hard to imagine a less meaningful exercise of democracy than to vote on a slate of between 30 and 120 nominees. Who is empowered by this system? It might seem to be the nominating committee, but in practice, what happens most of the time is that the de facto leader of each committee (who may be a staff member) ends up doing most of the recruiting, and the official nomination process is as empty as the election.

Staff Reporting to Committees

When board- and committee-centered congregations engage paid staff, they sometimes struggle to find language to describe how staff members should relate to one another and to the rest of the organization. Especially if the staff person leads a program area, like education, music, or youth work, "owned" by a committee, it seems natural that the committee should hire, orient, and supervise the new staff person.

Dial the clock forward ten years. The staff member is full time, still working "for" a committee (though by then he or she may actually handpick its members), and in conflict with another member of the staff, possibly the senior clergy leader. What is the process then? Do you assemble the two staff members and their respective committees to try to reach a solution? Do you all go to your mutual boss, the board, and ask it to judge the case? If the congregation elects both the committee and the board, does the congregation have to vote?

Having seen all of these methods tried, I have concluded that "a staff member reports to a committee" is one of those things that you can say in English but that makes no sense, like "rite of caster fish." Committees simply cannot supervise paid staff because they are not present when the work is done and they cannot easily speak with one voice. A staff member deserves a boss who works at least as many hours a week as he or she does. Others can participate in the evaluation process or in making policies about staff treatment. But a congregation that wants to remain sane will set its staff up as a single team and hold it responsible for sustaining its own working relationships. Designating someone to be "head of staff" or "leader of the staff team" and requiring the staff team to make its own plans, resolve its own conflicts, and carry out its own evaluations—inviting others to participate in all of these except the conflicts—gives the staff the space it needs to operate effectively.

Multiple Governing Boards

Some congregations have two, or even three, top boards, all responsible directly to the congregation. Sometimes the division reflects an old-fashioned mom-and-pop dualism: The board of trustees (pop) controls the money, while a program board (mom) does most of the work. Sometimes one board is said to be responsible for the "business" aspect of the congregation, while the other takes charge of the "spiritual" part. Have I made it clear yet that I don't like this way of splitting up the universe? Whoever controls "business" ends up having ultimate control of spiritual matters also.

A congregation can create as many boards as it wants, though generally the government will recognize only one of them as "the board" of the corporation. When two (or sometimes even three or four) boards stand together at the top of the organization chart, leaders are frequently in doubt about which buck stops where. In practice, multi-board arrangements tend to act out to excess the dualism their designers had in mind: Trustees manage the money without thinking about the mission, and the "program" board does just the opposite. When everyone gets along, communicates well, and pays attention to the whole, the worst consequence is a strong bias against anything new. At other times, the system can become a setup for the boards to fall into conflict that spreads to the congregation—because there is no other place it can be resolved.

It does make sense to have a separate board for a substantial subsidiary enterprise, such as a housing project or a nursery school, which requires more expertise and attention than the church governing board can give.[6] A congregation with a large endowment fund may want a separate board (or even a separate corporate entity) to counterbalance the temptation for the governing board to dip into the endowment principal to solve short-term financial problems. In general, though, it makes sense to put one board clearly at the top of the heap, responsible to the congregation for the performance of all others. If more than one board reports to the congregation, the congregation itself must be prepared to resolve differences between them. It is a rare congregation that is disciplined enough to oversee one board adequately, let alone two or three.

Jumbo Boards

Growing congregations sometimes expand their board proportionately—basing that action, I suppose, on a vague theory of proportional representation. Such expansion would make perfect sense if a board member's job were to represent a certain number of constituents. But if a board's job is to make sure the congregation achieves its mission, it needs to be the right size for that task. Boards with more than twelve or thirteen members find it difficult to think imaginatively as a group or to stay focused on a finite set of board priorities. Large boards, as a rule, tend to be more passive and less able to engage the staff as strong partners. Attendance becomes less consistent, a tendency that makes it difficult for the board to sustain a train of thought from month to month. In effect, the board becomes a miniature congregational meeting.

There is nothing wrong with miniature congregational meetings. Every congregation needs a way to gather all of the de facto leaders once in a while, including major donors, enthusiastic newcomers, and influential elders. Every congregation larger than 150 or so active members needs regular meetings in three sizes:

1. *As large a group as can be gathered as "the congregation"* at official meetings. The congregation adopts and amends bylaws and elects its officers and board. Depending on the polity or bylaws, some congregations also adopt mission statements, strategic plans, and budgets; select clergy; or approve public statements.

2. *A mid-sized group of forty to eighty* to be in regular conversation about the future. This group needs to be large enough to include a sampling of the congregation's viewpoints, subgroups, and areas of activity and small enough to have one sustained and fruitful conversation.

3. *A small group of six to eight—certainly no more than twelve*—to govern. This group makes strategic choices, ensures that the congregation's resources are protected and used properly, and shapes the agenda of the larger groups' discussions about the future. To me, it makes the most sense to make this group legally the board and to make it the primary partner and point of accountability for the senior clergy leader.

The defect of most jumbo boards is that they are too large to be effective as a board and too small to function well as the midsized group. One common solution, where tradition demands that the board be large, is an executive committee. This can be workable if the two groups differentiate their roles and powers clearly. For instance, the executive committee might be the clergy leader's primary partner, taking responsibility for many of the board's oversight tasks. The larger board might meet less frequently for an agenda focused primarily on planning. Unfortunately most bylaws simply say that the executive committee has all the powers of the board between board meetings—so full board meetings feature a long recitation of what the executive committee has already done. Board members wonder why they are needed, and executive committee members often become frustrated when they work hard to make decisions, only to see them overturned by a group whose members do not understand their work.

Sound values lead to jumbo boards: democracy, diversity, inclusiveness. But to include a large group in decision-making is not a simple matter of putting them all onto the board. Paradoxically, a congregation has its greatest influence when it distributes power to smaller groups of leaders. The whole group can then focus on a few important questions. As it finds and chooses answers, it can safely trust each smaller group of leaders to do the work its size equips it to do best.

ON TO SOME BETTER IDEAS

Having wandered for a season in the wilderness of questionable ideas, we can now move on to work toward something better. The simplicity of the board-centered structure is fine for small congregations that intend to stay small—in other words, for about half of North American Protestant churches and many urban synagogues and rural Orthodox and Catholic parishes. Congregations that do grow much beyond an average attendance of about 150 seem to go in one of two directions: One is the committee-centered structure, with its highly change-resistant system of triangulated fiefdoms. The other is the staff-centered model, which depends heavily on one strong leader who engages everybody else in ministry but keeps members at the periphery of the process of discerning and articulating mission.

Sadly, in many mainstream congregations, here is where the conversation about governance reaches a full stop. Too often, we see empowerment as a zero-sum game where empowering leaders necessarily disempowers followers. A few congregations, though, have pioneered modes of governance that honor congregational participation while charging ministry leaders to use and to share "permission" freely. For me, a good summary of the requirements of good governance in congregations could be phrased as a question: Can a democratic congregation and an effective governing board operate in partnership with a strong, permission-giving ministry-team structure? Some of the most vibrant congregations, across the spectrum theologically, are answering this question "Yes!"

4

A MAP FOR THINKING
ABOUT CONGREGATIONS

Analogies are useful but tricky. New Testament writers compare the church to a human body, a flock of sheep, a bride, and a vineyard. Synagogues are often likened to a house, a tent, or an extended family. None of these comparisons is meant to be exact or literal; a church may act in some ways like a herd of sheep, but a wise leader doesn't plan for that—poets do exaggerate sometimes!

In the same spirit of poetic license, it may at times be useful to compare the clergy leader of a congregation to a corporate CEO, its members to customers or stockholders, or its staff to the employees of a charity. We can draw many useful analogies between congregations, other nonprofits, and businesses, but ultimately congregations need language and ideas of their own. It is easy to say that "the church should run more like a business" without recognizing that in some respects, churches should and do run very differently. In talking about governance in congregations, we can't completely avoid borrowing language and ideas from other kinds of organizations, but it's also important to use words and images that remind us we are talking about something special.

Most leaders can see what they don't like about their current structure. It is not so easy to envision how that structure might improve or how it would work afterward. My intention in this book is not to prescribe a specific model of congregational governance but to offer a framework of images, language, and ideas that will help congregations to make choices about how to structure their decision-making. Those choices will vary, as they should, because the way a congregation makes and carries out decisions is a primary expression of its values.

MAPPING GOVERNANCE AND MINISTRY

In thinking about organizational structures, people often use charts. The most common kind of "organization chart" uses boxes and lines to show who is in charge of whom. Such charts have their uses, but to reimagine governance and ministry from the ground up, we need something a bit different: a conceptual map. An organization chart traces lines of power and control; a map, like the one in figure 4.1, marks out zones for participation and decision-making. It differentiates the roles of leaders and shows how they can work together to imagine possibilities, seek God's will, explore options, and get work done while remaining crystal clear about who makes each particular decision.

Our map begins with *governance* and *ministry*, two types of power that a congregation usefully can delegate in different ways. Governance includes top-level tasks of articulating mission, selecting strategies for getting there, making sure the strategy is followed, and ensuring that people and property

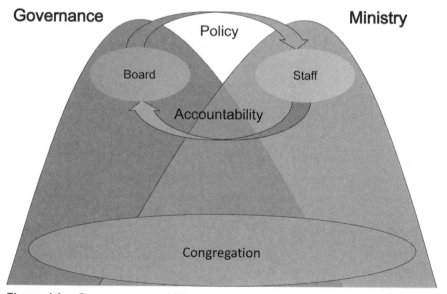

Figure 4.1.   Governance and Ministry.

are protected against harm. Ministry is everything else: the congregation's daily, practical work, including all the rest of the decisions about what to do and how.

At the top of each curve is its chief decision-maker: the board for governance, the staff for ministry. In this book, I use *board* and *staff* to designate the heads of these two loci of decision-making, even though I understand that congregations fill and name positions differently. The *board* is usually just that: a group of elected and appointed members, most of them unpaid, that has the general power to direct and oversee the congregation's work and resources. In *staff*, I include clergy, other paid employees, and all of the volunteers who lead or work in daily ministry.

Note that "chief" decision-maker may not be the "ultimate" decision-maker. In most systems, both board and staff report to other bosses: the congregation, presbytery, conference, or bishop. In a true organization chart, such entities would properly appear at the top. But this map is less concerned with keeping track of who reports to whom than with helping to assign spheres of responsibility and describing ways that leaders hold each other accountable.

Note that I am just defining terms right now, not giving advice. Congregations organize in many ways: Some insist on bringing every tiny matter to a meeting of the membership; others have a board of one with lifetime tenure. Often the same people play roles in both governance and ministry. But in this book, I call whoever carries the responsibilities of governance the *board* and anyone who manages and does the daily work of ministry the *staff*.

Defining *Governance* and *Ministry*

Governance means "owning" the congregation, holding and controlling its human and material resources, and making sure that they are used to serve its mission. A congregation's *mission* is not the same as its *mission statement*. The mission is what the mission statement tries to state. Even the best mission statement is an approximation, subject to improvement or revision as circumstances change and new light dawns. Good mission statements make clear what good the congregation means to do, whom it hopes to benefit and how, and what it claims as central principles and values. And so governance includes articulating mission, choosing major goals and strategies, delegating power to those who lead the daily work, and holding them accountable for their performance. Governance also means requiring that the congregation's money, property, and people be kept safe and that the congregation live in harmony with its own values. Governance connects the congregation's work with the concerns of various stakeholders: members, future members, donors, and volunteers; its wider community; its family of related congregations; and its ancestors in faith—the honored dead who are its greater "cloud of witnesses." Governance is holding the whole institution and its work in trust, voicing its intentions, and taking responsibility for its performance.

Ministry is the rest of what a congregation does—the daily work of building a community, managing resources, and transforming lives. Anyone whose job it is to lead a program, teach a class, serve food, lead worship, or help visitors to find a seat is part of ministry. So are those who provide indirect support by training others, writing checks, sweeping floors, and tuning the piano. In using the word *ministry*, I do not distinguish between ordained and lay, paid and unpaid, or "program" and "administrative" staff. I count as part of ministry anyone in the chain of practical activities that constitute a congregation's work. Ministry includes creating liturgies, curricula, and visitation schedules and making countless other long- and short-term plans. Ministry means making daily choices about money, time, and space. If ministry is to be more than a one-person show, it also requires writing job descriptions, setting goals, conducting evaluations, appointing paid and unpaid staff, and sometimes firing them. Ministry is the congregation's practical work of changing lives in ways that fit its mission, acting out its values, and achieving its goals.

A simple way to see the difference between governance and ministry is to look at the results each kind of work produces. Both governance and ministry, ideally, produce relationships, enthusiasm, and renewed faith. But each also generates a distinctive set of outcomes: Governance produces mission statements, minutes, policies, strategic goals, and lists of core values. Ministry brings into being worship services, study groups, mission trips, service projects, mowed lawns, happy children, and renewed hope. One too-simple summary might be that governance produces words on paper and ministry produces action. The reality is only somewhat more complex.

Board and Staff

Governance and ministry appear in figure 4.1 as two overlapping curves, with a bit of separation at the top and arrows running from the board to staff and back. The point is that, while governance and ministry are different and distinct, they do not operate in isolation from each other. They connect in two specific ways:

- The board speaks formally to staff by writing *policies* to guide their work. Through policies, the governing board (which legally could make nearly all decisions if it chose to) delegates authority to staff and gives them guidance about how that authority should be used. Having done all this, the board resolves not to meddle, hear appeals, require detailed reports, or respond to everyday complaints. In effect, the board sets a limit to its own agenda—deciding in advance that it will focus on its governance role instead of trying to supplant or duplicate the staff's work in the daily management of congregational life.
- Second, the board holds the staff *accountable*. Responsible boards match delegated power with accountability—neither writing a blank check to the staff nor holding it responsible for a result without first giving adequate authority to accomplish it. Having delegated power and identified high-level goals, the board monitors progress toward them and ensures that its policies are followed. The board always has the option of stepping into daily management in case of misconduct or malfeasance, but normally the staff's accountability to the board occurs on something closer to an annual than to a monthly rhythm.

Across the bottom of figure 4.1 is the congregation—not because it is less powerful than the other entities but because its members participate in all three zones. As the map suggests, the distinction between governance and ministry is more important to leaders than to members. Most members do not need to think about the difference between governance and ministry at all.

Three Leadership Roles

The overlapping curves of governance and ministry mark out three zones of authority that belong to the board, the staff, and the board and staff together. Figure 4.2 places these names into the different sections of the map and names them *oversight*, *management*, and *planning*:

- *Oversight* is the board's authority to hold the staff accountable. The board is exercising oversight when it reviews a financial audit, evaluates the congregation's progress toward its annual goals, or talks with the head of staff about performance. In oversight, more than any other aspect of its work, the board holds itself at a critical distance from the staff in order to give feedback from an independent standpoint.

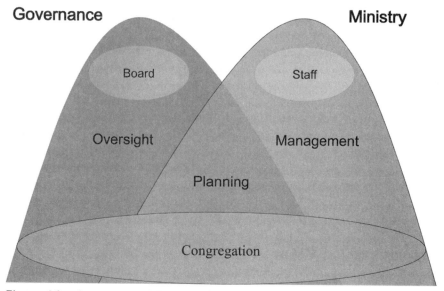

Governance   Ministry

Board   Staff

Oversight   Management

Planning

Congregation

Figure 4.2. Separate and Shared Roles.

- *Management* is the staff's authority to lead the work of ministry. Because all or almost all of the staff's management authority is delegated
  by the board, the scope of management depends on the extent of the
  authority the board has delegated. Within its management authority,
  the board expects the staff to make decisions and to take responsibility
  for them without asking for permission or approval.
- *Planning* is envisioning a future and making the big choices about how
  to get there. In contrast to oversight and management, planning is a
  "soft" kind of authority. To be effective, planning depends on wide
  support from board, staff, influential members, donors, and potential donors. A planning effort might produce a mission statement, a
  five-year strategic plan, or annual goals. After a wide process of discernment, plans flow to the board and possibly the congregation for
  approval. Implementing plans—and making many choices about *how*
  to implement them—becomes a staff responsibility.

Dividing authority this way permits the board, in partnership with the
clergy leader, to give priority attention to the congregation's most important
future challenges and opportunities. The congregation as a body can apply
its limited attention where it has the greatest influence. The staff—and
volunteers who work as staff—are freed to invent ways to achieve challeng-

ing goals without the dampening effect of a decision-making structure that questions everything at every point along the way.

COMMITTEES AND TEAMS

So far, we have paid attention mostly to the board and staff. But both board and staff need helpers, and because their jobs are different, they need their helpers organized in different ways. Figure 4.3 distinguishes *committees* of the board from *teams* for ministry. Committees help the board to govern; teams do ministry with leadership from staff. Many congregations call both kinds of groups "committees," but I prefer to use that word in the older sense of a group to which a parent body has referred, or "committed," a piece of business. A committee gathers information, drafts a policy, or prepares in other ways to report back to the body that appointed it.

A team is different: Teams exist to achieve practical results. A team might mow the lawn, arrange flowers, count money, or visit the sick. By this definition, the majority of what are called "committees" in most congregations actually are teams. Teams are more than simply crews of working drones: They make important choices about how they will accomplish goals. An education team might think with the education staff about curriculum and

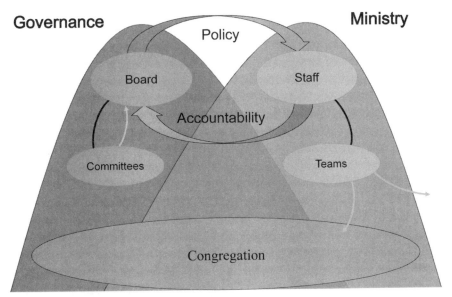

Figure 4.3. Committees and Teams.

help identify good teachers. A finance team might work with the office manager to choose safe practices for handling cash. Within the scope of what they have been asked to do and with the authority they have been given by the staff, teams think creatively about new ways to fulfill the congregation's plans.

People sometimes get confused about committees and teams, but the difference is not difficult to tell. As shown in figure 4.3, a committee is responsible to the board (or to the congregation), and its work product always goes back to its parent body. A team, in contrast, is responsible to the staff, and its work product flows outward to the congregation or the world.

Another way to see the difference between committees and teams is to picture the group of people each requires. Committees perform governance-related work assigned to them by the board. They usually sit at tables having orderly discussion. They make decisions by majority vote (or by another chosen method). Procedure is formal enough to make it clear exactly what the group has done or not done. Somebody takes minutes. When a decision has been made and written down, it is communicated to the parent body. Ideally, committee members would be reasonably patient, verbal people of diverse experience and understanding, all of whom are skilled at dialogue and abstract thinking and comfortable with work whose products take the form of words on paper.

The ideal team is constituted differently. A team needs to be systematically *un*representative, excluding everyone who lacks commitment to the task at hand or who has nothing to contribute to it. A team has a *leader* who knows how to do the work and is willing to accept responsibility for training, supervising, and coordinating others to achieve a stated goal. The team leader has a *supervisor*, who links the team to the staff structure and gives instructions about the work to be done and the results to be achieved. Unlike boards and committees, which are usually elected or appointed, ministry teams are *gathered* based on people's passion for the goal, with an eye to making sure group members have among them the gifts and time and energy and mutual commitment that the work requires.

Many congregations use the word *committee* for the gang that shows up on weekends wearing greasy coveralls and wielding screwdrivers and pipe wrenches—which to me is simply silly. Even sillier is to require that gang to sit around a table, adopt motions, and take minutes. Some congregations even criticize them for "not being a real committee" because they don't observe committee niceties or because they send one person for a one-person job. Many people who would run away if you asked them to serve on a committee respond gladly if you say, "I'd like you to do this job. Here are the resources you can use and a list of people who can help you. If you have a problem, let me know. I'll be your boss."

The team idea has become so popular that some congregations, in their eagerness to jump onto the bandwagon, simply rename their committees "teams" without changing their job descriptions, reporting relationships, or mode of selection. This creates a false appearance that things have changed more than they have, making it even harder to shift to a real committee-and-team structure later.

In the same vein, some congregations have thrown out the venerable word *committee* altogether, which to me seems wasteful. When a board appoints a group to rewrite bylaws, draft a budget, or propose a clergy candidate, I think it's a mistake to call it a team because that suggests that it is going to create bylaws, budgets, or a clergy leader in the same way that a shed-building team creates a shed. On the contrary, a committee's work product is a *proposal* that remains only a proposal until the board or other parent body acts on it. Once a congregation learns the difference between teams and committees, calling a committee a committee reminds everyone its job is to help the board to govern, not to govern in its place.

Committees for Governance

A true governing board has only a few committees. A board concerned primarily with governance would not appoint a committee to change the locks or to run the Sunday school because those tasks fall into the zone of management. The board has ultimate responsibility for building security and education ministry, but it discharges that responsibility by giving adequate authority to the staff, stating clearly the results it wants and does not want, and holding the staff accountable for its performance.

By this strict definition, what committees might a board have? Each board decides for itself, but if a board sticks to the principle that committees exist only to help the board to govern, the list will be much shorter than you might expect. A typical board might have four standing committees:

1. *A finance committee*, whose scope of work follows the same the limits the board sets for its own finance-related work. The board's financial focus is to plan the long-range future and to oversee the recent past, not to manage current work, and so a true finance committee educates board members, supports financial planning, and facilitates the annual audit. If the staff needs volunteers to help with finances (and it does), then it should create a team.

2. *A personnel committee* to help the board to create policies on personnel and handle grievances and other matters that the board must act on. Unfortunately, many personnel committees function as a personnel department—writing job descriptions, facilitating goal-setting and evaluation, and getting involved when there are conflicts. These are human-resource functions better handled by an HR team accountable to the head of staff.

3. *A governance committee*, which helps the board to maintain high standards of performance. An integral part of the board, this committee is responsible for helping the full board to live up to its role in governance, its meeting practice, and its expectations of board members. The governance committee leads an annual training session for new board members, to which "old" board members are invited, and facilitates an annual review of the board covenant.

4. *A nominating committee*, which works closely with the board to ensure that, when board vacancies are filled, the board will have the diversity of personal characteristics and experience that it needs. The nominating committee's function often is defined by the bylaws, in which case the board's policies will say only what the bylaws do not say already.

From time to time, boards also appoint temporary or ad hoc committees (also known as task forces) to draft policies or gather data for particular board meetings, so the board can have a better conversation. The committee's work is to support and educate the board, not to displace it or to make decisions it is too uninformed to make. The board should keep ad hoc committees and task forces on a short leash, requiring them to come back to the board regularly and to complete their work on a short time line. A good committee sets the stage for a well-informed board conversation and decision; a poor one makes its own decision and then dares the board to overturn it "after we did all that work."

In exceptional cases, a board might delegate authority to a committee to act on its own. The board of a church that owns a large retirement home, for instance, might have a committee to serve as a sub-board for the retirement home. Such arrangements complicate life for the board and run the risk that it will end up spending too much time managing a proliferating swarm of sub-boards. Unless there is a good reason to do otherwise, smart boards create a unified structure for *all* management decision-making, with one place where all management decisions come to rest.

In chapter 10, I talk in more detail through the choices boards need to make about committees. For now, I'll simply say, that normally, committees never act or manage on their own but only help the board to govern. The work product of a true committee snaps back, like a well-thrown yo-yo, to the hand that sent it forth. Boards that define committees in this way end up with a short list of standing committees and a series of ad hoc ones.

The transition to a structure that distinguishes committees from teams can be a challenge. Some traditional committees, such as finance, personnel, education, and property, may currently act both as committees (advising the board) and as teams (managing some aspect of program or administration). Some such committees need to learn new boundaries. Others need to be divided in two. Most boards need a finance committee, and most staffs need a finance team—and there is nothing wrong with having both.

Teams for Ministry

In contrast to committees, which write reports, make recommendations, and gather information for the board, teams produce practical results for the congregation and the world. Some teams (or ministries, as some of them are called) directly fulfill pieces of the congregation's mission, producing the primary results the mission calls for. Teams for worship, outreach, hospitality, and caring fall into the primary-results category. So do choirs and educational ministries. Other teams (or the same teams on a different day) produce supportive, secondary results: a clean building, a fund-drive mailing, a readable newsletter, an attractive garden. And of course all of them, potentially, invite people into mutually supportive and inspiring friendships, which through the power of good example may do more to transform lives than intentional life-changing programs do.

One benefit of differentiating teams from committees is that teams can recruit people to do things without asking them to also be involved in unrelated group deliberation. Teams do make decisions; a sound principle of management is that a team should take as much responsibility for choosing *how* to do its work as it can handle. But there is no reason a person with a heart for child care needs to attend meetings to interpret the insurance regulations on child safety—or that an insurance expert needs to care for children.

Teams free congregations from the limitations of the map theory of committees described in chapter 3. In committee-managed congregations, committees often act as gatekeepers, limiting initiative within a given area. "We have our hands full. In fact, we have trouble filling our committee as it is. How can we possibly take on something else?" A team structure, responsible to staff, is more expandable than a committee structure. A congregation with six new ideas for new-member outreach need not squeeze them mped membership committee. It can recruit six leaders charged with testing one idea each.

structure expandable, a good rule is never to start a team s with *the*: *the* choir, *the* youth group, *the* social-ministry s fellowship. Such names announce, right from the start, that there will ever be another. The old practice of naming women's circles and adult classes after their leaders may seem a bit aristocratic, but it does hold out the possibility that there might someday be one named for someone else! Unique names ("Jubilee Singers," "Vance," "Esther's Daughters") work against this one-and-only style of naming, keeping the door open to creating new teams in the same subject area and making easy points of entry for new people.

Teams make efficient use of leaders, paid and volunteer. To connect with a committee, you have to go to a committee meeting. But you can supervise a team leader with a periodic meeting or phone call and some e-mail. One staff person can oversee a dozen teams; a volunteer might manage two or three. Together, they can be responsible for the activities of some two hundred active individuals.

A common misunderstanding about teams is that they reduce lay power and initiative by putting volunteers under the direction of the staff. In some congregations, this feels like a violation of a sacred principle. I understand the worry, but I ask, Where is it more important to have congregational participation: in deciding what the congregation means to accomplish year to year or in deciding what to do from day to day? Most members want their congregation to achieve big goals more than they want a voice in small decisions. A team structure for ministry can be efficient—and democratic, too—because it is more capable of delivering what the congregation wants it to deliver.

Even in congregations that generally cling to volunteer control of day-to-day decisions, some of the happiest and most productive groups work under the staff. In many congregations, the most top-down leadership is found in the choir, where directors actually direct! But even choirs pause periodically during rehearsals to discuss whether they wish they were singing different music. Sometimes the director accommodates such preferences—not because it's better for the choir to choose the music democratically (the director may, in fact, have a better sense of the choir's capabilities, what's appropriate for the day or season, and what kind of music the congregation likes) but because empowered groups have more enthusiasm and more energy than passive ones. The essential qualities of an effective team—in contrast to a deliberative body like a committee or a board—are urgency, unity, passion, problem-solving ence for action over talk.

THE CONGREGATION

What, then, is the role of the congregation? As a deliberative body, the congregation is a powerful, if awkward, instrument of decision-making. As a voluntary association, it is a labor pool of sorts, providing workers without whom not much could get done. As a worshiping community, it holds a unique vantage point from which to seek after the good. Accordingly, across the bottom of figure 4.4, we see three roles for congregants to play: as *governors*, as *planners*, and as *ministers*. Congregation members readily see the difference between voting at a congregational meeting (governance), reflecting in small groups about the implications of neighborhood change (planning), and working in a soup kitchen (ministry). Usually they flow from one role to another without thinking much about it. It's the leaders who need to keep the boundaries between governance and ministry clear.

Symbolically, the chief lay and clergy leaders, at the top of figure 4.4, stand for the partnership of lay and professionals. Congregants pay atten-

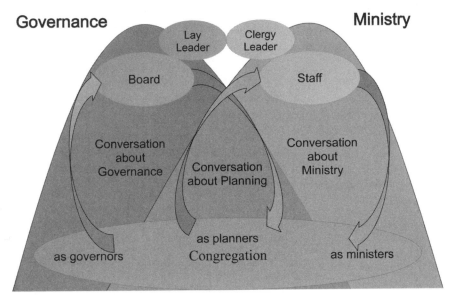

Figure 4.4. A Congregant's View.

to the way these leaders act, especially when they are together, as a sign
at all is well—or not.

Three Holy Conversations

Corresponding to the three roles of congregants in figure 4.4, arrows
leading to and from the congregation mark three "holy conversations":
about governance, about ministry, and about planning.[1] Each of these
three conversations has a vital role to play in helping leaders stay alert to
changes in the world around them and in bringing future leaders to the
surface. Each conversation includes elements of worship, prayer, and striv-
ing to discern God's will by reading the "signs of the times" and pondering
the congregation's history—both its local history and its wider history as
reflected in its scriptures and traditions. Lively congregations keep these
conversations going in a continual variety of formal and informal ways.

The *conversation about governance*, led by the board, includes preparing the congregation every year to do a good job of electing its new officers
and board members. Periodically, this conversation may include discussion about the mission statement, bylaw changes, or the calling of a clergy
leader. Once in a great while, decisions about mergers, building projects,
or denominational affiliation will be on the congregational agenda. As *governors*, the members play both formal and informal roles. The exact nature
of the formal role varies: Congregational meetings may be the supreme organ of governance, as in a synagogue or congregational-polity church, or it
may share that role with some part of the denomination, as in presbyterian
and episcopal systems. But in almost every case, the congregation plays a
powerful informal role. It may vote with hands and voices or mainly with
its feet and pocketbooks—but vote it does, and wise leaders pay attention.

The *conversation about ministry*, led by staff, consists of many separate
interactions about how to achieve results in various fields of practical work.
As *ministers*, the members comprise most of the congregation's labor pool.
A heavy dependence on unpaid labor is a distinctive challenge for congregations, and volunteers' high expectations make it imperative for leaders to
hold them in conversation. Parents' meetings, educational forums, surveys,
and program evaluations all are forms of conversation that help to inform
staff decision-making, especially when leaders collect, summarize, and feed
back what they think they heard, so members see that their participation is
appreciated and attended to.

The *conversation about planning*, pictured in the middle of the map,
takes place on several different timescales led by board and staff together.

Annual goals emerge from annual discussions. Every five to ten years, it makes sense to undertake a strategic planning effort that asks big questions about whether to continue ministry as usual or set a new course. As *planners*, members attend small-group sessions and town meetings to reflect on questions about the future or work on task forces to gather data and explore the practicality of ideas that emerge. The planning conversation invites members to help shape the congregation's identity, purpose, and relationships; in other words, to ask, What part of God's will is ours to do?

Two Planning Products

In figure 4.5, we see that planning generates two kinds of products, for delivery to two customers. A planning process—whether it is an informal board retreat or a large strategic planning process led by a committee and consultant—produces a *strategic vision* that includes a vision of the congregation's future and a short list of major choices about how to get there. The strategic vision goes for approval to the board and perhaps also to the congregation. The planning process produces also a complete *strategic plan*, plus a brainstorm of ideas about how it might be realized. We don't want to lose these ideas, but realistically, for the board to "adopt" the detailed plan, much less the brainstorm list, is a bit absurd, as if the board believed

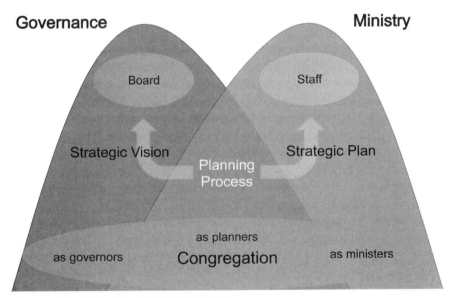

Figure 4.5.   Planning and Its Products.

it could foresee the future well enough to know what steps will seem appropriate in year 3 or year 4. So the planning committee's report has two parts: The strategic vision, running a page or two, goes to the board to be adopted. The strategic plan, with its specific checklists and timetables, goes to the staff for when it implements the plan.

Implementation, in a changing world, never goes according to a checklist but by trial and error. The board adopts a vision, and the staff tries this and that, keeping what succeeds, abandoning what fails. Each year, the board and staff agree on goals—the big steps they mean to take that year toward fulfilling the strategic vision. Planning is a process, but it also is a state of mind that informs daily management. Planning combines clarity about the outcomes with a readiness to risk, evaluate, and fail—and risk again. In chapter 8, I describe the annual and multi-annual planning cycles in greater detail.

WHAT "GOVERNANCE AND MINISTRY" IS NOT

Having laid out what I mean by *governance* and *ministry*, it may be useful to say a bit about what governance and ministry is not. The difference between governance and ministry is *not* hard versus soft, money versus faith, top versus bottom, or business versus people. Both governance and ministry concern themselves with faith and values, benefit from prayer and scripture study, and require decisions about how to deploy financial, capital, and human resources for the congregation's purposes.

Governance and ministry do not absolutely need to be done by different people, at different times, or under different leadership. It is quite possible to gather one group to do both, as most committees in committee-centered congregations try to do. But even in the smallest congregation, where the same twelve people seem to do everything, understanding the distinction between governance and ministry helps leaders to shift gracefully from one to the other. Some boards dedicate certain meetings to governance and others to ministry. The board chair chairs the meetings about governance, which mainly address policy and planning. The clergy leader leads the meetings about ministry, which might include a calendar review, a round-robin of reports, or a discussion about how to accomplish a cross-functional goal. In time, different people find they like one kind of meeting better than the other, and eventually there are two overlapping groups, one of which continues as the governing board, the other as a ministry coordinating team.

Governance and *ministry* might not be the best words to use in every faith tradition. If other words fit better in your setting, I encourage you to go ahead and use them. Some synagogues use *avodah* or simply *work* in place of *ministry*. Some churches prefer *eldership* to *governance*, or *pastoring* to *ministry*. These choices are important. Words connect a congregation with its roots and values, so wise choices make a difference. I use *governance* and *ministry* because they have worked reasonably well across a wide variety of congregations. If you find alternatives that work for you, I am interested to hear about them.

Finally, "governance and ministry" is not a "wall of separation" between board and staff. Figure 4.6 shows how different this idea—advocated by some nonprofit leaders—is from what I'm talking about. Wall-of-separation leaders say, "Board members should never talk with staff without the executive director's knowledge and approval" or "The board decides *what* to do, and the staff *does* it." One complicated system insists that the board confine itself to specifying abstract "ends," leaving "means" decisions strictly to the head of staff, subject only to the limitations set by the board's policies.[2] Such a black-and-white approach can be a useful form of temporary therapy when meddling by board members has become endemic, but it's rarely a good plan for congregations in the long run.

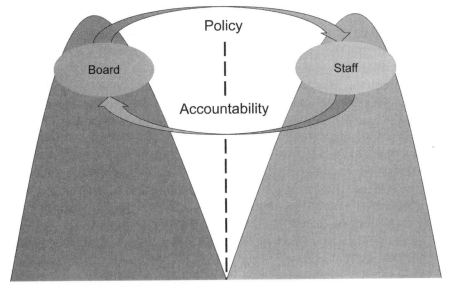

Figure 4.6. "Wall of Separation."

For one thing, few congregation boards can manage to articulate the mission or set top-level goals without full participation—actual leadership—from the senior clergy leader. And wise clergy look to their boards for wisdom and counsel, even about decisions that are clearly theirs to make. The most important choices require buy-in from everybody. A congregation pondering a move across town, a building project, or a proposal to expand its worship schedule to include a new ethnic group needs an inclusive conversation from the start.

In my view, is more important to be clear about the boundaries of authority than to draw strict boundaries between people. When the boundaries of authority are clear, it actually becomes easier for people to collaborate because they do not have to worry about losing power. In a healthy board-staff partnership, the board can invite the staff to help with board work without making the staff worry that the board will give them management direction. A clergy leader can take the board's temperature about a staff performance issue or a proposed change in worship without blurring his or her responsibility and power to address those issues. Board members can gratefully accept their pastor's leadership during a planning retreat without eroding their collective right to bless the final vision.

WEARING HATS

In place of the image of a wall, a better metaphor for governance and ministry in congregations involves hats. Each hat represents a different kind of activity: A board member has a board hat, but if he's a tenor in the choir, he takes his board hat off and wears his choir hat to rehearsals. The change may help remind him that board membership confers no musical authority: If the director says he's out of tune, then he's out of tune! A board member who happens to be active in a ministry activity takes that hat off so that at board meetings she can serve as an unbiased guarantor of the whole mission, not a representative of just one aspect.

Some nonprofits can keep their boards and staff physically separate, so each person is identified exclusively with one or the other and rarely needs to cross the boundary. Congregations sometimes try to do the same, but it's difficult because, especially in small and midsize congregations, so many people wear more than one hat. The hat metaphor serves as a reminder to respect the structures of authority appropriate to what you're doing at the moment and not to presume your personal authority will follow you when you take one hat off and put another on.

There is no one right way to organize a congregation; each community of faith must choose a structure right for its own values and beliefs and in harmony with the practice of its historic tradition and its larger family of congregations. What too many congregations choose, however, is a loose, ambiguous structure that is hard on leaders and creates a strong, unwanted bias against change. If the world were stable and the religious needs of people stayed the same from one generation to the next, then it might be fine for congregations to remain the same as well. But in the world as it is, congregations that persist at practices that worked in generations past soon find themselves in slow decline. Among those practices are the board-centered and committee-centered modes of governance that emerged early in the 1900s. In their place, congregations are experimenting with alternatives. The most successful of these efforts focus strongly on the congregation's mission rather than on organizational life for its own sake. They also have in common clarity about the difference between governance and ministry—about which buck stops where and how leaders are held accountable for their decisions. Equipped with a clear structure, congregations can identify their missions clearly, choose a strategy, get out from under their own feet, and move ahead.

5

THE JOB OF THE BOARD

As a conversation starter, sometimes I ask board members to tell me what their job is. I hear a variety of answers. Someone usually says, "We represent the members of the congregation. They elected us, and we should do what they would do." The board, in this political perspective, is like a city council or the US Congress: representatives elected by the people to make laws in their behalf. The comparison is not new: Civil government and congregations have exerted mutual influence in North America since colonial times. In the US national tradition, "we the people" exercise our sovereignty through representatives, and Americans tend to assume congregations should be organized that way as well. But "doing what the people who elected us would do" is no simpler for a board than for a legislator. Should a board do what its constituents want or what they *would* want if they understood the issues better and had spent more time thinking more deeply about the long-term implications? A problem with democracy in congregations (and elsewhere) is that future voters do not vote. If they did, at every meeting and election they would make up a majority—we hope! Because most congregations plan to be around for more than a short time, the board must represent not only current members but the disenfranchised future also. Clearly, this responsibility requires an understanding of the board's job that goes deeper than "we represent the members."

Board members sometimes say, "Our job is to give the members what they want." This idea depicts members of the congregation as customers and the congregation as a store. The customer is king, and the chief end of the congregation is to please the customer. Higher motives may exist alongside this one—just as a store owner may have other motives than to make a profit—but the board's overriding motivation is to keep the congregation voting "yes" with both its dollars and its feet. The key metrics of success are quantitative: membership, attendance, contributions, and participation. This perspective on the board's job explains quite a lot of what an effective board does—especially when it pays attention to the changing culture, tastes, and demographics of its service area and leads the congregation to refresh its program and recharge its appeal. But is this really the point of a congregation? Congregations do some of their best work when, instead of giving people what they want, they teach them to want something new. Longtime members often have their congregations to thank for the fact that they now volunteer to help the needy or take risks for social justice. Sometimes members are inspired to abandon a job that is just a job, at some sacrifice of income, in favor of a morally significant vocation. When people talk about such profound life changes, I sometimes ask them, What would you have done if someone had warned you how belonging to this congregation would transform your life? Often they admit they would have run the other way. The idea of "giving members what they want" fails to appreciate the value of a congregation that leads people to stop wanting some of what they want and to want new things they can't initially imagine wanting.

A third answer I hear occasionally to my question about the board's job is "We are ministers alongside the pastor." This is a powerful idea, personified in Protestant Reformed theology as the ruling elder, ordained to lead along with teaching elders, also known as pastors. In current Presbyterian practice, ruling elders are elected and serve terms like most other board members, but the rite of ordination (and the lasting honorary status it confers) makes ruling elders more than simple representatives. Elders, as one scholar puts it, rule "according to the guidance of their own nurtured consciences and not merely as spokespersons of particular interest groups."[1] While not so explicit in most non-Reformed traditions, the idea that a lay board member's work is a form of ministry is worth considering in any congregation. Making a board member part of the congregation's ordained leadership recognizes "gifts of the spirit" in the individual and acknowledges that boards need sometimes to lead constituent opinion rather than reflect it.

While the idea of board-member-as-minister deepens our understanding of a board member's personal role, it does less to clarify the work of the board itself. In order to work happily and in harmony, board members need to know with some precision what role they are to play and what results they should produce.

THE BOARD AS FIDUCIARY

When I ask about the board's job, someone (frequently a lawyer or a banker) often uses an obscure word that speaks rather deeply to the nature of the board's role: "The board is a fiduciary." And what might a fiduciary be? Many people connect this word exclusively with money, but the concept is actually much broader. A fiduciary (in Latin, *fiduciarius*, "trust," from *fides*, "faith") is anyone whose duty is to act in faithfulness to the interest of another, even at cost or peril to himself. A parent, for example, is a fiduciary for his or her children and must care for them no matter how much sacrifice that might require. The stewards in Jesus's parables who managed the master's property while he was absent are fiduciaries. The board of a business corporation holds the company's assets as a fiduciary for the stockholders. Because the stockholders' main goal, ordinarily, is to make money, the duty of a corporate board is to increase stockholder value. If the board seeks other goals—by pumping up executive compensation, making sweetheart deals with other companies owned by board members, or sometimes even trying to be responsible corporate citizens—they can expect to be accused of failing as fiduciaries.

A congregation's board is a fiduciary, also. Like a for-profit board, it controls property in behalf of its real owner. But who is the owner? Members of the congregation often answer this too quickly, "We members are the owners!" And the members' interest? Satisfactory worship, education, social action, and so on. The fiduciary duty of a congregation's board, in this view, is to know what the congregation wants and to provide it—a concept not so different from the political and commercial concepts of the board described earlier.

This way of thinking sometimes produces good results, but it is based on a false assumption. A congregation does exist to serve its owner—but the members of a nonprofit organization do not "own" it as stockholders own a business. Stockholders can vote to sell the corporation's property, pay its debts, and divide the remainder among themselves. A congregation—or any other nonprofit—that did likewise would be violating several state and federal laws. The most fundamental legal principle of nonprofit corporations is that they must use their resources exclusively to serve the purposes for which the state has chartered them. In the case of congregations, the charter purposes are relatively broad. For that reason, and because a congregation is exempt from many of the tax reports required of other charities, leaders sometimes forget that there is any limitation at all. But a congregation may not distribute its resources for the "personal benefit" of anyone—especially an officer or board member—except as reimbursement of expenses or fair compensation for services provided. For-profit corporations are required to benefit their stockholders, while nonprofits are forbidden to benefit their members.[2] To call the members "owners" under these conditions stretches the idea of ownership quite far.

Who Is the Owner?

Who, then, is the owner of a congregation? Who plays the role of the stockholders in a business? Not the members. Not the board. Not the clergy or the bishop or the staff. All of these are fiduciaries, whose duty is to serve the owner. Symbolically, we might say God is the owner, and that might be a correct interpretation. But God is too big a concept to guide decision-making helpfully. The specific "owner" that the board must serve is *this congregation's mission*, the small piece of God's will that belongs to it. Or to put it differently, the congregation's job is to find the mission it belongs to—the real owner for whose benefit it holds and uses resources. The primary measure of a governing board's success is not the balance in the bank, the shortness of board meetings, or the happiness of congregants. A congregation's "bottom line" is the degree to which its mission is achieved. The mission, like stockholders in a business, has the moral right to control the congregation's actions and to benefit from them. Because the match between a congregation's mission and a corporation's stockholders is so close, it seems to me helpful to say that the owner of a congregation is its mission.[3]

Fiduciaries for the Mission

An interesting corollary of this line of thought is that, when members of the congregation vote, they, too, vote as fiduciaries for the mission. Like the board, each member has a duty to make sure the congregation serves its mission—to vote as a fiduciary for the owner—even if that goes against the member's preferences or wishes. When a member's private interests are in conflict with the congregation's mission, the member's duty is to vote the mission.

And what is the mission? The great management consultant Peter Drucker wrote that the core product of all social-sector organizations is a "changed human being."[4] A congregation's mission is its unique answer to the question, Whose lives do we intend to change and in what way? What this means for a particular congregation at a given time is never clear or obvious, and so articulating mission is a continuing task. But a congregation that avoids that task—that simply seeks to please its members or keep doing what it has done in the past—falls short of its true purpose. Growth, expanding budgets, buildings, and such trappings of success matter only if they reflect positive transformation in the lives of people.

The board's role, then, might be summarized as "owning the place in behalf of its mission." To be sure, the board is accountable to the members who elected it and perhaps to other stakeholders as well—but achieving the mission is what the board is accountable *for*.

DUTIES OF BOARD MEMBERS

As fiduciaries for the mission, individual board members have certain legal duties: the duty of care, the duty of loyalty, and the duty of obedience.

Duty of Care

The *duty of care* requires board members to commit adequate time, energy, and attention to enable them to know the mission, understand the congregation's affairs, and act responsibly. One way to look at this obligation is to ask, If I personally owned the congregation—its property, its money, and its program—how much time would I devote to running it? How well would I feel I needed to understand its finances? What kind of assurance would I need that it was well insured, that no one was stealing from it, and that my money was being put to its intended use? No one board member will understand everything the board needs to understand—but each board member is separately responsible for taking "reasonable care" in governing. Taking care means that a board member who does not understand financial statements needs to seek out someone who can help decipher them and help find answers to the few key questions of greatest concern to the board. Board members unfamiliar with important program areas must seek out at least a basic understanding of how each area of ministry supports the mission. The board as a whole can help with this kind of learning by orienting new board members and allotting time periodically for the whole board to refresh its knowledge. The ultimate responsibility for taking care remains, however, with the individual board member.

Specifically, the duty of care requires thorough preparation for board meetings, regular attendance, and active participation. It also means voting when it is appropriate to vote. On some boards, "abstentions" have become so customary that the minutes show a count of zero abstentions when there are none. Abstentions are appropriate or even required in certain circumstances, such as when a member has a conflict of interest, but otherwise a board member who does not vote is failing to perform a duty. The congregation has a board to govern its affairs, and the duty of care requires every board member to understand the issues and to cast the vote with which he or she has been entrusted. Members who abstain should be asked to give a reason. In some cases, people abstain in order to reserve the "right" to undermine the board's decision later—not an appropriate reason or appropriate behavior for board members.

Duty of Loyalty

A board member owes the congregation a *duty of loyalty*. For a board member, one consideration must be paramount—the congregation's mission. Most obviously, a board member who stands to benefit from a board decision, personally or through a close relationship, must promptly disclose the conflict of interest. If the conflict is significant, the board member must withdraw, not only from voting but also from discussions leading to a vote. In response to recent abuses in the nonprofit sector, the IRS has begun to pay increased attention to conflicts of interest among nonprofit board members. While legal consequences for individual board members are still rare, a board that does not properly handle conflicts of interest risks costly "intermediate sanctions" against the congregation from the IRS, not to mention criticism or even lawsuits from anyone who claims to have been harmed by a biased board decision.[5]

"Interests" need not be selfish to conflict. A person who sits on two charitable boards can have conflicting duties to their different missions. A common example is the congregation board member who sits on the board of an independent school that rents space from a church or synagogue. While the missions may be sympathetically aligned, when it is time to set the rent, the institutions' interests conflict. The board member needs to step back from participating in at least one board's deliberations about rent.

The duty of loyalty extends beyond legal conflicts of interest. Personal preferences, friendships, rivalries, and bitterness from past divisions can cloud the objectivity of any board member. When the board is set up to have "representatives" from program committees or teams, partiality to one's own program area can be exacerbated or even made to seem legitimate. These kinds of conflicts usually can be handled simply, by acknowledging them candidly and understanding that each board member's duty is to set aside all partial loyalties in favor of the whole.

Wise boards have a written policy that defines conflicts of interest and requires board members to disclose them and to withdraw from debate and voting. A clear conflict-of-interest policy, in addition to protecting the congregation from harm, protects board members from unjust accusations. If the policy is fuzzy, then a board member might vote, supposing in good faith that the conflict of interest involved is trivial or that the proposed action is so clearly in the congregation's favor that no one could find fault. But assuming "no one could find fault" is risky. Someone always can find fault, and someone often will. When board members resist adopting a conflict-of-interest policy to protect the congregation from board members, I suggest they write one to protect board members from false accusations.

Duty of Obedience

The *duty of obedience* requires board members to comply with the congregation's foundational documents—which may include a charter, bylaws, and denominational rules—and applicable laws. Most important, board members must be obedient to the mission, even as they recast it in new mission statements from time to time. It is easy to confuse the happiness of influential individuals with the mission; board members need to be alert to times when the right action will make people *un*happy. The duty of loyalty is not to the congregation as a present group of individuals; it is to the mission.

Sometimes we speak of "this year's board" or "last year's board," as though each had a separate life. But a board, like the corporation it controls, is a continuing legal and moral entity. It inherits all the promises it has made, even if all individual board members are new. The board is the first guarantor of the congregation's good name and integrity; as such, it must "obey" past promises, including written and unwritten contracts and donor restrictions it has accepted by accepting gifts. Even unilateral promises, though not always enforceable by law, are moral obligations to which a board should adhere if at all possible.

When I was a young person serving on a church board, my elders made a lasting impression on me by the way they handled an awkward situation. It had come to light that the chair of the endowment committee, in conversation with a ministerial candidate, said he "saw no problem" with lending the minister money for a down payment on a house and added, "We can do that." He was a board member but had not been authorized to make such a commitment. Many boards would have apologized to the candidate and washed their hands of the matter. But one board member said, "If a person in a responsible position makes a promise for the church, we are obligated to make good on it if we can." That is what the board did, and I believe it was correct to do so—if not legally, then morally.

This story illuminates another aspect of the duty of obedience: Board members have a duty to respect the limits of their individual role vis-à-vis the board as a whole. Board members scattered through the social hall after a service are not the board. They become the board only at a duly called board meeting, and the board acts only as a unit. Individual board members, as such, have no special rights or powers except to participate and vote at board meetings. At meetings, board members disagree sharply, but once a vote is taken, the duty of obedience requires every member to speak with respect for the decision and the board's authority to make it. Some boards carry this obligation further and forbid members to disclose their disagreement to others in the congregation. I think this practice goes too far and violates the basic principle of openness about board business. But at the very least, a board member should say something like, "It was the board's responsibility to make this decision. I disagreed and said so, but we had a frank discussion and a vote, and now it's time to move ahead." If a board member's dissent is so strong that he or she cannot voice at least that level of support for the board's legitimate authority, then the time has come for that member to think about resigning.

The duties of care, loyalty, and obedience may seem almost too obvious to mention (so, incidentally, do about half of the Ten Commandments). But in our moments of reflection, we do not need a moral code to remind us of our duties. We need code-based morality for heated moments, when it suddenly seems reasonable to depart from everyday constraints. In such moments, a clear statement of the responsibilities of board members and clear policies that spell out what to do when issues arise become especially important. In extreme cases (typically, "gross negligence") board members may be held personally liable for actions of the board that violate the law or the foundational documents. Regular conversation about the legal duties of board members and a written covenant of board behavior are good ways to strengthen every member's native sense of what is right.

Important as the duties of board members are, a board is more than a collection of individuals, so from our reflections on the duties of board members, we move now to the duties of the board itself.

MODES OF BOARD GOVERNANCE

How should a board carry out its role? Bylaws and other foundational documents define the purpose, powers, and duties of the board. Unfortunately, beyond their general statement of the board's purpose (which often is quite thoughtful), such documents are often not much help. They frequently preserve ideas about boards that belong to an earlier era. They also tend to overemphasize problems because new provisions are most likely to be added during times of conflict. Over time, sections about how to address problems overwhelm the parts that describe healthy functioning.

Foundational documents appropriately focus on the legal aspects of a board's role, in particular on the extent and limits of its powers. But most boards have more power over congregational life than they possibly can use well on their own. Effective boards don't try. Instead they choose a few crucial areas where the board's contribution is essential and unique—and delegate the rest. To focus its attention, a board has to put firm boundaries around its own agenda. It remains responsible for everything under its authority—but controls some things directly, shares control of others, and delegates yet others fully. To achieve this level of self-discipline, a board needs a better-nuanced understanding of its role than foundational documents alone are likely to provide.

The board makes its most important contributions to the mission in three ways: by being a good *partner* to ministry leaders, by hosting an ongoing *conversation* about the future, and by creating a sound structure of *policy* to regulate decision-making.

Governance by Partnership

Creating and sustaining a strong partnership between itself and the main clergy leader is one of a board's most crucial contributions. In some congregations, the board hires and fires the clergy. In others, the congregation, regional authorities, or a combination share those powers. But in every congregation, the board has a unique opportunity to give support, feedback, advice, warnings, and encouragement to the clergy leader and to enhance his or her effectiveness as a result. Creating a good partnership is not a technical or legal project but a relational one. Some relaxed social time together helps but only if the board and clergy leader also work together gently and persistently to address misunderstandings and conflicts as they occur, so hurt and anger don't accumulate.

For the congregation, the most powerful symbol of the partnership of governance and ministry is the way the senior clergyperson and the most visible lay board member act when they appear together in the presence of others. President and rabbi, council chair and pastor, minister and clerk of session—these individuals, or their equivalents with other titles, reflect and represent the tone of the whole leadership. If possible, they should appear before the congregation often to affirm the importance of each other's role, to teach by example about healthy boundaries and effective conflict management, and to visibly enjoy their jobs. If their actual relationship is so bad that they can't do this, then they should make extraordinary efforts to improve it; if they still can't, then one of them needs to resign. If they can't choose which, then the board should help them. It makes no sense at all for a congregation to pay good money (or even mediocre money) for the privilege of watching leaders gradually whittle one another down to nothing.

Congregations without paid clergy—whether because they can't afford them or because they are lay-led on principle, like Christian Scientists and many Quakers—still need to nurture partnership. In small congregations, the difference between governance and ministry may be a subtle one. Small-congregation boards spend most of their time managing because there's no one else to do it. When they do find time to govern—perhaps on an occasional retreat—some board members will embrace the chance to plan and dream, while others keep their "ministry" hats on, continually tugging conversation back to urgent practical concerns. And there it is: the challenge to create a healthy partnership between two groups. The smallest congregation—just like a gigantic one with a large paid staff—can benefit from knowing that the tasks of governance and ministry are different and that a healthy partnership between them requires time and nurture.

A healthy partnership takes more than a good chart and rulebook. No paper structure is so perfect it eliminates the need for human skills. On the other hand, a better structure makes it easier for boards and clergy to build creative partnership and in the process lay the social underpinnings for success at anything the congregation chooses to accomplish.

Governance by Conversation

In theory, most North American congregations give their members an important role in governance—with less variation than you might expect based on differences in their historic polity traditions. But in practice, congregational business meetings make only a few significant decisions. In many congregations, membership meetings are routinized and scripted to the point that real decision-making rarely happens.

Congregations have to vote on certain matters, which may include electing members of the board, approving budgets, calling and discharging clergy, amending bylaws, and purchasing and selling real estate. But regardless of the congregation's size, attendance at congregational meetings rarely exceeds one hundred. Participation typically is skewed toward current officeholders and long-term, older members. Business items are presented as complex packages reflecting hours of preparation by staff, boards, and committees, discouraging an ordinary member from trying to affect them at the meeting.

The budget, for example, may consist of pages of small items carefully prepared by experts. The treasurer explains it all, making it clear, for instance, that "no one unfamiliar with the details of the Metzger Trust" could possibly intelligently question the "bridge loan from the temporarily restricted missions holding fund." "In laymen's terms," he adds, "we're borrowing (ha-ha) from ourselves."

After such an explanation comes an awkward silence, followed by a long debate about the postage budget, which decreased despite the fact that—as we all know—first-class stamps are rising. Is this thrift? A shift to e-mail? A mistake? Nobody knows, but this does not stop members from expressing their opinions. To be prudent—or possibly to salvage the appearance of congregational control—someone moves to add two hundred dollars to the postage budget, with directions to the finance committee to find a way to bring the budget back into balance. The motion passes; so does the budget. This is a most unsatisfactory, pretend kind of democracy!

Next on the agenda: the election of board members. This process is not much better. The nominating committee offers either a single slate or a competitive one. The single-slate approach suggests that, unless someone is angry enough to mount an insurrection, the nominating committee's wisdom is to be preferred to the congregation's. A competitive slate produces an annual crop of losing candidates who swear they never will subject themselves to this embarrassment again. It also makes for an appearance of democracy, but in the absence of real platforms or campaigning, the appearance rings a little false.

Can congregational meetings become more than empty pantomimes? I think so, but the key is not so much a new approach to business meetings but a better conversation between meetings. By the time a budget is balanced and spreadsheeted, it's too late to question its first principles. Once a slate of nominees or a clergy candidate has been presented, it's too late to suggest criteria by which they might have been recruited in the first place. For congregants to have an influence on congregational direction, they need to be brought into the conversation sooner.

The first step toward a budget, for example, is to choose a set of goals for the budget to accomplish. The first step toward the choice of a new clergy leader is to describe the role the congregation needs that leader to play in fulfilling its mission in the years to come. The first step toward the election of a board is to form some notion of the challenges the board will tackle and the scope of talents, passions, and experience the board needs, considering the vacancies created by the members going off. Behind all of these first steps is a vision—possibly a long-term vision, certainly a short-term one—of the new and different ways the congregation means to fulfill its mission in the future. That conversation about vision—not the postage budget—is where members of the congregation can make a difference.

Congregations, even small ones, are too thinly dispersed to manage their own agendas. They depend on leaders to pose well-chosen questions at a rate the larger group can manage—preferably before the leaders have made up their minds about the answers—and to invite the congregation into dialogue about those questions over time. I am talking about real dialogue, real conversation—not surveys, premature straw votes, or other mechanistic ways of bringing closure without making contact between people.

Chapter 8 offers some suggestions about how to accomplish such a conversation. In most congregations it would be a major step toward wide participation if eighty to one hundred members—the same number who now dutifully appear at business meetings—met throughout the year for conversation and discernment about questions of importance. Then when the board presents a budget, a slate of officers, and a few other crucial items for consideration at the annual meeting, it would also show how these agenda items and the rest of the board and staff's work over a year's time reflect the wisdom of the wider group.

Governance by Policy

Our conceptual map (see figure 4.1) suggests that one important way the board speaks to the staff is through policy. But what is a policy?

Many actions of a board control only a single event: Spend this money. Hire this staff member. Admit this family to membership. Let this organization rent the parish hall. Ineffective boards wait for business to be brought to them, deciding each case one at a time. This way of operating may make the board feel powerful, but a board that operates this way has long, frustrating meetings but little to show for them at year's end.

A stronger way for boards to exercise their power is by writing policies that define the board's own role, delegate authority, give guidance, and create accountability. Policies provide a framework for decisions to be made away from the board table. By policy, the board fixes responsibility for making decisions, protects human and material resources against loss, and sets standards for the conduct of the congregation's work. By policy, the board takes hold of the big picture, so that it can safely leave all smaller matters to be decided elsewhere.

A policy controls many events over time. A policy might say who can sign checks and under which conditions, establish a process for hiring staff, or create a guideline for the kind of group that can rent space in the building. Policy allows consistent, accountable decision-making and saves the board a lot of time and tedium.

Policy is not the same as precedent—though many boards believe they're making policy when actually they are deciding cases. Like medieval kings sitting as courts of last resort, such boards receive petitions and set precedents. Over time, they get so used to letting others spoon-feed business to them that they have no agenda of their own.

One way for a board to escape from this reactive posture is to resist deciding cases and insist on making policy instead. A board that means to govern by policy will question any agenda item that affects just one event. For example, a group might come to ask the board's permission to rent the social hall to a yoga teacher. The group talks about the teacher's background and credentials, her way of integrating yoga with the congregation's own tradition, and the plan for sharing space and furniture. It's all important, but it isn't policy because the board is being asked to say yes or no to only this one rental.

The board can respond in one of two ways. It can take the issue up, consider all the facts, and make a decision. In the process, board members will probably raise issues the petitioners did not think of, such as rental rates, janitorial services, liability insurance, and actual or possible conflicting uses of the social hall by groups that may or may not have been part of the conversation about yoga. No doubt, board members will express a range of thoughtful and offhand opinions about how a Hindu practice should or should not be appropriated by the congregation. And almost inevitably, the board will either vote without reflecting much on all these issues—or delay by seeking input from a wider range of stakeholders.

A well-ordered board handles such requests quite differently. Preparation starts well in advance, with a written policy about how to make decisions about rentals. Typically the board will delegate this power to the head of staff, who delegates in turn to a paid or unpaid rental manager. In its policy, the board tries hard to include everything it needs to say about rentals—their purpose, any types of rentals that are not permitted, and whatever other guidance the board wants to give. Having done all this, the board refuses from then on to accept rental matters onto its agenda, leaving them to the person it has put in charge. When people try to appeal rental decisions to the board (and they still will), its response is guided by specific questions:

- Has our policy been violated? If so, then we will address that violation with the head of staff.
- Do we need a policy we do not have, or do we need to change a policy we do have? If so, then when the time is right, we will review our rental policy. In the meantime, current policy—and decisions properly made under it—stands.
- Does this particular rental decision create a great injustice or a serious risk to someone's safety or our reputation? Only in such exceptional cases, the board may choose to seize direct control of rentals temporarily until such time as it can safely delegate them once again.

No board delegates everything. A few one-time decisions are so wide reaching in their implications—for example, moving to a new location or making a major change in program emphasis—that almost any board would choose to make rather than to delegate them. But such decisions are not common. Any agenda item that affects just one event should prompt board members to ask, Does this decision have such wide or lasting implications that it qualifies as an exception to the rule that boards ought to make policy instead of making management decisions? If so, then there might be an appropriate agenda item for the board. If not, the board will do itself a favor by allowing the decisions made under its existing policies to stand.

Governance by policy creates a boundary around the board's agenda—a basis to say no to most of the proposals, conflicts, and complaints that whirl around in every congregation. By creating places for decisions to be made away from the board table, the board frees itself to spend time on matters where it makes its highest contribution. In the long run, no list of one-off management decisions will matter more than the board's success at its main relational tasks—partnering with the clergy leader and engaging the wider congregation in conversation about the future. Policy creates a boundary that protects the board's ability to focus on its most important work.

Once the board has put a good structure of policy in place, tinkering with policy should not take up much of its time. But writing that initial set of policies is a tedious and complex chore. Chapter 10 walks through the creation of a book of policies adapted to the needs of a particular congregation. Appendix B gives an example of a complete book of policies to show how all the pieces work together to create a structure for the work of governance and ministry. After the structure is complete, the board can look forward to spending more time governing by partnership and governing by conversation.

BOARD SIZE AND COMPOSITION

What is the right size for a board? An oft-cited rule of thumb is that a board should be large enough to get its work done but small enough to work as a single team to communicate, deliberate, and function as a single body. A board needs to be large enough that its members bring various kinds of specialized knowledge: in congregational programs, organizational development, finance, real estate, law, and staff leadership. Each major group in the congregation needs to see at least one member on the board its members trust and who understands what they are trying to accomplish and how. These considerations, taken by themselves, might argue for a board of twelve or more, up to the full membership of the congregation.

But the larger the board, the more it is apt to have inconsistent attendance, weak preparation and participation, side conversations, and other signs that all of its members are not fully engaged. A great deal of research on the optimal size for a governing board has produced many answers, most of which fall between seven and twelve members. My own view is that from a group-dynamics standpoint the ideal size is seven and that considerations of workload and the need for diversity can justify a slightly larger group. It is very rare to find a board of more than nine that works as an effective, single team.

A group of seven (including everyone in the room, voting or nonvoting) finds it relatively easy to retain control of its agenda, to hear from every member, and to keep each member feeling 100 percent responsible for the board's work. Even from the point of view of democracy, a seven-member board has some surprising advantages. Unlike a larger board, it can be under no illusion that its members fully "represent" the congregation. Small boards know that, if they want congregational support (and they do need it, whether they like it or not!), they have to engage constituents in continual two-way communication through committees, surveys, town meetings, and informal one-to-one exchange. A large board has all it can do to achieve a quorum and bring board members up to speed, so they can discuss and vote. Having done that work, the board may feel democratic, even though the entire process has been internal to the board. A small board is continually reminded—simply by looking around the table—that it is too small to represent the congregation without communicating with the other members actively.

Reducing the board to seven members often is not politically realistic, especially in congregations with fewer than about 250 active members. Larger congregations, interestingly enough, more often see the value of a smaller board. It does become apparent in a congregation of two thousand members that a board of twenty-five represents no great advance of democracy over a board of seven.

Many secular nonprofits and some congregations with boards too large to function as a single team are frank in saying that they see the full board more as a way of honoring and encouraging large donors, while the management does the actual governing. This seems to me a much bigger defeat for participative governance than a small board would be.

A work-around for congregations where it is not feasible to shrink the board to manageable size is to appoint an executive committee and give it a more clearly defined job than most executive committees have. The typical executive committee makes all the decisions the board should make, plans board meetings to ensure that that those decisions will be ratified, and spends most of its time participating in management rather than in governing. A better way, in my view, is to think of the executive committee as the governing board—with the same purpose, role boundaries, and relationships as the "board" described in this book. The larger board then functions as a sort of permanent, empowered focus group, whose purpose is to stand in for the congregation as the board vets its upcoming decisions, ponders open questions, and discerns the congregation's mission and purpose.

The board's job is to represent the mission. In an institution with so many centuries of precedent behind it, this might seem to be a small task. But in our time, shifts in public attitudes have shaken faith communities to their foundations. Boards, in partnership with clergy, staff, and congregants, are stripping "mission" to its fundamentals, questioning many of our most familiar habits, and asking, Who must we be now? For work like this, no less than the best tools and the best techniques will do. And so I turn now to the board's most basic tool, the meeting, to sharpen it for challenges to come.

6

PRODUCTIVE BOARD MEETINGS

Many board members are dissatisfied with their current way of doing business. They realize they should be "looking at the big picture" or "setting overall direction," but instead they spend much of their time passively listening to reports and talking about pressing but ultimately minor decisions. Some boards float on clouds of happy talk about how well everything is going; others wallow in a bog of problems and complaints. Boards spend a lot of time talking about financial matters, even when some of their members cannot answer basic questions about the congregation's finances. Almost all boards hear too much from a few members and too little from the rest. No wonder so many board members doubt that they are making enough difference to justify their gift of time to the congregation.

The time involved is large. The next time you attend a meeting, count the people present. If there are twenty and the meeting runs two hours, it will consume a forty-hour workweek. One response to this alarming fact might be to rush through the meeting so that it ends sooner. A better response is to put only important work on the agenda and use procedures appropriate to what is to be accomplished. A short, pointless meeting is better than a long one, but a productive meeting trumps them both. If a board is going to use up forty hours of its members' time, it should accomplish a week's worth of good.

This is no small order. To be productive, a board needs to take control of its agenda, so it can devote its precious time to the best uses. It needs a repertoire of ways to meet, so it can match the most effective method to each stage in its deliberations about every topic. Having learned to do these things, it needs to institutionalize them, so it won't fall back on its old habits.

POOR ROBERT AND HIS RULES

For many people, *Robert's Rules of Order* is the starting point in thinking about how to run a meeting. This venerable resource is the official parliamentary authority for many congregations and functions unofficially as such in many others. *Robert's* has come in for quite a bit of criticism, some of it justified. Meetings run by *Robert's* can be dull and irritating, with a stereotyped agenda (call to order, reading of the minutes, officer reports, committee reports, old business, new business, adjournment) and much talk of motions and amendments and amendments to amendments. The more mysterious *Robert's* motions—to refer, defer, suspend the rules, adopt the previous question, and place on the table, not to mention arcane interruptions like the point of order, parliamentary inquiry, and question of privilege—are enough to tempt even the most tradition-minded board member to table the whole *Robert's* concept and begin from scratch.

While I understand and sympathize with these frustrations and share many of them, I must rise to defend Brigadier General Henry Martyn Robert, who is less to blame than people think. Quite a bit of the rigidity often ascribed to *Robert's Rules* is nowhere to be found in the book—the self-published 1876 original, the 1915 classic, or the even the endlessly expanded series of "revised" editions.[1] Robert himself is actually pretty flexible: He allows an assembly to adopt its own rules, to proceed as informally as it likes, and to follow any order of business it agrees upon. The original *Robert's* says next to nothing about boards, and the author surely would agree with his revising editors, who say that a small board (twelve or less) may discuss an issue without first putting a motion on the floor; receive a motion without waiting for a second; and talk until everybody has been heard without allowing motions (like the previous question), which, if passed, would squelch debate. The chair of a small board participates in the discussion and votes (unless the bylaws require otherwise) along with everybody else.[2] So far as Robert is concerned, even a large assembly can break into small groups, brainstorm onto newsprint, and burst into song—so long as everyone is given a fair chance to speak to the whole group before it votes.

Poor Robert wrote his rules after trying unsuccessfully in 1863 to chair a fractious meeting at First Baptist Church, New Bedford, Massachusetts, when he was a young lieutenant recovering from a fever. The congregation equipped him with "rules" that said vaguely religious things like "love and be kind to one another." Anybody who has poured such balm onto a church fight knows how combustible pious but ambiguous admonishments can be. Wrote Robert, "One can scarcely have had much experience in deliberative meetings of Christians without realizing that the best of men, having wills of their own, are liable to attempt to carry out their own views without paying sufficient respect to the rights of their opponents."[3] Robert had seen meetings railroaded by the determined few, and he wanted rules that would ensure that, in the future, each voice would be heard and each vote counted. Robert's purpose, if not every single one of his procedures, should be ours as well. In using *Robert's* with a grain of salt, boards should be careful to preserve the rights he wanted to protect:

- The right of the majority to rule
- The right of individuals to speak and vote
- The right of significant minorities (for Robert, one-third or more) to slow the process down so they can try to persuade others[4]

Although Robert's basic goals are as valid now as ever, his specific rules fall short of modern boards' requirements. For one thing, they are complex enough that "experts" sometimes use them to accomplish just the sort of railroad job that Robert wanted to prevent. Several simpler parliamentary manuals have tried to correct this problem, but so far, none has achieved wide enough acceptance to succeed as an alternative to *Robert's*.[5] Under any set of parliamentary rules, the chairperson needs to keep things simple and make sure that everyone can follow what is happening.

A second major shortcoming of *Robert's* as a guide to congregational and board decision-making is that it works best for "deliberative" meetings, where contending factions argue and the majority decides. But decision is only one useful result that can come out of a meeting. Other outcomes—creative thought and insight, deepened appreciation of personal differences, discernment of God's will—become more likely when meetings are conducted by less formal and contentious methods.

BOARD MEETING AS WORKSHOP

Often a creative "workshop" atmosphere provides a better way to start considering a question, leaving *Robert's Rules* for the decision stage. Workshop facilitation is an art in itself. I suggest a few of the techniques that have proved most helpful in board meetings.[6]

The Go-Around

To establish an egalitarian atmosphere, it is essential, early in the meeting, to bring every member fully into the discussion. A simple way to do this is by having a quick go-around. Ask a question that invites a one-sentence response—for instance, "What did you miss to be here tonight?" "How did this congregation touch your spirit in the past month?" or "Say one word that expresses part of how you're feeling as we start our meeting." The go-around accomplishes at least two things: It gives an opportunity for anyone who may be bursting with some bad (or good) news to get it out before it interferes with his or her participation. The go-around allows such news to surface early and gives others a chance to respond supportively.

A second major benefit stems from a fact of group psychology: If everybody speaks at the beginning of a meeting, even if some of them say, "I pass," then the group will share airtime more equitably from then on. The go-around helps to avoid one of the most time-wasting patterns boards experience, which is that the views of certain board members are not made part of the conversation soon enough. Sometimes the first sign of dissent comes when a member votes against—or worse, abstains from voting on—a motion that appeared until that moment to have had unanimous support. While it may *seem* efficient to move on, taking silence for assent, assent is not necessarily what silence means. After the meeting, members who held their peace may subtly—or not so subtly—undermine the board's decision. A go-around can be a helpful way to encourage board members to fulfill their duty of care by taking part in board discussion and their duty of loyalty by expressing their dissent at meetings of the board, not waiting until afterward.

The go-around is a good meeting starter and can be helpful now and then throughout a meeting also. For all their seeming rationality, boards are emotional systems composed of people who, at any moment, carry feelings, prejudices, attitudes, and preoccupations that control the meeting whether they are recognized or not. The go-around honors the complexity of a roomful of human beings and helps them to become a board more capable of thinking, feeling, choosing, and discerning as a group.

Small Groups

If group process were the sole consideration, the ideal board would have seven members. Any increase over seven increases the risk that some board members will feel less than 100 percent responsible for the board's work. Signs of this include absenteeism, nonparticipation in discussion, and failure to prepare. "Speaking before a group" is one of the most common phobias; for those who suffer from it, an audience of twelve can be quite frightening. If your board is large, you can still help it to gain some of a smaller board's advantages by dividing sometimes into smaller groups.

Suppose, for instance, that a board of twenty-five has an important decision to make. If a group that large begins with a motion and debate, in standard *Robert's Rules* style, it might hear at length from two or three members who are (1) comfortable speaking to a group of twenty-five and (2) already have opinions. If the motion was presented as the report of a committee, the "debate" may take the form of questions and criticisms for the committee representative, who speaks several times in order to explain, defend, or clarify the report. After the most opinionated members have spoken, a strong impression will have been created that one side or the other has the advantage—or that the group is evenly divided. At that point, someone "calls the question"[7] and a vote is taken. Often the decisive argument is that the board ought to respect (that is, approve) the work of its committee, which might make you wonder why the congregation needs a board, or that a majority of the board should rule, which might make you wonder why it needed a committee. Whatever the outcome, a large board that follows a formal, large-group debate model stacks the odds against creative interchange or increased understanding.

A better method is to break a big board into groups after the report but before the motion has been put. For this step, the chairperson may hand over leadership to someone else, either to make use of special workshop-facilitation skills or simply to punctuate the transition to a different kind of meeting. The facilitator asks the board to form for a few minutes into groups of two, three, four, or five. The first instruction to the small groups might be, "Please come up with three questions about the report we have just heard," or "State three religious values that inform your reflections on this issue," or "Think of a Bible story about a time God's people faced a situation similar in some way to this one."

After five or ten minutes (the facilitator should announce the time frame in advance and warn the groups when time is nearly up), ask one group to give *one* of its responses to the question. Rather than walking through a full report from each small group (a procedure likely to be so slow and repetitive that the board will never want to hear "small groups" again), the facilitator repeats the first response and says, "Whose group said something different on the theme of _____?" When the variations on the first theme are exhausted, the chair repeats the process—listing the major themes (not individual responses) on newsprint or a whiteboard.

At this point, the board returns, if it wishes, to a normal business session, knowing that each member, having spoken at least once in the small group, is more likely to speak to the full board and that the full range of opinion has at least been voiced somewhere in the room. Or it can postpone formal consideration until next month and perhaps commission an ad hoc committee to gather data or prepare a process for that meeting. A large group is still a large group, but even a brief detour into small-group mode improves its capacity to speak and listen.

Huddles for Staff and Volunteers

Another way of using subgroups for board meetings makes clergy hair stand up whenever I mention it: Why not hold a brief board session now and then without the clergy present? Strange as this idea may seem, it parallels a standard practice in the corporate world, where many boards have been exposed as passive rubber stamps for management. The Sarbanes-Oxley Act of 2002—a US federal law enacted in response to scandals at Enron, WorldCom, and other corporations—recognizes the important difference between board members who are and are not on the company payroll. Sarbanes-Oxley gives a special role to "independent" board members as guardians of governance, critics of management strategy, and arbiters of CEO compensation. Rules adopted under Sarbanes-Oxley by the stock exchanges require that outside board members be a majority of the board and that they meet regularly by themselves.[8] The rationale is simple: If nonemployee board members are to play a special role, then they need to meet alone from time to time.

Most of Sarbanes-Oxley does not apply to nonprofits or congregations directly,[9] but the logic behind separate gatherings of distinctive groups of board members is persuasive. In the secular nonprofit world, many boards hold a short "board huddle" without the head of staff at the end of each board meeting.[10] All volunteer board members have a brief conversation about how the meeting went and raise any concerns. Immediately afterward, the chair or other designated leader briefs the head of staff about any concerns or issues raised during the board huddle, especially anything touching on the board's relationship with staff.

This works for some congregations, but I suggest a different approach. Instead of asking anyone to leave, divide the board into two or more "huddle" groups for a limited time during the meeting. The groupings might vary from time to time, but one group should normally include the clergy leader and any other paid staff who may be present and perhaps the board chair. The other group or groups consist of volunteer board members. The agenda for this time is board self-management: How are we doing as a board? Are there interpersonal tensions among board members that are getting in the way? What went especially well? What would we do differently if we could? Are there topics we need to raise that are not coming up in the full group? Other items can be added to the huddle agenda by agreement.

After the huddle, the board reconvenes to hear from a reporter for each group. Issues that require further board attention—perhaps in a brief conversation on the spot or in a future board agenda—are noted in the minutes. Nonboard concerns are referred to be addressed one to one, within the staff group, or in some other setting.

The board huddle is not to be confused with an executive session, which is a meeting held to deal with sensitive or confidential matters, from which the board may (or must) exclude those who should not be involved in order to protect confidentiality or other important interests. Executive sessions may, and generally do, include the head of staff.

The board huddle is different. Staff members are not ejected but withdraw into a separate group, so volunteer board members have a chance to meet on their own. The board huddle has a defined agenda, and it is not appropriate to take official action until the full board reconvenes. Even if the head of staff is not a member of the board, such action would betray the trust that underlies the huddle practice.

Some congregations have good reason to worry that board members might exercise poor judgment in a huddle or that not everyone will be quite kind or candid afterward. These are important worries, and I would not initiate the huddle practice in the midst of a high conflict without skilled facilitation. On the other hand, *not* holding a huddle is no guarantee that everyone will use good judgment in the parking lot! The huddle practice may not be for every board, but it has helped some boards to raise and address important issues promptly, clear the air, and maintain trust.

Shared Study and Spiritual Practice

In many churches, board members expect the spiritual life of the board to start and end with a prayer by the pastor. Group prayer is fine, but I know of no tradition that requires prayer to be led by an ordained leader. I would encourage any board to give its clergy a year's vacation from praying at board meetings, so lay members can take turns doing it themselves. Synagogue boards commonly hear a *d'var Torah* (literally, "a word of Torah") from the rabbi at the beginning of board meetings, a practice I would recommend to anyone. The rabbi comments briefly on a Torah text, connecting it to something about the organizational life of the synagogue or even something on the board's agenda—preferably without taking sides. Here, too, I would encourage sharing leadership of spiritual exercises with lay board members.

One useful format for group reflection on a text is sometimes called African (or Lambeth) Bible study. A text is read three times, possibly by different readers, perhaps in different translations. After each reading, members respond to a simple question ("What one word or image stays with you from this passage?" "How does this passage touch you personally?" "How might this passage inform our work this evening?"). A small board can go around the table hearing a response from every member; if the group is larger, it can break into subgroups of three to five. With a leader who can keep the group on task, even a full three-reading study can occur in fifteen or twenty minutes—too much for every month, perhaps, but not too much to spend on bringing the stories of the larger faith community to bear on the board's work once in a while.

USING COMMITTEES

The committee is perhaps the most familiar form of small-group process used by boards. Most "committees" in churches and synagogues have charge of an activity, like education, worship, building maintenance, or social service. You know by now that if I ran the world, most of what are called committees in congregations would be called teams. In effect, they function as departments doing ministry.

But some committees really are committees: They don't exist to manage operational work but to help the board or other parent body to be more productive. The board, for instance, might be thinking about how to make more space for offices while preserving the option of providing extra space for worship in the future. After talking for a while, the board realizes that this issue is a complicated one, so it "commits" the matter to a small group—a committee—to look into it and report back. This is the old *Robert's* idea of a committee, and it's not a bad idea. A committee can often help its parent board to address a subject better than the board could do on its own, especially if the board is large or the subject calls for technical analysis. The best committees accomplish a great deal—generating and evaluating new ideas, enabling boards to make wiser decisions.

And yet for some time, the committee has been out of style. In an old cartoon by Charles Addams, a man and his son walk through a park and look at statues, each of which depicts a little clutch of people. "There are no great men, my boy," the father says, "only great committees."[11] We laugh. A great committee—how absurd! How could a committee possibly be good, or even great?

The Good Committee

There is reason to be skeptical. Some boards refer business to committees in a more or less frank effort to evade responsibility. "Good" committees go along with this. Many boards, for instance, confronted with the need to choose a carpet color for the sanctuary renovation will appoint a committee. The committee obtains samples, holds listening sessions, and reports back to the board. The board approves the recommended color (puce), piously intones its gratitude to the committee, and moves on.

What's wrong with this? The board correctly understands that picking a carpet color would be a poor use of its limited time, so it simply passes it to a committee, whose job is mainly to take heat for a decision guaranteed to be controversial. The board gives no guidance, no criteria for the committee to work with. And twice the board spends time talking about carpet without actually contributing to the conversation. One wonders why the board needs to approve the final choice at all. If the committee is so much more expert than the board, then why not simply let them choose and buy the carpet? Better yet, why not integrate the carpet-color experts into a renovation project team? The board then can instruct the team about the project's larger purpose, set constraints, and expect the project leaders to make all of the smaller choices in accord with those instructions.

For a carpet color, passing the buck to a committee may be relatively harmless (unless you really hate the color), but it's not so harmless when boards use the "carpet color" model to design new staff positions, write budgets, or create strategic plans. Mission-critical decisions—decisions like "What top priorities for program growth must next year's budget support?" or "What new ministry results will this renovation help us to produce?"—affect ministry priorities for months or years. If the board's job is to "own" the congregation in behalf its mission, then it should engage such choices itself, not fob them off on a committee.

The Great Committee

A "good" committee accepts its charge, completes it, and eases the board's stress. But for mission-critical decisions, the board needs a committee that is not just good, but great. A great committee scrutinizes the board's charge and demands more guidance if it needs it. Rather than relieving the board's stress, it helps the board to face its most important questions and address them after full and open conversation.

Ideally, a board would never hand a matter over to a committee without giving adequate guidance at the same time. This is not easy: It means saying up front everything the board has to say about the matter. What are the goals to be achieved and the criteria that must be met? Under what conditions would the board reject a course of action? Great committees do not spare the board this work. If the board's initial charge gives insufficient guidance, then they ask such questions as: What are the goals this budget must support? What are the principles that should underlie staff compensation? What difference do we mean to make in the lives of our young people through the behavior policies you want us to draft? How many people and what kind of programs do we mean to accommodate in our new building?

Sometimes, in response to questions of this kind, board members respond by identifying concrete options they prefer, such as a specific budget item, salary level, youth program, or a room they want in the new building. In response, a great committee asks, "What is important about that?" in order to get at the values behind board members' preferences. If the answer is still too concrete, the committee asks again, "What is important about *that*?" These are hard conversations; they can feel like squeezing the last drop of juice from a lemon.

In exasperation, board members might say, "We don't know what we want. That's why we appointed a committee." Really? The board has nothing to say about its underlying values, vision, and goals? Good committees accept this; great ones press on. If the board cannot or will not give a proper charge, then the committee may need to draft one for the board to approve.

Having obtained a values-laden charge, a great committee prepares for a great board conversation. Even if the board would like a simple recommendation it can vote on, a great committee resists quick closure on a mission-critical decision. It gathers data, analyzes options, and reaches out to experts and stakeholders. It does not dump all of its raw data onto the board table but presents a short list of the major options and explains why different values, visions, and priorities might lead reasonable people to arrive at different choices. It might paint a picture of each major scenario to dramatize its likely ministry results, its secondary consequences, and its costs. And it suggests a process that allows board members to talk about their values, learn what is most important in the data, and "live into" each of the scenarios before making a decision.

Good committees produce recommendations and get them adopted; great committees set the table for important conversations at the board itself. Great committees lead, not by getting their way, but by clarifying issues, gathering data, and posing questions that enable the board and the entire community to make their most important choices for themselves.

Boards are apt to be most grateful to the good committees because good committees make the board's life easier. Great committees make boards more effective. For a board to benefit from the help great committees offer, it has to clear management decision-making from its agenda and teach its members to expect at least one major conversation about a mission-critical decision each time the board meets.

POWERFUL AGENDAS

When I was a parish minister with young children at home, I made it known to all boards and committees that I would be going home at nine o'clock. At the beginning of each meeting, I reminded the group about my curfew and said, "If there's something on your agenda that you need me to be here for, please put it early." An interesting thing happened: From that day on, almost every meeting ended at nine. The simple act of stopping to think, "What are the most important items on our agenda?" was enough to sharpen every meeting's focus. When the time came to work on unimportant items, we went home instead.

My children are grown now, but when I plan a meeting or attend one planned by someone else, I still ask, "When will we go home?" and "What are the most important things we need to accomplish in this meeting?" Anyone can ask these questions! The best meetings shape their agendas around the most important items. The point is not to end on time (though that can be a side effect) but to use time well. The agenda names each issue—perhaps as a question—and says what the board will do about it at this meeting. If the intent is to have a good first conversation on an issue, then it will say so. If the board will vote, then it says that.

A good board agenda is like a meal with a main course. In the center of the plate sits a big, future-oriented question; around the edge are the side dishes. Such an agenda is not easy to achieve. The less important items on a board agenda generally are easier to understand and have strong advocates who want board action on them now. The most important items, on the other hand, are hard to understand, have few advocates, are seldom urgent, and do not lend themselves to quick decision anyway. To focus on its most important work, a board needs ways to move the unimportant, urgent items to the edge of its agenda—or off the plate entirely—and keep what is most important central.

The Consent Agenda

One helpful way of keeping "microitems" in their place is to divide the board agenda into two parts: a consent agenda and a discussion agenda. The consent agenda contains actions the board will take without discussion. Its purpose is to deal quickly with all of the necessary but routine things the board must act on. The consent agenda has become a widely recognized practice in the nonprofit world because it is a powerful way of streamlining board meetings and keeping the board focused on its most important work.[12]

The consent agenda requires every board member to be sent a packet of materials a few days before each meeting. The same person or team that prepares the agenda is responsible for the packet—typically this is the board chair, who consults with the clergy leader and others. The board packet contains the following:

- A reminder of the time and place of the meeting.
- A listing of consent agenda items, each with a brief explanation.
- A listing of discussion agenda items, preferably one to three in number.
- A page or two of background information about each discussion item.
- All reports, including minutes of prior meetings, financial reports, committee reports, and reports from the staff and ministry teams. Deadlines and page limits for reports help keep the packet manageable.

At the beginning of the business portion of the board meeting, the board chair says, "You have all received the board packet with the consent agenda. Does any member wish to move an item from the consent agenda to the discussion agenda?" If any member requests it, an item is moved. (By courtesy, advance notice should be given to the board chair if possible.) The chair then says, "We are ready to approve the consent agenda. Hearing no objection [the chair pauses briefly], all items on the consent agenda are adopted." Note that there is no discussion about *whether* to move an item to the discussion agenda!

What sort of items go onto the consent agenda? Approval of the prior meeting's minutes. Follow-up items, such as signing a contract for a project the board has already approved or shifting small amounts of money from one budget to another pursuant to plans already approved. Empowering the business manager to open a new bank account or to adjust deductibles on an insurance policy. Updating personnel policies to conform to changes in the law. Accepting people into or releasing them from membership. Certifying the congregation's membership so it gets the right number of delegates to regional or national meetings. In short, any item that the board must act on that is uncontested or that follows logically from a decision the board already has made.

Sometimes a board has to vote on something simply because the bylaws say so or because the board by policy has chosen to reserve a class of decisions to itself. But not every decision that a board must make is worthy of board time. The consent agenda helps the board to avoid chatting about matters whose outcomes are not in serious question. A few key points about the consent agenda are important to emphasize:

- All reports are sent in the board packet, not presented or discussed at meetings, so reports as such are not part of the agenda. This includes reports from the treasurer and clergy leader! If the board needs information in support of a decision it must make, then that decision will be part of the discussion agenda (see later). The information can be given as part of the plan for that agenda item.
- Contrary to a common misconception, a board does not normally need to "approve" or even to "receive" reports. "Receiving a report" is a common parliamentary mistake, needlessly declaring what is already obvious. Approving a report makes every word in it an action of the board—rarely the desired result.[13]
- In place of the common practice of committees, staff, and officers putting business onto the board's agenda by offering proposals in their reports, all business reaches the board agenda by a single route. With fewer items, the board chair can coordinate more thorough preparation for the discussion portion of the meeting.

Having disposed, in about five seconds, of what used to take all evening, our board moves on to something more nutritious.

The Discussion Agenda

The discussion agenda contains only two or three items, plus any consent items that have been moved to it. The result is that the board spends more time addressing topics it has identified in advance as important, no time listening passively to reports, and no time responding to issues that happen to arise during board discussion of reports.

The discussion agenda is the heart of the board meeting and includes one, two, or (at most!) three important things the board will have accomplished by the time it adjourns. Ideally, these items will be so interesting and attractive that board members will look forward to them. If a small group has spent time gathering data and planning a good process, then members will go home feeling pleased about how they spent their time.

For example, an agenda might say that the board intends to address one or two questions like these:

- What are our ministry priorities for the upcoming two-year period? We will have a first discussion about our priorities, with final approval expected next month, in time to guide the making of a budget.
- How well are we fulfilling our mission with regard to youth? This agenda item, part of our ongoing process of discernment about the youth, will consist of a one-hour workshop meeting with our special intergenerational committee on youth ministry. No board action is anticipated tonight until the committee's report next April.
- Shall we make room for more people by offering worship at one or more additional sites? The board will have an open-ended, twenty-minute conversation about an idea that might become a goal during the next decade.
- Should we be in the building rental business? Based on last month's preliminary conversation, the ad hoc rentals committee has modified its proposed policy. We anticipate a final vote tonight.
- How will the congregation respond to revelations that our bank has practiced racial discrimination in its lending? The board will hear an initial presentation by the treasurer, followed by a conversation focused on such process questions as: How will we gather data? What are our options? Who needs to be involved in this decision? What steps do we need to take before deciding?

By holding up one or two such questions as the central themes of a board meeting, the agenda creates a sense of urgency about what could otherwise appear to be routine reports or pro forma approvals. Big-picture issues tend to stay around for a long time, so board agendas can be planned months in advance. A yearly routine becomes possible—with predictable recurring events, like goal-setting, evaluation, and the creation of a budget. Along the way are chances for the board to have deep background discussions about the major points of the congregation's mission, its programmatic and strategic choices, and changes in the community environment. The result may not be shorter meetings, but a well-chosen centerpiece makes the work more likely to be worthy of the time invested. In place of a dull series of small items, each meeting is a feast with a main course.

"For Discussion Only" Items

Here's a political tip: The most important virtue any proposal can have going for it is that members of the board have heard of it before. People are naturally uncomfortable with change, and so the first time any idea comes up—no matter how familiar it may be to those who propose it—the full group finds objections more quickly than it sees advantages. If a decision has to be made right after a concept is presented for the first time, then the chances are against approval.

So if you want your idea to pass—or even to be seriously considered—it is not a good idea to begin by arguing for it. Arguing (however civilized and pleasant) activates the argumentative in people, which they employ to argue back. The best first campaign for a new idea is a "mentioning" campaign. Mention that you've heard about a new idea that another congregation (possibly in California, if you're not in California) has tried. The next week, mention that you heard about a congregation trying it in Iowa (unless you are in Iowa). The third week, simply raise the general issue. If you're lucky, somebody will say, "Haven't you heard? Here's what other congregations do."

I'm partly joking, but if you want your board to have an open-minded conversation, then a good way to make it happen is to introduce ideas, options, and questions long before decision is required. Plan some agenda items that will begin, "We do not expect to make any decisions about this today." Set a time limit, provide a manageable amount of information about the item, and let the conversation flow. When time is up, say, "As planned, we have not arrived at a conclusion, so we can declare this part of the agenda a success! We will return to this topic next month, with the benefit of the head start we gave ourselves today." If a committee has been working with the board on the agenda item, some of its members should be present for the board discussion, so afterward they can reflect back to the board about what think they heard board members say. In its next report, the committee can point out how the board's discussion influenced its work.

Under time pressure, familiar ideas tend to crowd out new ones, so making space for your board to think together without an immediate deadline helps the board to consider new ideas. A meeting that is only a meeting, where the first thing said is, "We will not make a decision today," may be more productive in the long run than the "efficient" meeting where a lot is done but not much is learned.

In 1876, Henry Robert's *Rules* offered a shared basis for civic and charitable participation in a time of concentrating wealth and growing cultural diversity. We face similar challenges in our time, raised to a new level. People come to congregations now for a wide variety of reasons, bringing different hopes and values. Often the board's first task, before a motion or a parliamentary debate is even possible, is to hunt for common ground.

For that reason, boards do well to focus more on consensus-building than on getting to a vote and getting home. Consensus-building partly is about finding compromises, but mostly it's about understanding others better in the hope of fashioning a proposal that might satisfy a wider range of hopes and interests. Often all it takes for two people to find mutually satisfactory solutions is for one of them to speak convincingly of what the other holds most sacred. Only when a board attends to every member's unique testimony and patiently returns to shared first principles can it move toward unity.

Or sometimes it will move toward several clusters of opinion. Diversity is real and does not always disappear because of a good process. In the end, a board that seeks consensus does not always find it. The board then faces a dilemma because, for many of the most important matters, a majority of those voting at a meeting falls far short of what is actually required to make decisions stick, to make a project happen, or to bring about significant change. Major choices have a tragic quality because acting to fulfil the mission almost always disappoints or angers someone.

That's where *Robert's* can be helpful. The framing of a formal motion signals that the time for "We will not decide today" is over. A proposed amendment tests whether, after all, we might possibly approach consensus. And finally we vote—an exercise of power rather than persuasion, a confession of our failure to find common ground.

When consensus fails, most people in our culture accept the right of the majority to rule, so long as it respects the rights of individuals. Those who find themselves in the minority may choose to join the board's decision, openly dissent, or even quit. In any case, a thorough process and a fair decision makes it more likely that the congregation will succeed in what it chooses to attempt, while earning the goodwill of those who wish it had done otherwise.

7

SIZE MAKES A DIFFERENCE

The most important factor in deciding how to organize a congregation for decision-making is its size because no fact about a group of human beings says more about it than its size. A group of twenty people behaves differently from a group of one hundred or two hundred or four hundred or eight hundred. As a congregation grows, its leaders need to renegotiate their roles. When it shrinks, they must abandon ways of working that worked when it was larger.

In general, the larger the group, the more its formal rules describe its actual behavior. Sociologists who talk about this difference sometimes use two German words—*Gemeinschaft* and *Gesellschaft*—informal, social "community" or "culture" versus formal, businesslike "society."[1] *Gemeinschaft* is what happens naturally whenever humans (or most likely other primates) form a group: Pecking orders appear based on age, sex, kinship, strength, longevity, and appearance. Favors are exchanged. Some people like each other; others don't. Soon a little commonwealth arises, with the subtle grades of rank and deference to be found on playgrounds everywhere. In smaller groups, the logic of *Gemeinschaft* explains most of the decision-making—even if the bylaws say it should be otherwise.

Gesellschaft holds more sway in larger groups. Bylaws, job titles, mission statements, salaries, and goals account for more of the decision-making—but not all of it. It's never safe to ignore informal hierarchies and networks because, even in the largest congregations, most decision-making still takes place in small groups, like boards and staff meetings. In those small groups, *Gemeinschaft* principles assert themselves just as they do in smaller congregations. In some ways, every congregation, regardless of its size, is both an institution and a family—only the proportions vary.

For clergy leaders, moving from one size congregation to another almost feels like a career change. Like many young ministers, I started my career in a small church, then moved to a larger one. Colleagues who had made similar moves warned me I would miss the close pastoral connections I had experienced in the smaller group, and that was true. What surprised me most, though, was the change in my leadership role. In the smaller church, I would meet with lay leaders, come up with a lot of good ideas, and end up with a long list of items for my to-do list. In the larger congregation, I would meet with lay leaders, come up with a lot of good ideas, and *they* went away with items for their to-do list. Sometimes they even thanked me for my valuable time! "If this is administration," I thought to myself, "I can live with it." Size does make a difference.

On the other hand, the risk for clergy of overestimating their authority is great, even in large congregations. An old story is well worth retelling: A promising young minister arrives at his first church, a large one. Everybody tells him that the organist is horrible. "We have been suffering with Gladys now for eighteen years, and that is long enough. She's a nice lady, but she never did play well. Since she turned eighty, she has only gotten worse. You are the head of staff, and we expect you to do something." Looking at the bylaws, the young pastor sees that he is indeed the head of staff, with power to hire and fire. After consulting with the governing board and getting their encouragement, he fires the organist.

At its next meeting, the board asks for the pastor's resignation. "We think you'll make a fine pastor somewhere," they say, "but not here. Until you came, this was a friendly church. But people are complaining that you seem to think you are the CEO. There probably are pastorates where you'll do well, but not here."

What happened? Informal networks kill silently, so it is not easy to retrace their steps. No doubt Gladys, like most church staff members, had a political constituency all her own. Her supporters did not speak up in the deliberations of the formal church—the first board meeting, where the focus was on her competence as organist. In that setting, it would have felt out of place to speak of personal affection or the fact that Gladys had provided music for hundreds of funerals and weddings and had woven herself deep into the fabric of the church's life. But in the informal congregation, such considerations no doubt dominated the agenda. In this case, it was the informal congregation whose priorities won out. *Gemeinschaft* is more important in small congregations than in large ones, but it never quite goes away!

SIZE CATEGORIES

For many Protestant churches, median attendance is a good measure of size (I use the median rather than the average because it is less sensitive to high attendance on holidays or low attendance when the weather is especially good or bad). Another useful measure—in both synagogues and churches—is the number of families who make significant financial contributions. Conveniently, the two numbers tend to be approximately equal, making it possible to use synagogue membership as a rough substitute for median attendance.[2] All such numerical metrics need to be fine-tuned with attention to the other factors that affect a group's effective size, like budget, buildings, staffing, program participation, and subsidiary enterprises. For many purposes, I count children twice, on the theory that each child contributes twice as much complexity as an adult. But at the moment, we are talking mainly about organizational decision-making (as opposed to staffing, seating, parking, or financial needs), so plain attendance figures serve us nicely.

In thinking about congregation size, I follow a free interpretation of the Alban Institute size categories, proposed initially by Arlin Rothauge in a 1983 Episcopal study of new-member assimilation and updated and elaborated over the years by Alice Mann and Susan Beaumont, among others.[3] Four size categories are of greatest interest because of their differing ideas about what it means to "join":

- A *family-size congregation* (median attendance up to 100) understands itself to be a group where everyone knows everyone. Formalities aside, you truly *join* a family-size group only after you know and are known by everybody—and especially by the "parents" or informal leaders of the group. In family-size congregations, job titles by themselves mean relatively little. The power of the parents comes from their long, trustworthy service to the congregation and its members.
- A *pastoral-size congregation* (100 to 250) is a place where everybody feels connected to the clergy leader. You can tell you're in a pastoral-size congregation easily: Just ask how things are going. Without missing a beat, they'll tell you how they feel about the pastor. (Note that they don't always say they *like* the pastor!) You join a pastoral-size congregation when you feel connected to the clergy leader.

- A *multi-celled congregation* (250 to 400) is a group of subgroups. People may or may not like the worship service or feel personally connected to the clergy leader. Most of them join the congregation by joining classes, choirs, committees, teams, or potlucks—each of which functions as a family- or pastoral-size group. A multi-celled congregation needs its clergy leader to maintain a good relationship with a family-size circle of group leaders, some of whom are members of the board.
- A *professional-size congregation* (400 to 800) looks and feels like an organization. Its members and participants join primarily because they trust the institution's integrity and competence. It gives real power to official leaders, whom it chooses at least partly for their competence. Professional congregations lose members quickly if their leaders seem inept, so they need their clergy to recruit, prepare, and offer coaching and support to other leaders.

Susan Beaumont has described categories for yet larger congregations: strategic (800 to 1,200) and matrix (1,200 to 1,800). The senior clergy leader's public performance skills grow in importance with the congregation's size, as do his or her ability to lead the staff team and maintain effective partnership with senior lay leaders and donors. When people join large congregations, they do so because they trust them to deliver on their promises consistently. For friendship and community, they look almost entirely to subgroups of the congregation. For a thorough discussion of these larger size categories, I recommend Beaumont's *Inside the Large Congregation*.[4]

Plateau Zones

Leaders often find size categories confusing, especially toward the upper end of each range. A congregation with a median attendance of seventy-five is officially family size according to the previous account, but it may behave in some ways like a pastoral-size congregation, and it may have members who are strongly committed to its subgroups. Three observations may clear up some of the confusion.

First, attendance numbers are only a rough guide to the category that describes a given congregation. The real difference between categories is the congregation's understanding of what "joining" means. Second, a congregation's size category is determined by its *idea* about joining—not by the way of joining that actually works best for its new members. Third, the mismatch between a congregation's idea of joining and what works is greatest near the upper limit of each size category, which Alice Mann has called the "plateau zone." In figure 7.1, plateau zones show as areas above each dotted line.[5] The family-size category, for example, crosses into its plateau when median attendance exceeds about fifty people. The pastoral plateau starts at about 200, and the multi-celled plateau begins around 350. Growing congregations tend to get stuck in the plateau zones; declining congregations sometimes stabilize below them.

In the plateau zone, life can be stressed and confusing. A family-size congregation with a median attendance of seventy-five, for instance, still believes that "we all know each other." In reality, it's likely to have fifty people who actually know each other—and twenty-five who don't, not all of whom are newcomers. The congregation may unanimously think it is a place where "everybody knows your name," despite this being true only for the core fifty. For the rest, the promise of a family experience is not kept. Growth tends to stop in the plateau zone because a newcomer cannot truly join until there is a vacancy.

In larger, pastoral-size congregations, something similar occurs. Most members, including newcomers, believe that the right way to join is to feel connected to the clergy leader. But if more than about 150 people attend regularly (or fewer, if the clergy leader is not active in creating personal

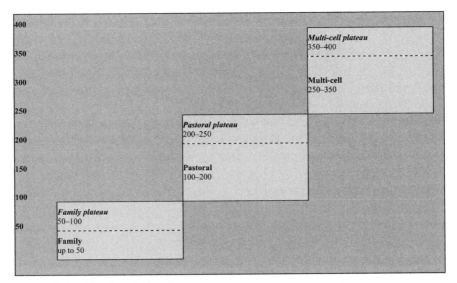

Figure 7.1. Median Attendance.

connections), then some of them are likely to feel disconnected. Often they express this feeling by complaining that the pastor or rabbi seems cold, distant, and aloof. Especially when the less-connected people are not new-comers but established members who felt closer to a prior clergy leader, their complaints can be a source of trouble. In a congregation that has vacillated for a long time at the pastoral plateau (200 to 250), the historical narrative may sound like this:

> We called a minister because she seemed so warm, bright, and caring. She attracted newcomers, and we began to grow. We added staff and started talk-ing about building a new wing. Then suddenly we found out that a group was meeting privately to complain about our pastor. They said she was cold and distant and cared more about growth and money than about people. They tried to get her fired. That failed, but pretty soon she left. We miss her, though honestly we are a bit relieved.

You can often chart the history of a pastoral-size congregation by this pattern. Whether the clergyperson stays or leaves, the pattern makes the pastoral plateau a tough one for growth-oriented congregations to break through. For declining congregations, on the other hand, the plateau may function as a safety brake. When attendance falls below about 200—the number of relationships most mortals can sustain—the remaining mem-bers feel more satisfied because the clergy leader can connect with them directly.[6] If demographic factors and the pastoral "fit" are reasonably good, then the congregation has a chance of stabilizing once again at pastoral size.

The multi-celled plateau follows a similar pattern: A congregation with median attendance of 375 probably has enough activities and programs to allow around 300 or 350 members to connect through subgroups. But to newcomers, it looks big enough that they expect a certain polish that is never quite in place. To satisfy newcomers' expectations, it must invest in paid staff at a level that is apt to seem unnecessary to leaders whose expec-tations are already met by the congregation's lifestyle as it is.

The concept of plateau may or may not apply to congregations in pro-fessional and larger size categories. There has been much debate about whether "barriers" exist at 400, 800, 1,200, or 10,000 people.[7] Because of the complexity of larger congregations, a thorough staffing and program assessment may be required in order to identify growth barriers and op-portunities. The larger the organization, the less likely it seems that growth will stabilize at predictable numerical plateaus.

STRUCTURING AT DIFFERENT SIZES

Keeping these ideas in mind, let's look more closely at the structures for decision-making that work best in congregations of the four size categories.

Family Size

A family-size congregation (see figure 7.2) is a single circle. The two most important roles are *parent* (shown as *P* in the drawing) and *gatekeeper* (shown as a smiley face). Small congregations usually have several parents—sometimes known as matriarchs and patriarchs—who share authority informally among themselves. The gatekeeper is a special parent who greets visitors at the door, sizes them up, and chooses how and whether to present them to the other parents. Before a newcomer can truly join, he or she needs a parental blessing, even if that newcomer has been selected as the clergy leader. The parents, whether currently in

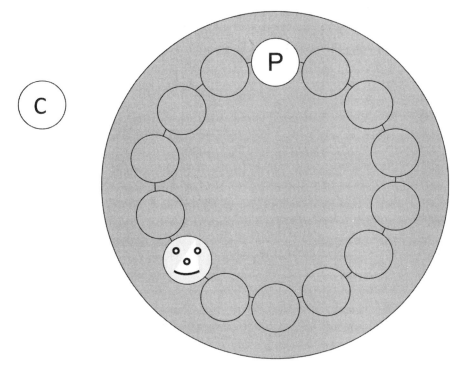

Figure 7.2. Family: Up to 100.

office or not, must consent to any major change or innovation. The governing board, unless it happens also to be a gathering of parents, ratifies decisions only after they are vetted by the parents.

The official structure of a family-size congregation often is a variant of the board-centered structure from chapter 3. But nonparent members of the board are making a mistake if they imagine that the board has power independent of the parents, even if some parents hold seats on the board. In family-size congregations, governance power resides with parents, though they may not be aware of having power at all. Good parents work to build consensus in the family and do not see a difference between their personal efforts and board or congregational decision-making. Good parents nurture younger leaders and hope to grow them into future parents—though they probably are thinking more in generations than in annual election cycles. Good parents care about their children and encourage growth and independence, at least up to a point.

But when circumstances require someone to act as the "owner"—for example, when a clergy leader is in trouble or the neighbor makes a tempting offer on the building—the parents network informally, outside the official channels. Once the parents have agreed on a plan, the board and congregation almost always ratify it. But if the governing board, or even the congregation, tries to use its formal power to act without parental support, then its plans generally fizzle.

The law generally recognizes the official structure, not the unofficial one. Nonparents (including denominational officials coming from outside the congregation) sometimes try to force adherence to the letter of the law. Sometimes they succeed, especially if their goal is to close down, merge, or liquidate the congregation. But as Roman Catholic bishops have found out when they experience a strong backlash against their decisions to close parishes, it's one thing to have formal power and another to make that power effective against local congregations and their "parents."

Astute viewers of figure 7.2 may have noticed that the clergy leader (marked as C) stands outside the circle of the family-size congregation. As a newcomer, that is where a clergy leader, if there is one, stands. Often the clergy presence in a family-size congregation is part time. It takes many years, even for a full-time clergyperson, to "join" a system based on trust and longevity. Sometimes clergy do stay long enough to become parents themselves. In such cases, it's important to remember: Parent status is a personal honor, not an automatic perk of the position. The next clergy leader starts outside the circle and stays there for a long time. Especially for new clergy, freshly educated to believe in their authority, this time of exile can be hard.

The most successful partnerships with clergy in family-size congregations start with an acceptance by the clergyperson of the limitations of the clergy role's authority. Wise clergy look for ways to make a contribution that supports the parents' understanding of the mission and negotiate for their support. This negotiation takes finesse because many parents think sincerely that all power lies with formal leaders and the congregation as a whole and not with them. It is rarely useful to dispute this charming self-delusion.

Family-size congregations readily promote newcomers into roles of leadership, often putting them in charge of ministry activities and onto boards. New leaders learn, though, that their license does not include experimenting with new methods on their own. One function of the board-centered structure is to require nonparents to check in frequently by making board reports. The board knows the accepted limits and enforces them. Only the parents as a group have the power to initiate true innovation, and the road to parenthood is paved with long, closely supervised service in accepted ways. The first step for a newcomer who wants to try something new is to secure support from a parent, who can then persuade the rest. This rule applies to clergy just as much as to lay leaders.

In a family-size congregation, the idea of a group for governance that is separate from the group that does the work of ministry can feel insulting, almost heretical, to those who have earned their place in leadership by long and faithful service. This attitude can make it difficult to create space for mission-focused governance—which is a shame because family-size congregations need to think about their mission and their future just as much as larger ones.

One solution is to separate governance from ministry conceptually rather than having separate groups. One board meeting (or part of a meeting) can be dedicated to governance and another to ministry. The board of a small church in Maine, whose members read an earlier edition of this book, bought actual hats from L. L. Bean, some of them emblazoned with a big red *G*, others with a big green *M*. Board members switched hats as a way of signaling that they had shifted (purposely or not) from talking about governance to talking about ministry. When the shift was intentional, the board shifted leadership as well—the pastor chairing meetings about ministry, a lay leader chairing those for governance. The hats were a way of recognizing that a small-church board can never completely wash its hands of "management" or even "micromanagement"—but that now and then it can still lift its eyes to the horizon and reflect about the future, so long as it respects the natural authority of parents.

In a family-size system, personal relationships trump roles, bylaws, and contracts. Wise clergy patiently discover the half-conscious network of relationships that actually governs and the equally opaque system of authority that gets work done. The most frequent error clergy and boards make in family-size congregations is to assume authority they don't have—by thinking, for example, that a major change will happen because they got the congregation to adopt it or that they can change the way the congregation makes decisions simply by tinkering with formal structures. Clergy partner most effectively with family-size congregations when they and other leaders work with parents rather than apart from them.

Pastoral Size

In the mid-1950s, Dean Samuel H. Miller of the Harvard Divinity School, speaking to an all-male graduating class, most of whom were destined for pastoral-size churches, is supposed to have said, "Gentlemen, when you get into the parish, don't use your authority . . . until you have some!" It's still good advice. In a pastoral-size congregation, the authority of clergy is based on personal trust, which can develop only over time and with help. The board and clergy leader who build relationships of trust among themselves and then invite the congregation to join them can together lay the groundwork for productive ministry.

In pastoral-size congregations, official roles like "rabbi" or "minister" carry more weight than in the family-size category because the pastoral-size idea of joining is "We all feel connected to the pastor." (Where there is no pastor, one or a few "parents" step in to play a similar role.) When it works, the pastoral-size concept looks like figure 7.3, with the clergy leader at the center, connected to each member like a hub and spokes. Feeling connected to the congregation through the pastor—which was only tolerated in the family-size group as an exception—is the rule here. The board's role is also more significant because the congregation is too large to function as a unit—socially or for decision-making. Still, in figure 7.3, the board is shown off-center, seen in its relation to the pastor more than for its own distinctive role.

All rules have exceptions. Some members of pastoral-size congregations do not feel connected to the pastor. Some feel connected only indirectly—through their spouses, for example. A few may feel connected through subgroups, as represented by the family-size grouping near the bottom

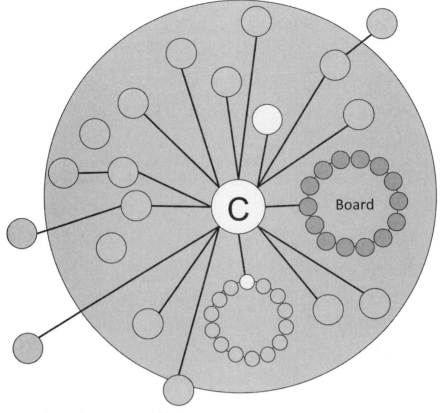

Figure 7.3. Pastoral: 100–250.

of the diagram. A choir, a social-outreach effort, or a class sometimes be-comes a primary point of loyalty for members. Because this way of "joining" violates the rule that everyone should be connected to the pastor, family-size congregations often treat people who connect through subgroups as second-class citizens. Subgroup leaders who inspire such loyalty may even be suspected of divisiveness. A strong taboo on subgroup loyalty is one way congregations keep themselves at pastoral size. To break through the pastoral-size plateau (200 to 250) in order to evolve into the multi-celled category, a congregation needs to embrace subgroups as a fully honored point of connection for new people.

Many clergy leaders understand this and encourage subgroups for the purpose of promoting growth and other worthy outcomes. Unfortunately, their efforts run against the natural *Gemeinschaft* of a pastoral-size group, which expects everyone—especially the pastor—to behave according to the hub-and-spoke arrangement in the diagram. Rather than applauding clergy for developing small groups, congregations in the pastoral-size plateau are more likely to attack them for not forming enough positive personal connections. A cycle similar to the one described earlier for family-size congregations is often seen in pastoral-size groups that push repeatedly against a ceiling of around 250, get into a fight about the clergy leader, and then cycle down again. Declining congregations often find a comfortable landing at around 100 to 200 in attendance, where the pastor can connect with everyone directly.

The board in a pastoral-size congregation occupies an awkward spot. The pastoral-size culture encourages board members to behave as a collection of individuals, each connecting to the congregation through the clergy leader. This idea often leads to heavy emphasis on praise and criticism of the clergy at board meetings, making it difficult for the board to offer strong, cohesive leadership of its own. But a congregation with as many as 500 members (corresponding to the top pastoral-size attendance of 250) is far too large to function as a single body for decision-making. To have meaningful influence, it needs its board to shape the congregational agenda by identifying the most critical decisions and providing substantive leadership. The board can hardly play this crucial role if its members speak to the congregation as individuals, expressing personal opinions without reference to board actions or positions. The larger the congregation, the more it needs its board to sort out a few truly critical decisions to be made by the congregation and to accept responsibility for making or delegating all the rest.

Lay and clergy leaders in pastoral-size congregations, much more than in family-size ones, need to be committed to each other and to have each other's back. The clergy leader needs the board to help pick priorities—and to run interference when success at sticking to priorities produces a crescendo of complaints. The board needs the clergy leader—the one person everybody knows and recognizes—to help focus attention on decisions it has made and on the questions it has chosen for wide congregational discussion. To support each other in these ways, both clergy and board members set aside their personal preferences in favor of their joint success as leaders.

Contrary to the hub-and-spoke mentality of the pastoral-size ethos, effective family-size boards and clergy leaders develop and commit to a collective viewpoint as a team of leaders. They may even come to feel that the mission calls the congregation to accomplish something that its members don't yet want—like growth, diversity, a social justice goal, or renewed appeal to younger generations. Neither partner can accomplish changes like these on its own. Together, they can choose a manageable rate of change and work together to accomplish it. The board's primary role is to build consensus and give official sanction to the chosen goals. The clergy leader builds the ministry-team structures that can implement the goals. All this requires a level of cohesion and group discipline that is not easy to achieve.

The pitfalls are many. Clergy, young and old, may be seduced into accepting too much responsibility for implementing major changes before the board has finished getting buy-in. (That's what happened to the young minister who fired Gladys the organist.) The board may find it tempting to expect the clergy leader to miraculously part the waters of resistance and lead the congregation without pain or struggle into implementing changes just because the board desires them. (This can happen when board members misunderstand figure 7.3 and think that the clergy leader, because he is so central, must have lots of power.) To lead change effectively, the board and clergy leader—plus the "parents" of the congregation's family-size subgroups—need to partner formally and firmly, in the process putting themselves somewhat at odds with the relational *Gemeinschaft* of a pastoral-size congregation.

Leaders who understand this may be tempted to move quickly into a governance change process to legitimate and formalize their efforts. This can be helpful. But especially in pastoral-size congregations, structure change is rarely a good idea in the early years of a rabbinate or ministry. The pastor's first task is to become the pastor—to join the congregation on its own terms by creating a relationship with "everyone" (that is, with at least the 150 or 200 most-connected people). Without those relationships, the clergy leader is in no position to promote substantial change or even to last long in the position. Board members can help the clergy leader to create relationships, especially in the crucial first three years. Relationships are the glue that bonds a pastoral-size congregation together. Unlike a family-size group, it needs its members to bond not only with each other but also with official, designated leaders—starting with the clergy leader and including the board also. Some of those bonds may be affectionate, others pastoral or intellectual. The one indispensable element is trust.

Multi-celled Size

In congregations that regularly see 250 to 400 people on a weekend, joining through a subgroup becomes the rule and connecting through the clergy leader the exception. Newcomers in multi-celled congregations don't generally stick around unless they join a subgroup. As figure 7.4 suggests, not everybody gets the memo. Some attach to the clergy leader directly; a

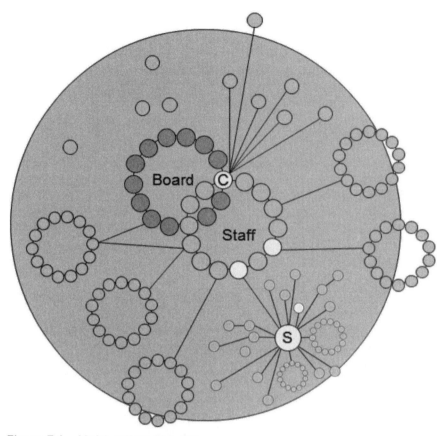

Figure 7.4.   Multi-celled: 250–400.

few seem not to be attached at all. One group of people in the diagram—
perhaps a large choir or education ministry—has grown to pastoral size
because of their attachment to a charismatic member of the staff, shown on
the diagram as *S*. But most subgroups are family size: small classes, choirs,
ministry teams, potluck groups, and mission-trip alumni.

   Leaders—many of them paid—organize, support, and tactfully disband
these subgroups, so there will always be enough fresh points of connection to accommodate newcomers. Members may say that the congregation
"feels like one big family" or that a clergyperson "makes me feel personally
cared for" in the large auditorium. On this scale, such feelings come more
from a symbolic sense of inclusion than from concrete connections. Happy
members of small groups are quite ready to attribute their strong sense of
belonging to the congregation as a whole, even though the groups are the

"families" that actually give care. Subgroups bond participants to one another, and the paid and unpaid staff who resource the subgroups bind them to the congregation as a whole.

The staff team emerges, in the multi-celled size category, as a separate group with power, opinions, and an agenda of its own. The staff team's unity is an important form of "glue" holding the congregation together. Dissension among staff is the most frequent cause of serious conflict in multi-celled (and larger) congregations, so one of the clergy leader's most important jobs is to attract, inspire, and unify a strong staff team. A new clergy leader needs to "join" the staff group, whose longer-tenured members exercise considerable influence.

As the staff emerges as a distinct entity, so does the governing board, with the clergy leader as a full participant. Clergy-board cohesion and commitment, so valuable in pastoral-size congregations, becomes utterly essential in the multi-celled environment, where centrifugal forces are quite strong. Cohesion does not mean that disagreements in the boardroom have to be suppressed. On the contrary, boards need to be constantly alert to the dangers of conformity and "groupthink." Nor does it mean board members who vote in the minority should keep this secret from the congregation. But all board members and the clergy leader do need to speak continually, respectfully, and loyally about the board's legitimate authority. The board speaks for the congregation's mission. To keep mission in the driver's seat of a complex and differentiated congregation, the board needs all the support it can get from its own members, from the staff, and from the congregation.

Some multi-celled congregations implement, in their organizational structures, something like the full "map for thinking about ministry" in chapter 4, with separate governance and ministry decision-makers. More commonly, the board retains some of its management functions and resists creating a distinct ministry decision-making structure. This partial separation of governance and ministry, suggested in figure 7.4 by overlapping board and staff groups, takes a number of forms. Some boards (especially large ones) have an executive committee, which acts as a sort of kitchen cabinet for the clergy leader, helping with management decisions while also managing the board's agenda. Another approach is to create a program council or leadership team comprised of staff and program leaders, plus perhaps some officers or board members, to do some of the reporting, calendar clearing, and conflict management work to free the board to govern. Over time, such partial steps allow one group to act more like a governing board, while the other exercises a degree of management autonomy along with staff.

This almost-but-not-quite situation creates special challenges for lay-clergy partnership. The staff of a multi-celled congregation has a lot to manage. From a staff perspective, the persistent notion that the board can helpfully participate in management can feel like play-acting. In addition to their program and administrative work, staff members spend time preparing for boards and committees to make simple, out-of-context management decisions. The board's reluctance to delegate management authority to staff means every staff member lives under two chains of command—one of committees leading up to the board, the other of staff members leading to the clergy leader. As a result, the clergy leader can feel caught between two worlds—the board's world and the staff's—that can feel rather alien to one another even when they get along.

Short of a full governance change process, boards and clergy leaders can build trust by way of an annual planning process like the one described in chapter 8. Once goals and strategies have been agreed upon, the lack of a single ministry decision-making structure creates less tension for the staff. And after a few rounds of such planning, leaders may feel ready for a more comprehensive governance-change process like the one described in chapter 9.

Professional Size and Beyond

Even in large congregations, *Gemeinschaft* does not go away. Trust and relationships still matter, even though the apparatus of *Gesellschaft*—job titles, formal agreements, goals, and roles—matters more than it does at smaller sizes. Most actual decision-making is still done in small groups—the board, the senior staff, committees, teams—where personal authority and pecking order matters. From year to year, for instance, a clergy leader's quality of life varies with the quality of his or her relationship with a succession of board members and board chairs. Too often, congregations of all sizes harm themselves by carelessly electing people to board roles to reward long service, to appease a valued "parent" or encourage a promising "child," or—worst of all—on the theory that antagonism might be useful as a counterbalance to clergy leadership. Such mistakes can be especially costly in large congregations, where people join because they trust the institution's integrity and competence. Consistent execution of ambitious plans is of the essence, with less margin for error and incompetence than smaller congregations. Large congregations need to get their money's worth out of their clergy and are smart to elect lay leaders who will support, not undermine, them.

Selecting leaders—clergy, staff, and volunteer—for their competence and willingness to work with other leaders is especially important in professional-size and larger congregations (four hundred to eight hundred and up). Members join large congregations not only because of inspiring worship or small-group experiences but also because they come to trust the institution to create such quality experiences consistently. Members of large congregations vote with their feet and do not tolerate incompetence or aimlessness for long.

A multi-celled organism can only grow so large before it must evolve and differentiate its organs for decision-making and for action. The professional-size structure shown in figure 7.5 resembles the full map of governance and ministry (see figure 4.3) because large congregations cannot leave as much to chance. Here staff and board have differentiated fully; the board a family-size democracy with the clergy leader at the table, the

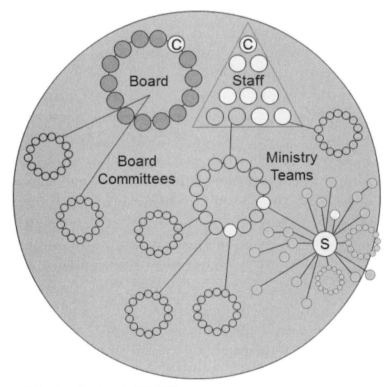

Figure 7.5.   Professional: 400–800.

staff a family-size, hierarchical work structure with the clergy leader at the head. Committees help the board to govern. Ministry teams, under staff direction, carry out the programmatic and administrative work. Often a co-ordinating body—a program council or ministry leadership team—gathers leaders for the kind of regular reporting, calendar clearing, and coordination that consumes so much board time. Organizational refinements that are a good idea in the multi-celled size category—including differentiating governance from ministry—become minimum requirements for congregations of professional size.

We all can learn from the whole spectrum of congregation sizes because a healthy congregation, however large or small, is both a family and an institution. The family is tended, as a rule, by long-term members, small groups, and laypeople. Clergy, new leaders, and denominational executives more often advocate for formal institutional behavior. Family therapists like Edwin Friedman and Peter Steinke have taught that the informal, family nature of the congregation actually controls much of its behavior.[8] Church growth advocates have shown us how small-congregation informality may need to change if a congregation is to grow—or to achieve whatever mission it is called to. Wise leaders understand and learn to enjoy this double truth and keep both sides of it in mind as they consider how to structure their decision-making work.

8

LIFE AFTER
GOVERNANCE CHANGE

Before planning a vacation trip, most people choose a destination. Before embarking on a governance-change process, it makes sense to picture what life in your congregation will be like afterward. Along the way, you will make many decisions about the specifics of your governance model: how big the board will be, what committees it will have, how to structure the staff, what authority to delegate to them, how to keep the board and staff in sync with one another, and how to keep them both in touch with the congregation. However, it will not be possible to draw a final picture of your congregation's governance model until you have created it.

On the other hand, before your board appoints a task force to design a change in governance, it probably will ask for a preview of daily life under the new model. Changing how your board, staff, and congregation make decisions is no small matter and cannot be accomplished by decree. Lasting governance change requires dozens of free agents to engage voluntarily in new behavior. Holding up a picture of the result you hope for—even though details will change—helps draw leaders into the process at the outset. In this chapter, I sketch what "governance and ministry" might look like. Only you can draw the final picture.

ANNUAL CYCLE OF PLANNING AND EVALUATION

One goal of a governance change is to free the board to spend more time thinking about the future while empowering staff to get things done efficiently right now. The annual cycle in figure 8.1 shows how this can happen. The board's work runs across the top part of the diagram; across the bottom is the staff's work. In the middle, on the level that begins with *planning retreat*, are activities that fall into the shared zone, where board and staff work together. Because figure 8.1 depicts a cycle, you might imagine wrapping it around a cylinder so that it repeats year after year.

A key annual event is the board's planning retreat. The senior clergy leader always participates, and depending on the planning focus in a given year, the board invites others to participate as well. The retreat agenda includes devotions and socializing; time for thoughtful and expansive conversation; and also time for practical work, like orienting newcomers and divvying up tasks and roles.

As always with retreats, the ideal is to meet away from usual haunts— somewhere where, if the phone rings, it's not for you. For the same reason, a clear agreement to limit cell-phone use is a good idea. Staying overnight helps separate the retreat from daily work and fosters flexibility of thinking. These benefits are hard to imagine ahead of time, but they make a big difference. As a retreat facilitator, I have often heard board members say, "I voted against spending the money to meet off-site. But I was wrong. This retreat will pay for itself many times over."

At the retreat, the board creates two major products: a set of *open questions* about the congregation's future and an *annual vision of ministry*. Both

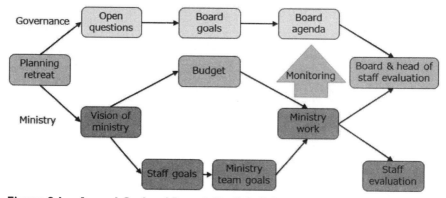

Figure 8.1. Annual Cycle of Board-Staff Collaboration.

are official actions of the board. Both take the form of lists—a list of future-oriented questions and a list of goals for the coming year or so. Both lists are short—ideally, no more than three items apiece.

Why so short? Because congregations suffer from attention deficit disorder; two or three questions are the most they can hold in their collective sights at once. And the list of priorities in the annual vision of ministry has to be short because, when a list of priorities gets long, it is no longer a list of priorities!

Responsibility for work on open questions belongs to the board, and responsibility for accomplishing the annual vision is owned by the staff, but neither works in isolation. The diagram in figure 8.1 highlights four key points of connection between governance and ministry: the annual retreat, the budget process, board monitoring of staff activity, and the annual evaluation of the board and head of staff. These are not, of course, the only moments when the board and staff connect; there are many others. To take a few obvious examples, the clergy leader normally attends board meetings, and sometimes other staff do so as well. Board members participate as volunteers in ministry activities. And as the board adopts, reviews, and modifies its policies on staff activity, board members seek assistance from the staff members who are most familiar with specific pieces of the work.

Each congregation adapts the cycle of board-staff collaboration to accommodate its fiscal year, meeting and election dates, holidays, and other givens. Sequence is more important than exact dates. A congregation with a fiscal year that starts July 1 might hold its planning retreat in February, so the results can influence the budget and staff planning for a program year that gears up in September. The board and head of staff might do their annual evaluation at a short retreat in August. It is not necessary—or possible, usually—to schedule everything to dovetail logically. What is most important is that high-level planning work precede the budgeting and goal-setting it is meant to influence and that evaluation follows both.

Having taken a quick tour of the annual cycle, let's walk through it once more, examining each step more closely, starting with the two main products of the planning retreat: open questions and the annual vision of ministry.

Open Questions

Open questions are a powerful tool for facilitating congregational participation. I believe in congregational participation, not mainly for pragmatic reasons, but because of something like what Martin Luther called the "priesthood of all believers": the belief that every one of us is born equipped to receive the promptings of the Spirit—in the form of ethical insight, compassionate awareness, and practical wisdom. To choose the right direction, a congregation needs to pay attention to its members, prospective members, and neighbors, even if that makes decision-making less efficient or more complicated.

Open questions are a way for boards to open themselves up to congregational influence. Boards are often criticized for being secretive or closed. Some boards work to counter this impression by posting minutes, publicizing their decisions, and inviting comment, but such practices rarely satisfy the critics. Telling people louder and more frequently what you have already done does not convey a sense of openness.

What does help is to tell people about questions you are thinking about before you make your mind up about answers. It takes courage to announce truly open questions. Leaders who admit they don't have all the answers cannot hide behind a façade of certainty. That's why most leaders like to resolve all their own uncertainties and disagreements before going public. Some congregants prefer this, too, because it frees them to be critics rather than decision-makers.

Posing open questions is worthwhile, though, because nothing prepares people to accept change—even radical change—more effectively than several opportunities to talk about important questions in a meeting where the first thing said is, "We will not be making a decision about this question soon." A board that has the courage to announce open questions creates a huge space for dialogue and mutual influence.

Open questions—sometimes called "frame-bending" or "adaptive" questions—call for a wider, longer conversation than a quick goal-setting process can accommodate. Often the most important open questions facing congregations are versions of the "questions of congregational formation" identified by Gil Rendle and Alice Mann:

- Who are we?
- What has God called us to do and to be?
- Who is our neighbor?[1]

Good open questions are localized, specific versions of these questions posed before the board has made its mind up about answers. Open questions create space for "balcony work," where the board and its conversation partners step aside from the press of daily business and reflect together about the future. Good open questions respond to a change in the ministry environment, to ways of working that don't work anymore, or to a chance event that calls attention to an opportunity for ministry that existed all along.

The open questions shown in figure 8.2, chosen by the boards of actual congregations, illustrate how the most useful questions arise from specific situations. Good open questions can't be answered with a *yes* or *no*. Instead of "Should we _____?" "Can we _____?" "Will we _____?" the best open questions ask, "What shall we _____?" "How shall we _____?" and "With

What difference does this congregation mean to make in our denominational community?

Whom shall we invite to join us as worshipers, and how do we mean to change their lives?

What is our "brand"? How do we wish to be known by others in our city?

What groups of people that we are not now reaching do we mean to reach? What special efforts will we take to reach them?

Is this church ready and willing to undergo a significant size transition? If so, how will we build enthusiasm and plan for such a transition?

What difference do we want worship to make in the lives of the variety of people who now come to us?

How can worship help us to maintain congregational unity in a time of change?

What changes to our physical plant, staffing, and organizational structures will we make in order to make room for more people?

As we make significant changes, how will we meet the needs of the current congregational members?

Now that we are smaller, how will we refocus our ministry to make it vital and sustainable?

How will our church express the social justice principles that led us twenty years ago to found our successful ministry in Guatemala (or *our nursery school, our retirement community, our AIDS living apartments, our food pantry*)?

What new identity will build on our reputation as "the Norwegian church" (or *the workers' church, the gay synagogue, the Republicans at prayer*)?

What does it mean in this time to be a church that "integrates children, parents, elders, singles, and families into all aspects of congregational life" as our mission calls us to do?

What are the core values for which we would sacrifice unity?

How will we earn the trust of our potential donors in our church's competence at using their gifts?

What are the core values that will shape our stewardship of money, and how shall we express those values in our future budgets?

What is our ministry to people in the community outside the walls of our church?

Figure 8.2.   Examples of Open Questions.

whom shall we _____?" They raise the kinds of questions whose answers shape a congregation's ministry for years to come.

What are your congregation's most important questions? Perhaps you face a choice whether to abandon, renovate, or replace a building that has been your major symbol of identity. You may wonder how to serve a neighborhood whose residents are different from the members of your congregation. Perhaps you have a nagging sense, as Jonah did, that God is calling you to make big changes, but your congregation (like Jonah) does not want to talk about it. The board could simply make up its mind, announce a solution, and invite feedback. Sometimes that works, but for major issues, such an approach more often only unites people for and against the board. A quick, action-oriented leadership stance rarely activates the wisdom of the whole group. For little things, that's fine, but for a few of the congregation's most important challenges, the board's highest contribution is to frame a question that states the issue clearly and to announce that, for the coming year, it plans to hold the question open for sustained, reflective, and inclusive conversation. The board draws on the results of these conversations when it develops the vision of ministry in future years.

Open questions often raise anxiety, so choosing a short list of questions— up to three, in most cases—is important. When the board announces its choice of open questions, it also says what future plans might possibly come out of the conversation about each question, who will decide those plans and when, and what opportunities members will have for input in the meantime. If the board has already decided to exclude some options from consideration, then it says so frankly. Drawing clear perimeters around an open question in these ways helps to create a "container" for the conversation. A container reduces anxiety and helps members to participate in civil and constructive dialogue.[2]

Keeping a short list of important questions open at all times helps the congregation see its board as open to influence. A well-run congregational discussion of an open question generates far more interest and excitement than the typical business-meeting fare of reports, budgets, and elections.

Annual Vision of Ministry

Open-question work bears fruit in many ways, including helping when the board selects its annual vision of ministry in future years. The annual vision, you will recall, contains the congregation's list of top-priority goals. Instead of simply snatching these goals out of thin air each year, a board that has been working on open questions sets its goals out of a deeper sense of God's will, the congregation's gifts, and changes in the wider environment.

Figure 8.3 shows how this worked over a three-year period in a fictitious congregation I call Bourne Street Church, located in a suburb called Arcadia, near Algo City. For a long time, people at Bourne Street have occasionally said, "We really ought to have a ministry in Algo City." But despite sporadic efforts, nothing related to Algo City has ever seemed to gain momentum.

Several years ago, at the annual planning retreat in year 0, the minister suggested it was time to stop feeling guilty and do something. Realizing that its previous efforts had suffered from both low commitment and unwarranted self-confidence, the board admitted that it really didn't know much about Algo City. So instead of looking for another quick-fix project, the board decided to initiate a multi-year effort. To launch a learning process, the board posed, as its first open question for year 1, "How will we engage in ministry in Algo City?" The board set this question as the main agenda item at four of its meetings in year 1. It also created a discernment committee that met regularly with the minister for prayer and scripture study, to gather data, and to reflect on future possibilities. With help from the committee, the board held two holy conversations about Algo City in the course of year 1. A Catholic nun who ran an agency in Algo City spoke at one of the conversations. At the other, the outreach director of a larger church in the same suburb as Bourne Street spoke about how his church had addressed suburbanites' fears about urban involvement.

Not content with conversation, the board also chose, as one of the three goals in its year 1 vision of ministry, to "Build deeper personal and institutional connections with leaders in Algo City." Acting on this goal, the minister joined an Algo City interfaith organization and invited members of the church to come with him to meetings and work projects. Through this affiliation, Bourne Street members met a number of city leaders and discovered that several of Bourne Street's members were more involved in Algo City than they realized. The board's discernment committee recruited some of these knowledgeable members to help plan and to attend the board meetings and holy conversation gatherings on Algo City.

	Year 1	**Year 2**	**Year 3**
Open Questions	How will we engage in ministry in Algo City?	How do we intend to change the lives of older adults who choose to join us on the journey?	What changes to our organizational structures will we make in order to become an effective "professional-size" church?
	How will we transform the lives of young people through our youth ministry?	What worship presence will we offer in Algo City?	What is our distinctive ministry with the people who will live in the five hundred new homes to be built in our neighborhood?
Annual Vision of Ministry	Build deeper personal and institutional connections with leaders in Algo City.	Initiate an effective and visible ministry in support of children's education in Algo City.	Plan for a new worship location in Algo City.
	Plan to add a second worship service that will attract about the same number of people as our current service.	Initiate a second worship service that attracts about the same number of people as our current service.	Initiate curriculum changes to implement the faith development vision approved by the board.
	Take steps to increase positive multigenerational interaction in our church.	Develop a faith development vision to guide our teenage youth ministries.	Increase the church's capacity to serve elderly members by offering companionship, practical assistance, and off-site Bible study.

Figure 8.3.   Open Questions and Annual Visions of Ministry.

In their evaluation at the end of the year, the board and minister discussed the board's progress at learning about possibilities for ministry in Algo City and the minister's progress in leading the church into deeper connections with Algo City leaders. All agreed that, while the two efforts were deeply intertwined, it had been helpful that the board's and minister's responsibilities were separate and clearly defined.

Questions and Visions, Year by Year

In each of the next couple of years, as you can see in figure 8.3, the board adopted other goals related to Algo City. In year 1, the goal was simply to build connections. At its planning retreat for year 2, the board invited the discernment committee to join them at the planning retreat, and the board decided, on the basis of its open-question work during year 1, that a ministry in support of children's education in Algo City would be the best match for Bourne Street's talents and Algo City's needs. At the retreat, board members suggested a number of good ideas for an educational ministry in Algo City. Rather than selecting one, the board chose to say that, by the end of year 2, they expected that the church would "initiate an effective and visible ministry in support of children's education in Algo City."

The board also wondered whether, in addition to serving people in Algo City, the church might find a way of inviting people to worship with the Bourne Street Church. After some discussion about why "those people" do not simply come to Acadia, the board posed, as an open question for year 2, "What worship presence will we offer in Algo City?" The board appointed a year 2 discernment committee to plan conversations on this question.

The minister accepted the year 1 committee's recommendation that Bourne Street "adopt" an Algo City public school, where they could offer tutoring and supplies. He also appointed Dorothy, a former committee member, as the unpaid director of the "Algo City education ministry." Dorothy began to organize a team and worked with the minister to set goals and a budget, which the minister put into his proposed budget for year 2.

The year 1 discernment committee, its work finished, had a dinner party and disbanded. One of its members joined the year 2 discernment committee, another joined the board, and three others accepted Dorothy's invitation to join ministry teams for hands-on work in Algo City.

At their next evaluation, the board and minister celebrated the successful start of the new ministry. At the planning retreat for year 3, they agreed there was no need to set any further goals related to it at the board level.

The educational ministry had become part of Bourne Street's ministry and would continue under staff direction.

During the three years chronicled in figure 8.3, the Bourne Street board posed other open questions and set other goals: creating a second worship opportunity at its location on Bourne Street, building intergenerational community, and strengthening the church's ministries with youth and elders. All these goals were chosen by the board at its annual planning retreat based on reflection and learning that had taken place in the course of the previous year.

Some of the board's goals were more specific than others. In year 2, for instance, it said the new worship service should attract "about the same number of people as our current service." The board included this requirement because its members knew that one of the most common pitfalls in creating a new worship service is to aim too low, so the new service is so obviously second class that it attracts a group of fifty to one hundred and then never grows. Music and education leaders often resist doubling their effort to create comparable programs in the new time slot, especially when budget planners resist paying them to do it! The board wanted to close the door on halfway measures by requiring a result that could only be achieved by offering a full-service worship opportunity.

The board decided not to specify the style of the new worship service or the type of intergenerational, youth, and elder ministries to be created. At one point, the minister, hoping for political cover, asked the board to give him more direction, but an influential board member looked him in the eye and said, "Surprise us."

The process for creating the vision of ministry changes from year to year. In some years, the top priorities may be so obvious that the board creates its vision quickly and spends most of its retreat time on other purposes. Some possible goals may turn out, in the course of board discussion, to be too ill-formed to package into goals and hand them over to the staff. Some of these the board may choose to frame as open questions for the coming year.

Worrying about Measurement

Worries about measurement, raised too early in the planning process, can inhibit boards from saying what they mean because it would be hard to measure. Board members schooled in the SMART system of goal-setting (Specific, Measurable, Actionable, Realistic, and Timely) sometimes let measurement considerations influence the selection of the goals themselves. But many things a congregation properly wants are hard to measure.

Often the more accurately you state a goal, the less precisely you can measure it. When the staff sets goals, the SMART standard is appropriate. But the board's first job is to state its goals exactly, not to worry about how to measure them.

In youth programs, for example, it's easy to measure registration, attendance, dropout rates, and dollars raised. Harder to measure—but more important—are such things as the number of volunteer hours given and young people's knowledge about scripture and tradition. Most difficult of all to measure are the actual outcomes of a ministry with youth: ethical life choices; spiritual depth; compassion; and adult observance, service, and affiliation.

The board's primary planning task is to say, in its strategic plans and the annual vision of ministry, what outcomes it is seeking. It should not limit itself to outcomes that are easy to measure. Instead, it should state its goals as exactly as it can and require the staff to come up with some way to measure them that satisfies the board that the goal has been achieved. Measurement does not have to be exact or quantitative—and for many goals, it can't be. John Carver put it well: "A crude measure of the right thing beats a precise measure of the wrong thing."[3]

A nonquantitative measure of youth ministry effectiveness might be to interview alumni of the high school program and ask about their volunteer commitments, faith practices, and beliefs. Quantitative measures are useful, too: A youth ministry that produces good results is twice as good if it produces those results for twice as many youth. But without qualitative evidence of the program's effectiveness, the quantitative data do not mean much.

THE BOARD'S YEAR

The purpose of distinguishing clearly between open questions and the annual vision of ministry is to draw a line between the board's responsibilities in the coming year and the staff's. The board's work is largely organized around the open questions; the staff accepts responsibility for implementing the vision of ministry. Board and staff interact a great deal along the way without confusing who is responsible for what.

Board Goals

Having posed its open questions and adopted an annual vision of ministry, the board proceeds to plan its own work by setting goals and an agenda, as shown in figure 8.1. A board that delegates management authority to

staff reduces greatly the number of day-to-day decisions it must make because, for most decisions, appropriate authority already resides away from
the board table. A board that uses the consent agenda process, described
in chapter 6, reduces the meeting time spent listening to reports to zero.
For many boards, these two changes alone eliminate most of what they currently do, opening the way to a twelve-month agenda plan.

Each meeting has a major focus. At most meetings, the main topic is
related to an open question. Other major pieces of board work, such as
nominations, board development, shared learning, policy review, and end-
of-year evaluation, all need time slots also. Creating a year-long agenda
helps the board resist slipping into management because board members
see that future-oriented, mission-focused work is more interesting and has
a higher impact. With longer lead times, ad hoc committees can prepare
for excellent board meetings by gathering data, inviting internal or external
experts, or planning special workshop meetings. Some boards appoint a
committee for each open question, as the Bourne Street Church did for its
Algo City question. One goal every board can have is to make its meetings
satisfying and worthwhile.

Other goals may have to do with the board's own process and disciplines.
It may decide, for instance, to create or renew its covenant of expectations
for board members or to implement one of the other practices described in
chapter 6. Another goal might be to make sure every board member has a
basic understanding of the congregation's finances. The board builds whatever goals it decides on into its agenda for the year.

Unexpected developments may require changes, but it's much easier to
stay on track with major goals when a plan is in place to start with.

Open-Question Work

A crucial part of the board's agenda is to connect with its constituents.
Although the congregation is not the "owner" in the same way stockholders
are owners of a business corporation, they share with the board responsibility for ensuring that the congregation serves its mission. How, then, can the
board stay in touch with the congregation and benefit from its wisdom? It
certainly should post its minutes and announce decisions it has made, but as
I have already suggested, this is not enough. A better way is to hold a series of
events designed to give the congregation opportunities to talk about the open
questions that the board identifies and to express other ideas and concerns.

Most members of the congregation will not be well-versed in the distinction between governance and ministry and cannot be expected to confine

their comments at board-sponsored events to board business as distinct from staff work. Congregational gatherings, whether they are organized by board or staff, produce a mixture of ideas. Leaders have to sort it out and explain when necessary who will be responsible for handling which suggestion. For that reason, both board members and staff should attend open-question events.

The whole repertoire of possible discussion methods and facilitation styles comes into play in open-question work. Breaking into small groups for part of the time helps everyone to have a voice. Having some way to collect data is a must. I'll mention a few specific formats that work well in a variety of settings.

World Café is a simple, highly adaptable process for getting people into conversation and collecting thoughts. As participants arrive, they find a room set up with small tables, each with four chairs. Unusual décor—a checkered tablecloth, a vase with flowers, perhaps a little café lighting—helps set the tone. Each table has paper and colored pens for writing. After an introduction and some ground rules ("café etiquette"), the facilitator states a question and the people at each table talk about it, making notes as they wish, for a stated time (perhaps ten or twenty minutes).

When time is up, everybody moves to a different table for a second round of conversation. Optionally, one person stays put as the "table host." Each round of conversation can have a new question, or a question may be repeated so that people have a conversation on the same topic with a new group.

Finally, the facilitator (often with a couple of assistants to help scribe results on newsprint or whiteboard) harvests insights and ideas. At the conclusion of the evening, there may be time for conversation in the whole group. (For more information about World Café, check out www.theworldcafe.com.)

Focus groups gather people who have something in common. For example, parents of third-graders might discuss how they would like their children's lives to be changed by their participation. Neighbors might be invited to discuss the impact of expansion plans. A simple focus-group agenda that allows plenty of time for uninterrupted conversation generally is the best plan for a focus group.

Parlor meetings are like focus groups, only for diverse ("max-mix") groups. The whole congregation might be gathered for dessert in homes, for instance, with an effort to ensure that each group has variety in terms of age and length of membership. The advantage is that people get to hear perspectives they may not have heard before. This can encourage creative thinking and also helps prepare the congregation for the fact that the board's decisions cannot be designed to satisfy just one group.

Expert meetings gather people who have knowledge or experience relevant to an open question. For instance, many open questions have to do with social-service activities that the congregation initiated many years ago. A preschool, for instance, that began as a co-op nursery school for children in the congregation thirty years later may be a profitable enterprise with a clientele mostly from outside the congregation. The open question may be about how the nursery school will be related to the congregation in the future. Such situations often have many complex dimensions that require educational, financial, building, and community-development knowledge to address.

In advance of an expert meeting, it is often helpful to commission one or more short white papers covering some aspect of the facts. In the nursery school case, one white paper might address the local day-care market, another the financial aspects for the congregation, and a third the current and projected building costs. The same group of "experts" might gather once or more to see if they can agree on a common set of facts that the board can use in responding to the open question. From the outset, it should be made clear that the board, not the experts, is the decision-maker.

Town meetings are gatherings of the congregation to discuss open questions or other topics of importance. Unlike a business meeting, a town meeting is for discussion, not action. It is also not a chance for leaders to "sell" members on the board's prior decisions. A good town-meeting format is small-group discussion followed by large-group discussion. Town meetings are especially helpful once the board has framed a number of proposals to test which might achieve consensus.

Using any method, open-question work calls for authentic listening by board members, or the congregation will quickly lose trust in the board's openness to influence. It helps to ask board members who are present to identify themselves, so that participants know whom they can speak to if they have afterthoughts. Recording important points from the conversation confirms that the board is listening as well. After any open-question gathering, the board communicates in writing to the congregation about what it heard. When it makes a decision, it references the results of the town meeting in the report. Even those whose input did not carry the day are reassured by the clear sign that the board listened.

THE STAFF'S YEAR

While the board focuses on open questions, the staff's work is guided by the annual vision of ministry. Staff members spend most of their time on routine tasks and can devote only a small part of their time to achieving forward-looking goals. The scarcity of discretionary time makes the annual vision of ministry all the more important. By helping keep the staff's attention focused on the congregation's growing edge, the annual vision of ministry helps to ensure that, when a staff member has discretionary time, it will be used to achieve goals that move the congregation forward.

Staff Goals

After the board adopts the annual vision of ministry, the staff translates it into goals and objectives. If the vision of ministry says, "We will make room to welcome more people," then the staff might say, "After the first of the year, we will add a second session to our children's Sunday school and double the number of parking-lot greeters skilled at hospitality to families with children." Setting staff goals shortly after the planning retreat helps to ensure that they will be consistent with the board's priorities expressed in the vision of ministry. The head of staff plays a strong role in deciding on staff goals and is ultimately responsible for the result. The staff may have other goals as well, so long as they adhere to the priorities in the annual vision.

The larger the staff, the more subgroups of staff set their own goals. In large congregations, the senior staff team adopts goals as a group, and so do teams of paid and unpaid staff who direct ministry in each major area. Some multi-site congregations practice matrix management, where each staff member belongs to both a site team and a functional, congregation-wide team, such as music, education, or operations. Individual staff goals support the goals of whatever staff groups he or she belongs to. Volunteer ministry-team leaders set goals in conversation with their supervisors, just as paid staff do.

Counterbalancing this neat hierarchical mindset is the fact that staff and volunteers at "lower" levels know more about their work than those at "higher" levels do, so the board and senior staff rely on creativity and insights that can come only from the periphery. Politically, each staff member belongs to two groups that are in tension with each other at least some of the time: One group is the staff team, with its interest in alignment and accountability. The other is the natural constituency surrounding every staff position. The staff and volunteers who gather around music, education, social justice, or administration differ in their worldviews, goals, and comfort zones. The staff relies on every member to encourage his or her constituents to support its goals—and also to communicate frankly about pushback from the trenches. Managing the tensions between alignment and creativity, unity and participation, is a key to staff success, especially when setting goals.

Sometimes the board's vision of ministry requires a clear departure from familiar ways—by choosing one style of worship over another, for example, or declaring a clear stance regarding who may be accepted as a member. In such cases, the staff and ministry teams must fall in line, even though that means the loss of valued volunteers. More frequently, the board's vision calls for a less dramatic shift—to diversify the worship offerings or to welcome a new group while continuing to support old-timers. The staff's goal-setting task is to find ways to accomplish board-adopted goals while managing the feelings, preferences, and energy of the available workforce of volunteers.

Goal-setting is most formal at the top. Paid staff members' job descriptions and performance goals are kept in writing. Goals for supervisors and professionals will be more abstract and complex than those for staff in support or service roles. Some performance goals relate directly to goals set by the board or staff, while others are more personal, calling for improvement in the basic functions of a job. A staff member whose performance is unsatisfactory will be confronted with improvement goals, either at the annual goal-setting time or at any other time. Staff goals, in other words, include but are not limited to those that help to accomplish the vision of ministry directly.

Ministry-team leaders function as staff and in collaboration with their supervisors create written goals as well. Including ministry-team leaders in staff goal-setting honors their importance and gives them an opportunity to clarify the scope and limits of their jobs. It is also a good chance to balance the results expected against the resources available.

The Operating Budget

The operating budget is part of the congregation's plan for accomplishing, among many other things, its annual vision of ministry. Many boards assume that budgeting is their responsibility—in the standard process, a board committee gathers requests from staff members, committee chairs, and other leaders and assembles it into a spreadsheet for approval by the board. There are two main problems with this process. One is that the head of staff never approves the budget. This undermines accountability by giving the head of staff a ready excuse for failing to achieve any goal. The other major problem is that this budget process is driven too much by spreadsheets and too little by vision. We need a better way of making budgets that puts responsibility for creating the budget in the same place as responsibility for achieving the vision of ministry: the staff.

Congregational budget-makers frequently divide into two camps that approach the task in different ways. The first camp is likely to include children of the Great Depression, experts in finance, elementary school teachers, and people anxious about their own financial situations. Their first priority is to make sure that the budget balances and that the congregation makes no plans or commitments it is less than 100 percent certain it can meet. They squint over budget sheets like bookkeepers of old with their bright lamps and sleeve garters—I call this camp the Green Eyeshades.

The second camp typically includes young clergy, upscale decorators, affluent retirees, college professors, and commission salespeople. They firmly believe that with God (or even without) all things are possible. They say, "We are a congregation, not a business." This camp can be identified at budget meetings mostly by their absence. When lassoed into talking about money, they glaze over. Staring at a distant sunrise, they float over the surface of numerical reality—I call them the Rose-Colored Glasses.

The division between the Eyeshades and the Glasses is as old as Mary and Martha, Moses and Aaron, Job and Job's wife. It is as deeply rooted in our culture as the duality of secular and sacred, temporal and spiritual. There is nothing wrong with it, so long as both groups value the other's contributions and see themselves as members of one team. But too often, the boundary becomes rigid—one group always thinks of ways to spend more money; the other always calculates the reasons we can't afford it.

The standard budget process often sets up friction between the Glasses and the Eyeshades. The first step is for a board budget committee to ask program units to request a budget for next year. The program units (full of rosy thinkers) ask for more than they expect and then some. Budget committee folk (strapping on their eyeshades) put all of the requests into a spreadsheet as a "dream budget." Usually even the dream budget ends up trimmed, so that it resembles the Green Eyeshades' own, fiscally sound dreams.

The fund drive, predictably, falls short of the "dream" goal. How could it not? Calling a goal a dream almost guarantees that you'll fall short. The finance committee sharpens its pencils and begins grinding the dream down to a practical nub.

The program people rise up, asking, "How can we say we can't afford what God has called us to accomplish?" The finance people answer, "Good stewards live within their means." The Eyeshades with their pencils and spreadsheets do battle with the Glasses with their blunt-end scissors, opera glasses, and pink feathers. Eventually, together, they come up with a budget, but there has to be a better way!

A better way begins with the annual vision of ministry, understood as the first draft of the budget, though it may contain no numbers at all. The vision of ministry confronts the question most budget debates address only indirectly: Which aspects of our mission will be top priorities this year? Only after the board adopts the vision of ministry (usually at a formally called meeting after the retreat) does the call for proposed budgets go out to program units. The call does not ask for a "dream" budget but for a budget that will help accomplish the vision of ministry.

The budget itself may be assembled by a budget team of volunteers (who may look a lot like the old spreadsheet crew that runs the standard budget process) and presented to the board for approval by the head of staff, who says, "I believe this budget is a reasonable plan to achieve our vision of ministry." Or possibly, "I see no realistic way to fund the vision we agreed on, and so I recommend we trim our vision to fit our means."

With a budget created in this way, the annual fund drive can be based on the vision of ministry as well. Contributors are asked for amounts that, if most of them say "yes," will make the vision possible. The board, clergy, and staff make it clear that the vision is not just something they hope to shoot for; it's a goal they mean to reach. Year after year, people learn that, when the congregation asks for gifts, it means what it says. If the members give what is asked, the results promised—the vision of lives changed through ministry—will happen.

MONITORING AND EVALUATION

Goals mean little without accountability. *With* accountability, they mean a great deal. People do respond to feedback about their work when it is given firmly and consistently. Congregations cannot use some of the incentives used by business corporations—bonuses, layoffs, promotions, and demotions. But that does not mean they cannot motivate hard, focused work by stating clear objectives and practicing accountability. When leaders lead, the group will follow.

The challenge is to create a culture of accountability without spending too much of the board's time on oversight or setting up an adversarial relationship between itself and staff. A board that overemphasizes its role as a watchdog can induce ministry workers—paid and unpaid—to draw their wagons into circles or (switching metaphors) to fly below the radar, achieving autonomy by hiding information.

To be effective at its oversight role, a board must learn to focus. In creating an annual vision of ministry, the board names its top concerns. By creating one structure for ministry decisions, it minimizes the number of people it must supervise. A board with one direct report—the head of staff, who is accountable for the performance of all other staff—can do a much better job of supervising than a board that tries to oversee a dozen programs and six staff directly. A clear goal-setting and evaluation process for one head of staff is an efficient way for the board to ensure that the whole ministry is goal directed.

But for this to work, the board has to trust that the whole structure is functioning properly. As fiduciaries, board members are responsible for the proper handling of money and property, the safety of those who participate in programs, and the lawful treatment of staff. It is not enough to trust one person without verifying. And so board oversight has two parts: monitoring and evaluation. By monitoring, the board ensures that the congregation is in compliance with laws, bylaws, and board policies. Through evaluation, the board assesses individual performance (including that of its own members) against previously agreed standards and goals.

Monitoring

Most monitoring is passive—the staff provide periodic reports about their progress toward the annual vision of ministry and on their compliance with board policies. Board members are expected to read the reports, raising questions if they have them, and not taking board time unless there is board business to be done. The board may ask its finance or personnel committee to vet reports in their areas of expertise—not to relieve board members of the duty to review them but to ensure that they are clear and relevant to policy requirements. Reports from staff (including volunteer leaders of ministry teams) appear in the board packet. In setting standards for the packet, the board emphasizes that reports should focus on policy compliance and progress toward the vision of ministry rather than on advertising the zeal and busyness of those reporting.

Evaluation

At the last stage of the annual cycle comes the evaluation of how well the congregation and its leaders fared. Many people flinch at the mention of evaluation, and with reason. Research shows that, in many workplaces, the main effect of employee reviews is to hurt productivity by annually lowering morale. In congregations, staff evaluation too often is conducted as a popularity poll with anonymous respondents rating staff performance on the basis of subjective impressions. In effect, staff members are encouraged to feel that they report to dozens of semi-invisible bosses who can invent new things to blame them for at any time. This approach raises stress even for popular staff members and does little to improve performance.

A second reason to dislike staff evaluation is that people who are in conflict with a staff member often propose evaluation as a way to express unhappiness. For the staff, this ploy turns evaluation into a harbinger of doom, like the arrival of the priest in an old movie. Evaluation is a poor way to deal with conflict, whether the conflict is really about staff or (as is often the case when a staff member is criticized) the congregation itself is divided over an underlying issue.

A third reason to dislike evaluation is that supervisors often wait until they have decided to fire someone before engaging in evaluation seriously. As a consequence, evaluation becomes associated with the notion of "building up a file" to protect against lawsuits or other conflicts after discharging an employee.

Understandably, some clergy and staff erect rigid boundaries around themselves and refuse to be evaluated or (more often) simply never get around to it. Volunteers do the same thing, sometimes expressing surprise at the very suggestion that their performance ought to be evaluated. In frustration, boards sometimes insist on punitive or inappropriately quantitative systems of evaluation in the hope of cracking down. Such rigid, unilateral approaches to the subject of evaluation often express underlying tensions needing to be addressed directly—perhaps with the help of a consultant— before evaluation can become healthy and constructive. Increased emphasis on evaluation is rarely a good first step in conflict management, though it can be helpful in stabilizing a relationship that is working reasonably well.

To be constructive, evaluation has to become a routine, nonthreatening part of congregational culture. This can happen when leaders stick to a routine of serious, periodic evaluation and set an example of openness to feedback and respond to it by learning and improving their performance.

Staff Evaluation

Staff evaluation is a staff responsibility. Each staff member's direct supervisor takes responsibility for the evaluation process and report. For hourly wage staff, the evaluation process should be as private as possible, consistent with gathering appropriate input. For program staff leaders, the supervisor might enlist key ministry team leaders in an evaluation session. In every case, the individual staff member and his or her direct supervisor sit down for a conversation about how the work is going. This is a chance for the supervisor to express appreciation for the staff member's contributions and to lay the groundwork for goal-setting in the coming year.

Staff teams that have set team goals also evaluate the group's progress toward achieving them. In these discussions, the focus is on group, not individual, performance. The question for a team evaluation is, How did we do? not, Who gets the credit or the blame?

The board, by policy, requires the staff to engage in evaluation, but the staff owns its own process. The "customer" for staff evaluations is not the board or a committee but each staff member's own superiors, beginning with the direct supervisor and ending with the head of staff. Others can and should participate by giving input, and the board may appropriately require the head of staff to provide a summary of senior staff members' evaluations. Raw data from surveys about staff performance should not be published; doing so empowers the least constructive respondents to have disproportionate and negative impact on morale.

Board–Head of Staff Evaluation

The head of staff, in addition to participating in evaluation with the senior staff team, evaluates and is evaluated by the board. At the same time, board members evaluate themselves. The governance committee, if there is one, structures the board's process each year. Each member might complete a written self-evaluation of his or her performance as a board member. The questionnaire might also ask about the member's contribution to achieving board goals set the previous year. Some boards also ask each member to rate every other member. The committee tallies the results and gives each member both an individual report and a summary of all responses. On the day of the evaluation, board members meet in groups of three to talk about the performance of each as a board member during the year. The governance committee gathers the results of this discussion, including any items that might inform future adjustments to the board covenant or board goals for the coming year.

Having had this conversation, the board will be in a good frame of mind for its evaluation conversation with the head of staff. One way to start is with written input from each member and the head of staff responding to simple questions about what they need from one another, what they are grateful for, and where they would like something different. The governance committee summarizes the responses, leads a conversation, and writes a brief report of major comments and concerns. If others report directly to the board, then the board engages in a similar process for each of them.

In addition to relating to the board and leading the staff, the clergy leader has a wider role that includes contributions as pastor, preacher, and public figure. Every three years or so, it is appropriate to evaluate the clergy leader's efforts in this wider sphere. Unfortunately, "clergy evaluation" is much easier to do poorly than well. One important safeguard is to entrust the process to a small committee, whose members have the confidence of both the clergy leader and the board. In consultation with the clergy leader, this group decides how to gather more input and other data and writes a summary report of the results to the board. The report should not magnify complaints, sweep widespread concerns under the rug, or forget to pass along appreciation. One helpful guide to evaluation of clergy and others is Jill Hudson's *When Better Isn't Enough*.[4]

Evaluation Principles

Despite the pitfalls, evaluation is important to effective partnership from the board and head of staff on down. Accountability requires an atmosphere in which people give each other feedback. When evaluation is done well, it clears the air and motivates improvement. It can also sharpen awareness of differences between an individual's sense of calling and the congregation's emerging vision, leading to adjustment or even to separation. Regular evaluation helps to surface issues while the relationship is good enough to make it possible to work on them. Although a unilateral (or even mutual) decision to end a partnership is rarely easy, avoiding problems to postpone the pain makes it no easier.

Adhering to sound principles helps make the evaluation process helpful. To be constructive, an evaluation process should include everyone who holds responsibility and have the following characteristics:

- *Scheduled*: Evaluation takes place by the calendar, not in response to problems.
- *Mutual:* Everyone gives and receives feedback.
- *Goal centered*: Previously established goals are the basis for evaluation.
- *Individual*: Evaluation asks, Am I meeting the expected standard for my job? How am I contributing to our goals?

- *Collective*: What progress have we made toward our goals? How do we need to adjust course? How are we fulfilling our vision for this particular program area?
- *Backward looking*: What did I accomplish? How well did we do?
- *Forward looking*: How can I improve? What should we do differently next time?

Nothing can make evaluation easy all the time; sometimes difficult words need to be said and heard. But with a healthy process, evaluation helps leaders and staff members pull together toward shared goals. A comprehensive guide to staffing and supervision—written for large churches but useful for anyone who wants to be a better supervisor—is *When Moses Meets Aaron* by Gil Rendle and Susan Beaumont.[5]

STRATEGIC PLANNING

The concept of strategic planning, born in the military during World War II, became popular in congregations 1950s and 1960s, when life seemed to have stabilized into a new and lasting pattern. The idea was that a committee of experts would spend several months developing a ten- or twenty-year plan with checklists of programs to be started, buildings to be built, and staff to be hired.

Today, strategic planning is still useful, though instead of focusing on ways to follow proven paths of growth, it is more apt to ponder the dislocating changes in society that have made congregational leadership so much more challenging. In addition to occasional bouts of "long-range" or "strategic" planning, management experts now recognize the need for continual "strategic awareness," "adaptive thinking," and even "strategic management." In a world where easy answers are simply not available, we do not have the luxury of keeping planning in a box and taking it out just now and then. We need a planning frame of mind; we need to plan all the time, not just once in a while. That is the purpose of the annual cycle described in this chapter.

A strategic plan contains the longest-range plans—though in my experience, few congregations can realistically plan further ahead than five or ten years. A strategic plan answers the question, What major choices have we made about how we will fulfill our mission? Because strategic planning happens in the middle section of the map, it involves everyone: congregation, board, and staff. A congregation might form a strategic-planning committee every five or six years. The team's job is to engage the whole community in "holy conversation," leading to a fresh sense of the congregation's identity, calling, and relationships.

Figure 8.4 shows how a strategic-planning process fits into the annual cycle of planning and evaluation described in this chapter. The strategic-planning process started in year 1. The board appointed a strategic-planning committee, which identified a short list of "driving questions" to guide the planning process. After a year-long process of data-gathering and holy conversation, similar to that described earlier for the board's open-question work, the planning committee presents its report, which includes, in addition to a strategic vision, some high-level plans for program, staffing, capital investment, and annual budgeting.

As mentioned in chapter 4, the planning committee has two primary audiences for its report: When it presents its strategic vision, it is talking mainly to the board. When it proposes major changes in location, buildings, program emphasis, or staffing, the board is also probably its main audience for those recommendations. If the plan includes timetables, budgets, miscellaneous ideas, and other such specifics, then the staff is the principal audience. The planning report should recognize these differences, so that it can address the appropriate part of its recommendations to the proper audience.

In addition to the strategic vision, the planning report contains recommendations for how to achieve it. These recommendations are addressed to the staff, which will be responsible for organizing ministry teams to do the work and for developing milestones and measurements for their progress reports to the board.

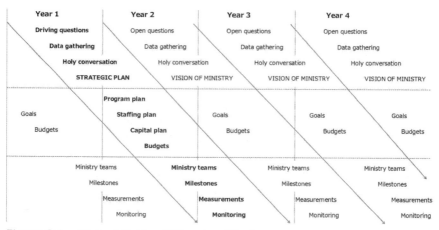

Figure 8.4. Annual Cycle of Planning Work.

Meanwhile, the board is busy working on next year's open questions. With a strategic plan in place, the open questions typically say, "What big steps will we take next year toward implementing our strategic plan?" Each year's vision of ministry may reflect little more than a progress plan toward the realizing the strategic vision.

You may be wondering, What is the difference between "driving questions" and "open questions"? Answer: There's no difference, except that *driving questions* is the term used in the wonderful strategic-planning guide *Holy Conversations*, and *open questions* is the term I used for annual planning in this book. You can use whichever term you like!

ANNUAL WORK PRODUCTS

Congregations grant their boards and clergy leaders different kinds of power. To boards, they grant the ultimate responsibility for articulating mission and ensuring that the congregation's resources are cared for and directed to fulfill that mission. Boards also have inherent limitations that arise from being a group, being volunteers, and meeting only a few hours a month. Effective boards focus on a few work products that will make a serious difference over the long haul. These include, in declining order of importance, the following:

- Creating a short list of annual goals for the congregation.
- Approving a budget that supports those goals.
- Writing a five- to ten-year strategic plan.
- Endorsing a useful, lasting statement of the congregation's mission.

Like effective boards, effective clergy focus on a few primary work products. These include, in declining order of importance, the following:

- Building trust by keeping promises and setting a good example.
- Gathering and supporting a cadre of paid and unpaid ministry leaders who work together to create positive results.
- Excelling in at least one of the primary pastoral skills of preaching, teaching, organizing, and the care of souls and showing adequate proficiency in all the rest.

When such partners sit together, they don't worry about interfering in each other's business. Instead, they focus first on their own contributions, then on helping one another. The clergy leader offers the board leadership and insight. The board offers the clergy leader wisdom; political support; and firm, compassionate feedback. Such a partnership requires clear boundaries and mutual understanding and support. Standing side by side before the congregation, lay and clergy leaders let the people see how partners honor one another's roles and help each other—not because there is no boundary but because the boundary is so clear it can be safely crossed.

9

EXPLORING GOVERNANCE CHANGE

One approach to changing the organizational structure of a congregation is to reprogram it like a computer. The board appoints a bylaws-revision committee, which goes into seclusion like a group of old-time hackers in a garage. The group members scour the Internet for free resources, read some books about the latest new ideas, and punch out a set of bylaw changes and a new organization chart. Then they roll out version 1.0 of their proposal. Like version 1.0 of anything, it turns out to have bugs in it. Some congregations simply reject the changes. Others, like so many users of new software, vote them in, only to experience incompatibilities or crashes later on.

A congregation is not a machine; it is a living system. As such, it has a strong inclination to persist in doing what has become familiar. In a plant or animal, biologists call this inclination homeostasis, from the Greek for "staying the same." In organizational systems, the unwritten law is, "When we don't know what to do, we do more of what we know."[1] The imposition of good ideas from outside is not enough to cause a congregation and its leaders to modify ingrained daily habits. Systems can be extremely clever about undermining anyone or anything that tries to change them from outside. On the other hand, a system can change itself quite readily in response to inner forces. It may change in response to the shared unhappiness of its leaders. It may change to achieve the same old results in a new situation. Or it may change because it catches an exciting glimpse of new results—results that fit so powerfully its inward sense of mission as to disturb old comforts and make the status quo untenable. Bylaw amendments may be necessary for systemic change, but they are definitely not enough. The secret to enduring change is to engage the system's own deepest motivations—including its resistance to change. A system changes willingly when it sees change as a necessary way to continue being what it truly is.

OVERVIEW OF THE GOVERNANCE CHANGE PROCESS

A process like the one shown in figure 9.1 stands a better chance of producing systemic change than an approach focused only on changing the bylaws

Year 1	1	Board appoints governance task force (GTF)
	2	Leadership workshop on governance
	3–4	GTF writes and presents governance vision for board approval
	5–11	GTF engages in "iterative process" of policy-writing:
		GTF seeks board input on a policy topic
		GTF drafts a group of policies
		Board reviews and affirms policies
		GTF seeks wider review and input
		GTF revises policies and repeats the process
	12	Board adopts proposed policy book for the trial run
Year 2	1–2	GTF disbands, and board appoints governance committee
	3	Planning retreat
	4	Board adopts first vision of ministry (VOM) and open questions (OQ)
	5–7	Board elections and training
		Implement new plan for board meetings
		Staff sets team and individual goals
		Board explores OQ (full year)
	8	Board and head-of-staff evaluation (no VOM or OQ in place)
	9–12	Staff works to achieve VOM (full year)
		Governance committee facilitates frequent check-ins and adjustments and an evaluation near the end of the year
Year 3	1–2	Staff and Board work continues
	3	Planning retreat
	4	Board adopts second VOM and OQ
	5–7	Board elections and training
		Staff sets team and individual goals
		Board explores OQ (full year)
	8	Board and head-of-staff evaluation (against first VOM and OQ)
	9–12	Staff works to achieve VOM (full year)

Figure 9.1. Governance Change Time Line.

or the organization chart. This process has been tested by a variety of congregations, each of which has carried it out differently. It takes longer than most people expect because it aims to change both structure and behavior, roles and attitudes, language and understandings. Systemic change requires wide participation and starts by asking questions rather than providing answers. After a brief overview, we'll walk through it step by step.

When the board decides the time is ripe for a governance-change process, it appoints a governance task force (GTF) to lead the process, which begins with a workshop for the board and other leaders. At the workshop, leaders talk about what they value in their current structure, what they find difficult or frustrating, and what they hope for from a new way of organizing. Someone presents concepts from chapters 3 and 4 of this book and a change process adapted from figure 9.1. By the end of the retreat, the board should have a better sense of whether the time is right to start a governance-change process and what the scope of the GTF's charge should be.

The GTF's job is to draft a governance vision statement and a book of board policies. At each step, the GTF reports back to the board and asks for affirmation (not adoption) of its work to date. Affirmation is a yellow light—permission to share the partial proposal with a wider group of leaders, then with all interested members. At each iteration, the GTF adjusts its proposal and shares a revised draft with the board. Repeatedly along the way, the GTF explains the process to a wider circle of congregational leaders.

Once the GTF has developed a reasonably complete set of policies and the board has affirmed them, the GTF asks the board to approve the new structure. Depending on the nature of the proposed changes, the congregation may need to approve parts of it as well, such as bylaw amendments. The congregation should not, however, vote on board policies, as this would have the effect of making them congregational policies beyond the power of the board to change. If there is something in the GTF proposal that requires congregational approval, then that should be accomplished in a way that leaves the board in control of its own policies.

Optionally, the board may choose to call the first year under the new structure a "trial run" to underscore that it is serious about continual evaluation and improvement. Once its proposal is adopted, the GTF disbands, to be replaced by a board governance committee, with some GTF members continuing in the new role.

From this point on, the work of the board and staff begins to resemble their future "Life after Governance Change," as described in chapter 8. The governance committee coaches and monitors the board and staff as they change their behaviors. Toward the end of the year, it leads an evaluation of the congregation's progress toward adopting its new model. Based on the evaluation, the governance committee may recommend adjustments and perfecting changes for approval by the board.

For some time, reverting to the old behavior is a continual temptation for leaders—especially when they become anxious. Leaders find the new ways awkward and continually discover situations in which the new structure calls for behavior that surprises them because they have not internalized the full implications of the new governance model. The governance committee continues to assist with board development and training. The first full evaluation session between the board and head of staff takes place a year after the board adopts its first annual vision of ministry.

Making the new behavior automatic takes yet another year or two. At that point—three years from the beginning of the process—leaders' first thought, most of the time, will be to follow the new structure rather than the old one. Enculturation of new leaders, updating of covenants, and the shoring up of effective practice when it sags—these tasks remain on the board's and staff's agendas indefinitely.

GOVERNANCE CHANGE, STEP BY STEP

Now that we have seen the governance-change process in overview, we will start again and walk through it more deliberately, beginning with the process before the process—deciding whether it is a good time to be considering a change in governance at all.

Questions to Ask before Starting

Governance change is not always a good idea. There is no perfect time, to be sure, but sometimes it is a good idea to wait. Before you dive into a governance-change process, you might ask the following questions to help you determine whether this is a good time.

Who Wants This Change?

Before moving ahead with a change process, you need support from a significant group of lay leaders and staff. If your clergy leader is strongly committed to continuing your current structure, then it is not constructive to begin a process that is likely to increase demand for a new one.

If the main reason you are interested in governance change is that one person (especially if that person is the clergy leader) read this book, then the next step is obviously to buy more copies! One of the hazards of reading a book or going to a seminar is that you can find yourself alone in your enthusiasm.

Another hazard is to become so convinced of a specific "model" that you have a hard time listening to others who are just starting to consider the question. It is important to tell others why you are initiating a change process, but it is even more important to gain a broad base of support by listening to others.

Admittedly, if you wait for throngs to rise up and demand a governance-change process, you will wait a long time. But if only two or three of you want change, that's not enough. If interest in restructuring is lukewarm, then it might be best to initiate some education or self-examination rather than a full process. You might want to hold a "discussion that is only a discussion" for leaders to talk about what is going well in your decision-making process now and what they would like to improve. Some of the ideas presented later for the initial governance workshop work equally well for a preworkshop meeting. Agreement about the outcome or goals of a change process is not necessary or desirable; at this stage, all that is needed is agreement that a process is appropriate and timely.

Why Is This Question Coming Up Now?

Sometimes when leaders are in conflict, they decide that structure is the problem and hope that a change will make things better for them. If the conflict is severe enough to involve rudeness, personal attacks, or secret meetings, then it is best to address the conflict first. Otherwise, some people will see the governance change process as a stealthy way to get the upper hand—and they may be right! When the question of governance arises as a way to resolve differences over clergy or staff members or about worship, social issues, or building policy, the best option is to resolve the conflict under the existing rules. Rebuilding a boat while it is sailing is difficult; rebuilding it while it is on fire or when a mutiny is under way is pretty much impossible.

What Else Is on Our Agenda in the Coming Year or Two?

If you have a building program coming up or you need to make challenging decisions soon about worship, morality, or social justice, then that is a caution sign. A congregation can have only two or three big things on its agenda at a time. Governance may need to wait its turn.

Who Is Your Clergy Leader?

During the first three years of a new ministry or rabbinate, I would question any push for governance change. During this crucial time of relationship-building, congregations are prone to see a governance proposal as cover for a power grab by one side or the other of the new relationship. In general, waiting is the wisest course. An exception might be made for a congregation that has already decided on a governance change before the new clergy leader arrives. Even then, I would not be surprised if, three years later, some members blame what they don't like about the governance model on the clergy leader.

On the other hand, it is *not* necessarily a caution sign if your clergy leader is close to retirement, is about to go on a sabbatical, or is with you as an interim while you search. Such moments in a congregation's life are often good opportunities to rethink the lay-clergy partnership while the partners have some space in their togetherness. In the case of a sabbatical, the scope and general direction of the proposed change should be agreed upon before the clergy leader leaves. If agreement cannot be reached, then the process should be suspended. Conversation may continue (how could it not?), but no decisions should be made until after the sabbatical.

During an interim, coordination with the search committee is essential, so that prospective candidates know that a change process is underway and how it might affect the clergy leadership role they are considering. It is much better to begin a change process during the interim than to spring it on a leader chosen for a role that is about to change.

When Did We Last Reorganize? How Do People Feel about That Process and Its Outcomes?

If the congregation still holds bad feelings from its last bylaws revision process, then it is helpful to put those feelings to rest before starting something new. In the last reorganization, one person or a small group of members may have created and proposed a set of bylaw changes. With pride of authorship, they put their work before the congregation only to see it bent, folded, mutilated, and rejected—or adopted in a form that did not leave them feeling good. After such a process, some people may want to revisit the original bylaw proposal, while others have learned to associate reorganization with tiresome parliamentary debates or other unpleasantness and want to avoid the subject altogether.

Most of these cautions are merely that—yellow lights that may or may not indicate the need to postpone governance change. If your current structure discourages initiative, abuses volunteers, or contributes to a morbid sense of drift, then the question is not whether to explore changing it but when. In the meantime, a quick-fix approach may be in order to solve any problems that are so severe that they prevent the congregation from addressing its most urgent issues—leaving a more comprehensive change process until it can get the attention it deserves.

Governance Workshop

When the time is right, a good way to begin thinking about governance is to gather leaders for a workshop to educate them on the subject and to take stock of their interest in exploring a change. In preparation for the retreat, the board appoints an advance committee. The advance committee's job is to plan a process for deciding whether to have a process. It often makes sense to appoint an advance committee to help in deciding *whether* to proceed with a major change and another to take the lead in deciding *how* to implement the change. The first committee should include people who are inclined for and against the proposal, but the second can consist only of those who can wholeheartedly commit to its success. (One governance advance committee called itself the "John the Baptist committee" and cried out from time to time that it was *not* the governance committee.) In some cases, where the board is pretty sure it wants to go ahead with governance change, it makes more sense to appoint one group to see the process through from start to finish.

Hiring a consultant to facilitate the workshop—or even the governance change process as a whole—can be a help. Be sure, though, that you know how your consultant will approach the task. Some consultants promote only one specific system of board governance; all consultants worth considering have ideas about what works and what doesn't. You will want to know that your consultant's ideas are compatible with yours and that he or she can listen with respect to the ideas of others. For your initial governance workshop, you will want a facilitator who can strike a balance between *process* (letting you have your own discussion without pushing a narrow agenda) and *content* (offering language and ideas that will help you have a better conversation). Perhaps the most helpful trait to look for in a consultant is curiosity—about your congregation and its history, values, and traditions and about the hopes and expectations your leaders bring to the governance discussion. It is better to muddle awkwardly through your own conversation than to be force-marched expertly through someone else's.

At the retreat, starting with some mixer or team-building activities helps introduce newcomers to the group and creates a comfortable atmosphere for everyone to participate. Prayer, text study, singing, and ritual—as appropriate to your tradition—help place the work of the retreat in a larger picture. Such practices remind participants that, in every time and place, people have strived to gather worshiping communities in just, effective, up-to-date ways. Some personal sharing helps to recognize the unique experiences that color each participant's perceptions about leadership, decision-making, money, and power. "Opening the room," so that all ideas are heard with respect, builds trust.

Before talking about change, it is good to spend some time describing the status quo. Using old minutes (or memory), leaders can estimate how much of the board's time is spent on management decisions, reports, and other matters.

It can be fun to break up into groups and ask each group to draw an organization chart for the congregation as it actually operates. An organization chart should answer certain questions about each position; for example: Who appoints someone to do this job? Who is responsible for making sure someone does it properly? Who can fire the person? Who approves the necessary resources—money, building space, and staff? After the groups have finished, they post and present their charts. Enjoy the differences rather than trying to reconcile them. Look at each chart appreciatively—as a source of information about how people see and describe the congregation.

Sometimes in the course of these activities, real differences appear in board members' descriptions. Rather than pushing to resolve differences, explore the reasons for the different perceptions. Your congregation may have changed, and leaders' perceptions may be drawn from different eras. Or current and past board leaders may feel defensive in the face of what feels like criticism. A reminder that the whole board shares responsibility for its practice can help to take leaders off the spot. The most useful product of a conversation about the status quo is information about areas where board members want to spend more time or less time. This information can be a useful guide to changes the board is ready to consider.

Including an educational component in the retreat plan adds grist to what, to some participants, might otherwise seem a tiresome diet of pure "process." Someone might prepare to present your polity tradition in comparison with others. Edward Long's *Patterns of Polity* may help the presenter identify the core values behind your style of governance.[2] When I give presentations at governance workshops in congregations, I use material from chapters 3 and 4. I encourage readers to borrow content from those chapters as a way to stimulate conversation among leaders about the governance approach that fits your congregation. Another presentation might include information about your congregation's size and its history of growth and decline, based on chapter 7. Are you organized to be larger or smaller than you are? If there is a mismatch, is it intentional or just a leftover? Asking people to prepare presentations is a good way to make sure a variety of voices are heard.

To help participants look ahead, a presentation based on the conceptual maps in chapter 4 and the roles of the board in chapter 5 can be helpful. Be sure to emphasize that the proposed process is an open one, designed to enable your congregation to create a structure suitable to its needs and traditions. Pay attention to the points that draw particularly strong positive or negative responses. Of course, you'll have to choose what to present so that it fits the time you have and leaves plenty of time for participants to talk!

Wind up the retreat by seeing if the group can agree on a rough statement of goals for the governance-change process. Then ask, How big a change is this? Is it worth a full governance process? Share a plan for a full governance process like the one in figure 9.1 and explain why major shifts in the behavior of a system take a longer time and broad participation to achieve. See if the group can reach consensus about the kinds of improvements they want. The advance committee writes up the results of the retreat, which become part of the board's agenda at its next official meeting.

Some leaders may incline toward a strict view of your denominational polity—assuming, in effect, that only what is customary is permitted. If possible, set these concerns aside for now and say what you want to do, leaving questions about how to harmonize your plans with polity rulebooks for later. Even the most prescriptive polities allow more flexibility than people sometimes assume.

Appointing the GTF

Assuming that the board decides to go ahead with a full governance-change process, its next task is to appoint a governance task force (GTF). The choice of personnel for this group is crucial. GTF members need the congregation's trust and must be able to set aside factional loyalties and preconceptions if they are to participate in a truly open process. A good size for the GTF is five members, at least one or two of whom are also members of the board. The clergy leader (or a trusted representative, in a large congregation) should be an active member and participant.

A good method for appointing the GTF—or any group that needs wide trust and respect to fulfill its purpose—takes two board meetings but is well worth the time. At the first board meeting, the chair introduces or reviews the concept of brainstorming (all ideas are welcome, no criticism or praise, "building on" ideas is permitted, "improving on" is not). Using newsprint, brainstorm a list of qualities the GTF will need. The GTF's job has an introverted, policy-wonk side and an extroverted, process-facilitation side. In appointing members for the GTF, the board will want to make sure it has people with both kinds of skills. Close the brainstorming session, and discuss which items on the list are most important and generally agreed upon. Edit the list accordingly.

Finally, assign board members the homework of coming to the next meeting with one or more potential nominees in mind. Urge members *not* to ask permission from the nominees but simply to nominate the best. Any member may bring any number of nominations; all are encouraged to bring at least one. After the first meeting, e-mail the list of qualities to board members with a reminder of their homework. Ahead of the next board meeting, send another reminder.

At the next meeting, pass out 3" × 5" cards, and ask members to write each nominee on a separate card. Appoint a teller team to tally all the nominations and list them on newsprint or whiteboard. If someone gets more than one nomination, show the number, but list the names in random or alphabetical order. Discuss (initially in subgroups, if the board is large) which group of four—plus your clergy leader—would make the best GTF. When the board has agreed on a set of nominees (and an alternate or two), charge someone to contact each one. Before asking them to serve, be sure to show each nominee the list of desired qualities, explain how they were chosen, and show them the list of other nominees. Boards that use this process often experience a rate of acceptance that surprises them!

Planning the Process

After it is selected, the GTF's first task is to plan the process it will follow. While the outline in this chapter is a starting point, the process for a particular congregation must be customized to fit the scope of the changes to be considered and the schedule for program planning and board elections, which will affect the best time to roll out a new mode of decision-making.

The plan should specify the areas of governance that will be looked at, the concerns or goals to be addressed, the occasions when leaders or members can have input, the approximate date when the task group's recommendations will be acted on, and the body that will act. After it has drafted a proposed process, the GTF presents it to the board. Once it is approved, the GTF publicizes the plan widely and repeatedly. It almost never hurts to overdo publicity. People will accept a great deal of decision-making by leaders if they are told well in advance—and reminded frequently—what is under consideration, when they can have input, who will decide, and when. By the time of the final decision, every interested person will have had a chance to express his or her hopes and concerns, and the vote itself will be an anticlimax.

Governance Vision Statement

Shortly after the governance workshop, the GTF articulates a *governance vision statement* that sets forth the principles and goals of the governance-change process. In theory, the board might have given such a statement in its charge to the GTF, but in practice, boards generally appoint committees to do things they are unclear about. So a good first step for the GTF, as for most committees, is to clarify and restate its own charge for board approval. As a starting point, it has whatever charge the board did give, plus data from the newsprints at the governance workshop. After reflecting on this document, the GTF at one church described its vision this way:

> The congregation of the —— Church elects a board to function as its governing body and a minister to serve as its spiritual, programmatic, and administrative leader. The goals of this governance-change process include
>
> - enabling the board to spend more of its time discerning God's will for the long-term future of the church,
> - empowering the minister to lead the staff efficiently and responsibly to fulfill the church's mission and goals endorsed by the board, and
> - creating a clear policy structure that allocates responsibility for decision-making and ensures that church resources are protected and that its activities support its mission.
>
> The intended style of leadership will be consultative, collegial, and inclusive. Clarity about ultimate responsibility and authority will exist along with a democratic and egalitarian spirit. All church leaders are expected to practice transparent decision-making, healthy conflict management, and mutual support in their respective roles.

The governance vision statement serves primarily as a guide and communications tool for the governance-change process and might find a permanent home as a preamble to the board policy book.

Once it has drafted and approved the governance vision statement, the GTF goes to the board and asks for affirmation. The concept of "affirmation" may seem strange to a board accustomed to voting motions up or down. Affirmation does not freeze the text or put the policies in force. Affirmation gives permission for the GTF to proceed with further policies on the basis of the ones already affirmed. The GTF can also present affirmed policies to a wider audience. This procedure avoids confusion in the congregation, which will tend to assume that the board is in at least general support of anything its committee (the GTF) presents more widely. Affirmation does not mean the policies are permanent or set in stone. The GTF may bring revisions to the board later on as it creates a consistent body of policy. Nothing takes effect until the board approves the whole package after the drafting process is complete.

Along with the governance vision statement, the GTF may choose to add a statement about the scope of any major changes that seem likely to come under consideration. Major changes might include reducing the number of board members or how they are elected or consolidating multiple boards. Even if you're not sure what you will decide to do about them, raising possibilities while they are still only possibilities helps lower their shock value later.

WRITING POLICIES

Most of the GTF's work can be organized around the task of drafting policies for the board to approve. This task is so large and important that the next chapter is devoted to it. Writing a logical, consistent set of policies can become rather fascinating, introverted work. The biggest risk is that the GTF becomes so focused on policy-writing that it neglects the larger aim, which is to familiarize the board and other leaders with the new governance model as it evolves and to secure their support. That's why a mix of introverts and extroverts is helpful on the GTF.

The governance vision statement constitutes the first step in creating a full policy book, and the first step in a sequence that repeats until the work is complete. Here is a sequence of policy subsets that has worked well in many congregations:

- *Governance* policies say how the board will operate.
- *Delegation* policies give authority to staff.
- *Guidance and Limitation* policies say how the board wants the staff to use the authority it has been given—and how it may *not* use it. This is often the most complicated set of policies. For policy-making purposes, it can be subdivided into:

  Personnel Decisions
  Care for Paid Staff
  Care for Members and Guests
  Care for Resources

- *Oversight* policies lay out a plan for board and staff to stay in touch, so that the board knows whether all is well.

Is this the best sequence for you to use? Not necessarily. No two congregations are alike—each finds something a bit different to be anxious about.

You may get a clue about this at your governance workshop! But if there is no strong reason to do otherwise, I suggest building the policies themselves in the sequence given here. You can always loop back or jump forward if you need to.

By dividing the policy book into a well-ordered sequence of subsets, the GTF helps board members and others to absorb, reshape, and finally accept the policies at manageable speed. The final policy book, by the time it is approved, has been affirmed in pieces by the board and shared with the wider leadership. By following consistently in every round the principles and values articulated in the prior rounds, and by letting what it hears from others influence its work, the GTF builds trust not only in itself but also in the model it is building.

The Iterative Process

The GTF's work follows what a computer programmer might call an "iterative" procedure: a repeating process where each round produces a result that is the starting point for the next round. The GTF initiates each round by choosing a subset of the full policy book. For each group of policies, it takes several steps, which I have identified here as they are labeled in figure 9.2:

1. *GTF Preparation.* The GTF thinks about the questions the subset of policies must answer, alternative approaches, or perhaps even some alternative draft language.
2. *Board Conversation.* The GTF goes to the board and asks them to talk for a few minutes about the policy subset the GTF is about to write.
3. *GTF Deliberation.* The GTF decides how it intends to address this subset of policies.
4. *GTF Drafts Policy Subset.* The GTF completes the draft (perhaps with the help of a small drafting subcommittee).
5. *GTF Approves Policy Subset.* The GTF approves and recommends it to the board, taking care to acknowledge the board's input and whether it was followed.
6. *Board Affirms Policy Subset.* This gives the GTF a green light to share the affirmed language more widely.
7. *Wider Conversation.* The GTF presents the affirmed policies to an appropriate group of lay and staff leaders.

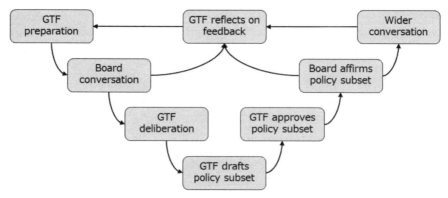

Figure 9.2. Iterative Policymaking.

8. *GTF Reflects on Feedback.* The GTF reflects on feedback from the board and the wider conversation and perhaps adjusts its policies in response.

9. *GTF Preparation.* Based on the results of the first iteration, the GTF begins again with the next subset of policies.

This process repeats several times—once for every policy subset. Once it gets going, the GTF is receiving three kinds of feedback all the time: board comments on the next subset to be drafted, board comments on the prior subset, and comments from the wider leadership about the policies the board has affirmed. In response to any of this feedback, the GTF may choose to loop back and rewrite some policies. Alternatively, the GTF can say, "Give us another chance to show how the policy we have proposed will help us to fulfill our mission." In this case, the same policy subset might go through more than one iterative cycle.

An iterative process has several virtues. It honors the role of the GTF as architect in chief of the new governance model. It enables its client, the board, to play a strong role in shaping the new structure in a reasonable amount of time. It gives the GTF several opportunities to seek input and demonstrate its openness to influence. And finally, the whole process is a "mentioning campaign" (see chapter 6, under "'For Discussion Only' Items") that keeps leaders and the congregation aware of the emerging structure they will be asked to live by. Getting a cross-section of leaders involved along the way helps them to see the new structure as a means for achieving the congregation's mission.

If the iterative process goes well, somebody will ask, when it comes time to actually approve the policy book, "Didn't we vote on this already?"

This is a good sign! It indicates the congregation has begun to feel it owns its new governance model. (Unfortunately, no amount of outreach and conversation will prevent at least one person, prior to the final vote, from saying "Nobody asked me!") To some leaders, the whole process will seem tedious because at every step they will hear some of the same questions and concerns. Members of the GTF may correctly feel that they are having the same conversation with each larger group of people. This repetition is a normal cost of lasting system change.

Midcourse Corrections

The GTF does not need to create an utterly complete policy book. Some policies—for instance, the board's covenant of expectations for board members—it should skip because it is better for the board to write this for itself. The GTF can offer to help with that conversation or let the board and governance committee do it in the first year under the new model.

Sometimes the process gets stuck. Like a contractor who encounters a forgotten burial ground, the GTF may accidentally spade up a dormant conflict. In many congregations, for example, the older women's organization is like a leaky time capsule, holding decades of unfinished business in male-female relations. Understandably, its leaders can be skeptical of efforts by the board to define their place in the new structure. The GTF might possibly resolve such issues with a masterstroke of policy—more likely not. In such cases, the GTF might choose to acknowledge that the issue is outside the scope of its charge. It can leave a blank space in the policy book, suggesting that the board work out a solution with the parties concerned. When that is done, the GTF (or later on, the governance committee) can draft the necessary policies.

Do We Need to Amend Our Bylaws?

Some changes may require amendments to the bylaws or other foundational documents. The best procedure, I have found, is to draft the policies first and leave bylaw amendments for last. Leaders are often surprised at how little bylaw change turns out to be necessary. Sometimes they find, on reading their bylaws closely, that provisions they have diligently followed for years are not there at all. When amendments are needed, it is usually to change the size or method of selection of the governing board, to eliminate lengthy lists of standing committees and their duties, or to change misleading language—saying, for example, that the board or its officers "manage" the congregation. Once the basic plan of governance has been affirmed based on the board policies, such amendments are not difficult to frame.

One frequent mistake is worth mentioning. Sometimes, in frustration with the problems of the governance structure they have, congregations do something called "suspending the bylaws." I am not sure where this idea comes from—maybe it is an extension of "suspending the rules," which is a bit of *Robert's Rules* arcana meaning to do something slightly outside normal parliamentary procedure.[3] Suspending the bylaws is more like suspending the Constitution: If it ever happens, then I hope to have some bottled water in the basement. A congregation that suspends (or repeals) its bylaws is governed instead by the nonprofit corporation statute of its state or province, which may have some provisions that would come as a surprise. If someone proposes suspending the bylaws, I would encourage them to cool off and think of a safer way to make the needed changes.

In some denominations, the most fundamental rules of governance can't be changed by the congregation at all. Change is usually still possible, though it may take some imagination to effect. It is important to adhere to those provisions that are actually mandatory. Fortunately, many denominations have in recent years made their polity manuals more flexible.

Should We Collect Old Policies?

To many people, the obvious first step in writing an updated policy book is to collect all of the existing policies. If you do, you are likely to find that only some of them are truly policies, written to control decisions over time. Others turn out, on inspection, to be case law—the board's response to a single event, which then was interpreted as a precedent, whether the board intended it that way or not. One purpose of a policy book is to remove this ambiguity.

Some existing policies may try to answer every possible question about a subject, such as building rentals, staff benefits, or kitchen cleanup. Under an improved policy structure, the board will adopt the "biggest" policies in any area and let the staff make smaller decisions, including writing any further policies that may be needed.

Understandably, those who have invested time and energy in the board's existing policies are sometimes anxious that their work not be forgotten. In my experience it is a waste of time for the GTF to collect and review existing policies at the beginning of its work. The GTF is not simply writing new policies to pile on top of old ones. It is creating a new structure that defines which decisions the board will make by policy and which it will delegate to others. Existing board policies, made without the benefit of such a structure, may or may not fit into the new board policy book.

Polishing the Policies

Once the policy-writing process is complete, the GTF collects, edits, and refines the policies themselves, making sure their language is clear and consistent. This is a good point to ask an attorney with experience in nonprofit law to review the policies in relation to your bylaws. The board will need to see the final language of the policy book well in advance of the meeting where they will be asked to adopt it. The motion to adopt should specify a future date to ensure that the responsibility for making any particular decision is as unambiguous as possible.

Champing at the Bit

Long before the policies are fully drafted, leaders will begin to act as though they already have been adopted. Some governance ideas have a viral quality. Despite the plan to live under the current system until the switch is thrown, new concepts sprout up in old places. Board members ask, "Is this what we should be talking about?" Staff members ask, "Would it be okay for us to decide this on our own?" Anyone can ask, "What are our priorities this year?"

These are good signs! And there is nothing wrong with making incremental changes, so long as everybody understands that, until the new policies have been approved and put into effect, all changes have to comply with the existing allocation of authority.

YEARS 2 AND 3

Officially, governance change begins when the board adopts its policies. The behavior change the policies require takes longer. Over time, the board, staff, committees, and teams experience a major shift, not only in the way decisions get made and work gets done, but also in *which* decisions get made and *which* work gets done. Strategic questions that have floated in the air for years will now be posed officially, addressed openly, and turned into priorities for action. Opportunities for ministry will open up on a new scale because responsibility for taking action on priorities is vested in the same place as the power to make things happen. When all goes well, the pace of congregational life picks up, along with its efficiency. Individuals feel increased stress because it's clearer what they are accountable for doing. Long-standing performance problems quickly become more obvious. It's exciting, and it's hard.

Changes for the Board

How, exactly, life will change depends on the details of the proposed new structure. According to the time line in figure 9.1, the board adopts its policies at the end of year 1, effective at the beginning of year 2. After the planning retreat, the board adopts its first annual vision of ministry and open questions. Assuming that the new board members are elected at this time (which may or may not be the case), the board has an opportunity to train them from the start in the new model, starting with a twelve-month plan for board meetings.

An important consideration in designing the board's work during the transition is to make sure board members have an opportunity to experience the benefits of the new structure. Paradoxically, in order to achieve its goal of spending more time thinking about the future, the board has to write policies. Unchecked, too much policy-writing at board meetings could attract board members who *like* tinkering with policies—the wrong group, on the whole, to usher in the board's new, future-oriented life. Realistically the board will need to spend some time refining policies, but as much as possible, it should spend time on future-focused work instead. It should plan large blocks of time through the year for conversation and reflection and for reaching out to the congregation. The GTF (and then the governance committee) can lift some of the wordsmithing burden and free the board for its more important job.

Partway through year 2, the board and head of staff hold their first evaluation session. Unless goals have been previously agreed upon, this cannot be a complete evaluation, but it's worth going through the motions, if only to assess how the board and head of staff are doing at establishing their new roles. The governance committee will have been monitoring this along the way and might well participate in this first evaluation session.

As the year 3 planning retreat approaches, the board will want to spend some time drawing together what is has learned from its discussions about open questions through the year. As it draws tentative conclusions about its new vision of ministry, it can decide whom to invite to the planning retreat, which data to gather, and what kind of process will be best for the particular priorities that are rising to the surface. It never hurts to be transparent about what the board is working on, even when it is not ready to present a polished report, so that those who have strong feelings can express them along the way instead of afterward. The year 3 planning retreat initiates the second cycle of collaboration.

In year 3, the board–head of staff evaluation session can be done properly because a board-approved vision of ministry will have been in place for more than a full year. The evaluation is mutual, though it is not perfectly symmetrical. Board members evaluate their own performance and that of the board itself at the same time as they evaluate (and receive feedback from) the clergy leader.

Changes for the Staff

When boards turn their attention away from management to pay more attention to discernment, strategy, and oversight, the first group to feel a painful pinch is apt to be the staff. Congregation staff, accustomed often to a style of work that emphasizes preparation for committee meetings, may be surprised how much simpler it is to make decisions than to prepare for others to make them. Staff members may also be surprised how weighty it can feel to be responsible for outcomes.

One temple administrator put it this way: "Before, we had a problem getting anyone to provide oneg refreshments after service. A committee was in charge, but it didn't happen. Occasionally the board talked about it, but there was nothing they could do. Now we still have a problem getting anyone to bring oneg refreshments. The difference is: *I feel responsible!*"

And that is just as it should be. A board that takes responsibility for governance puts pressure on the staff (including volunteers who act as staff) to take responsibility for ministry. In congregations shifting from a board- or committee-centered model to one that entrusts the staff with a more central role in daily management, people often ask, "Who will do all of the work we now do in committees?" A simple (and sometimes disappointing) answer is that the work will be done by the same people who do it now. Congregations depend heavily on volunteers, and making staff accountable for ministry does not change that. Lines of accountability change, but groups of laypeople who teach children's classes, organize for social action, or weed the garden will look much the same before and after. The first major task for the staff is to organize existing lay leaders and volunteers as part of the staff structure. Lay members of the congregation need to continue to lead, as well as to work. The staff needs to recruit and develop not only volunteers, but leaders, too.

Building the Team Structure

One practical step that many congregations have found useful is to hold a series of meetings to organize the new team structure. A first meeting might include the paid staff and volunteers who hold (or will hold) major program, outreach, and administrative leadership responsibilities. Prepare some 6" × 8" sticky notes and a large, empty wall or whiteboard, and invite the group to design a structure that connects all of the activities and services that will fall under "ministry." At the top will be the head of staff, the senior staff team, and other paid staff and volunteer leaders. At the bottom are notes representing the activities you need to manage—or, better yet, the ministry outcomes you want to produce for people. By thinking in terms of results rather than programs, you will be more likely to find novel, streamlined alternatives to your current organization chart. The only constraint is that everyone on the chart has to be connected to the head of staff, directly or indirectly. You may not have enough staff to fill every position near the top—that's okay. In fact, calling attention to the need for volunteers to fill such leadership positions is one of the good outcomes of this meeting.

The second meeting is larger—one congregation called it the Great Big Meeting. Invite everyone who is active in ministry and everyone you hope to recruit. Show the organization chart produced at the first meeting (and approved by the head of staff), and have everyone gather in groups according to their places in the chart. Ideally, everyone would be at a table for six or eight, with a staff member or staff-appointed volunteer leading the discussion. Topics for discussion might include the following:

- What resources, permissions, reimbursements, or other support do you need in order to do your work effectively?
- What questions do you have about how your work under the new governance model may differ from how it has been previously?
- What goals, plans, or projects do you have underway or under development that you want to be sure the staff is aware of?
- What suggestions do you have about how to make our transition more effective?

Collect all of the questions on one wall, combining those that overlap. Some questions can be answered on the spot; all can be answered in a follow-up e-mail. Still others will require temporary working groups to solve them.

It may take a while for committees that become ministry teams to realize that they are free of the responsibility to hold monthly meetings, keep minutes, file reports, and otherwise act like a committee. Some of these behaviors might be useful for some teams but not all. Some teams are permanent; others can go out of existence when their work is done. The staff is free to create new groups to fit new tasks. Each ministry team need not be representative of the whole congregation. In fact, a team should systematically exclude anyone who is not in favor of accomplishing its task!

When staff members are delegated power and responsibility for ministry, their work shifts in many ways. The staff team will need patience and forbearance while its members develop new skills and habits. A budget for staff training, planning, and retreats is an important part of a successful governance transition. The board needs continual reminders that its role is to tell the staff what ministry results it hopes for, not to intervene whenever the staff stumbles. A board that has been willing in the past to listen to complaints about staff members will no doubt be tested by members hoping—often with the best intentions—to bypass the staff team by going to the board. The board needs to develop immunity to such attempts and a willingness to let the staff make its own decisions and its own mistakes. Every role will have new boundaries and new duties during the trial run. It is important to be both kind and firm in nudging people into new ways of responding to familiar situations.

EVALUATION AND YEAR 3

Toward the end of the year 2, the governance committee invites the board, staff, lay leaders, and congregation as a whole to evaluate how well the congregation has addressed the concerns and achieved the goals that motivated governance change in the first place. The governance vision statement articulated by the GTF just after the initial governance workshop is one basis for evaluation, along with other goals articulated later. As with any evaluation, achieving preexisting goals is only one positive outcome; another is to learn to desire a different goal. It is not the main point of the evaluation to measure people's happiness. One sure result of success in any change process is that some people will become less happy. Congregations do not exist to make their members or their leaders happy; the important measure of success is whether governance helps to produce the results called for by the congregation's mission. This criterion is not easily measured, but a rough estimate is better than a thousand "metrics" that amount to nothing but opinion polls.

The governance committee presents a written report of the evaluation. Because its members have an obvious stake in the success of "their" structure, the governance committee should take care to summarize all feedback it receives, including criticisms. During year 3, the governance committee keeps evaluation of the ongoing governance-change process itself at the center of its agenda. All year, and especially in its annual evaluation, an effective board continually asks, How well are we playing our governance roles?

Change can be joyous and exciting, but it is rarely easy. It takes something like three years, from the first decision to inquire into governance change, before the behavior called for by the new structure is the first idea that comes to mind. Even after that, new leaders will need to be acculturated and helped to unlearn habits they acquired in other congregations, in other nonprofits, and at work. The effort is worthwhile, though, if it creates a congregation that is better able to say what difference it means to make in people's lives and to accomplish what it sets out to accomplish.

⑩

POLICY CHOICES

No board should adopt a set of boilerplate policies. Congregations are too varied and their ways of organizing too imprinted with their values for generic policies to fit. Strong boards don't outsource policy-making even to their own committees. If a subject is too trivial for the board to address with policy, then it should be delegated to the staff. If a policy is too technical for the board to understand, then the board should educate itself so that it can carry out its own responsibilities. A committee might assist by providing information, developing discussion questions, or drafting policy alternatives. But the board always is responsible for its own policies and should write, not rubberstamp, them.

In a normal year, policy work should occupy only a small part of the board's time. But during a governance-change process, when the board needs to create a whole new set of policies at once, policy-making temporarily becomes a major chore. One way to make it manageable is to get the governance task force (GTF) to do some of the work. Another is to divide the task into pieces. Instead of drafting all the policies at once and dumping them onto the board table, the GTF makes policies in batches, feeding them to the board bit by bit at a pace the board can handle. The GTF can also reach out to the wider leadership to seek input as the policies are written, so that when the finished product is approved, it bears the stamp of wide participation and is more likely to receive support.

This chapter has two parts: The first addresses what, for many congregations, is the most challenging governance-change topic: delegation to the head of staff. For many congregations, this is the most challenging policy choice of all. Other policy choices depend on the leadership structure for ministry and especially on knowing who the head of staff will be.

The second part of this chapter walks through all the other major topics of board policy. In appendix B, you can see a completed set of policies, from which you are encouraged to adapt and borrow but only after you have had a good discussion about the policies that will best serve your congregation and its mission.

DELEGATION TO THE STAFF

In many congregations entering the governance-change process, the "elephant in the room" is staff authority. How much of what kind of power should the board delegate? How should we expect paid staff to work with volunteer leaders in ministry? What process of goal-setting and evaluation will promote high staff morale and creativity while achieving the board's goals and ensuring that its policies are honored? No one answer to these questions fits all congregations, but certain benchmarks are worth considering by any board as it makes choices about staff authority and structure. Effective delegation policies will balance *authority*, *guidance*, and *accountability*.

Congregations often give people—most often, volunteers—authority without holding them accountable. Think of the longtime treasurer who can do just as he likes because no one wants to think about replacing him. With paid staff, we do the opposite—holding them accountable for things they can't control. Worship attendance is down? People must not like the music! (But the music director better not bring a guitar into the sanctuary.) It's not fair to hold people accountable for outcomes without giving them enough authority to make that reasonable. Authority and accountability are two essential elements of proper delegation to be kept in balance.

The third element—guidance—is the one that for some reason we most often avoid. Instead of telling people what we want, we wait until they give us something and then criticize. We would do better to give all of our advice up front, including prohibitions, hopes, advice, and aspirations. It is hard work, but good delegation demands giving guidance in advance as much as possible instead of later in the form of criticism.

Effective delegation policies also accomplish the following:

- They minimize the number of individuals and groups that report directly to the board, so that the board can concentrate on planning, policy, and oversight.
- They encourage staff to form a strong and self-sufficient team whose members take individual and joint responsibility, manage their own relationships, and resolve their own differences.
- They create a single structure for decision-making about ministry.
- They encourage wide consultation but avoid triangulation by placing the final decision for each class of decisions in one place.

With attention to these goals, a board can create delegation policies that encourage the firm, just-right boundaries that give even leaders who are less than perfect a good chance at creating and sustaining fruitful partnership.

Global Delegation

Policies that delegate the board's authority to others are at the heart of effective governance by policies. The simplest way to start is with a "global delegation" policy, which empowers the staff to make *all* operational decisions not reserved explicitly to the board, assigned to someone else, or prohibited by policy. (By *staff* I mean whoever has been designated as the head of staff or ministry decision-maker. Who this should be is a separate question, discussed in this chapter under "The Head of Staff.")

"Global delegation" provides a safety net to ensure that the congregation has a legitimate way to make all of the novel decisions life tosses up to be decided every day. How should the thermostats be set? Can we take down the lawn sign about last year's humanitarian crisis? May the youth group play the organ? No board has the foresight and imagination to anticipate all such questions in its policies; what it can do is to vest someone they trust with the power and responsibility to decide them as they come up.

Having adopted global delegation, the board could simply stop—leaving *everything* under the control of staff—in which case it would plan to accept whatever the staff did, so long as it did not violate the law, the bylaws, or some other higher source of authority. Most boards are not comfortable with quite that much freedom of staff action, so they adopt more policies to limit, guide, and direct the head of staff. To make those policies stick, they then adopt policies about how they will hold their staff accountable.

This procedure—delegating all of the authority, then taking some of it back—does not necessarily result in giving any more (or less) authority to staff than any other method. How much authority the staff has depends on the limits the board sets. But it does create a leak-proof container to ensure that someone is always responsible for taking necessary action. When board policies are silent, the staff has both the authority and the responsibility to act. This can be rather energizing, especially compared to the timid, wait-we'd-better-ask culture that prevails in many congregations.

The Head of Staff

Who should be the "head of staff"? In a congregation large enough to have a clergy leader, the simplest and most common structure is to make him or her the head of staff. There are other ways, but the more variety I see, the more partial I become to the simplicity of one head of staff. When the board speaks to or hears from "the staff," it is talking to one person, who represents the whole ministry structure. (Other staff or lay leaders will sometimes actually do the talking, but the head takes responsibility for what they say.) An advantage of this straightforward system is that the board has just one "direct report" to oversee, which minimizes the board's time spent directing, guiding, and evaluating staff and mediating differences among them. One direct report is also easier to hold accountable because there never is confusion about who is responsible for staff failures or successes. Clear accountability makes the board more powerful.

Being head of staff fits some aspects of the clergy role better than others. It fits the fact that, symbolically, the clergy leader is the head of the congregation—regardless what the bylaws say—and is seen as such by many members and all passersby. Even in congregations where clergy have little power to make decisions, the role itself confers moral authority. In the long run, what the clergy leader pays attention to will grow; what he or she ignores will shrink. Moral authority is persuasive rather than compulsory—but effective. Congregations rely on volunteers, and only moral authority mobilizes them. To use authority productively, the clergy leader needs things only the board can grant. Money, building space, staff time, and power to direct the work of others—without these, all the rights and privileges of ordination amount to very little. The clergy leader as the head of staff and the board as holder of its material resources are natural and necessary partners in the congregation's leadership.

Manager or Clergyperson?

Like many managers today, a clergy leader is not first of all a manager but a member of a profession—a priest, pastor, minister, or rabbi. He or she may lack specific managerial skills, like supervision, finance, budgeting, and project planning. Board members, who may be expert managers themselves in other industries, may see the clergy leader as unqualified to head the staff. Most congregations say on surveys that they want their clergy to spend time on worship preparation, study, writing, pastoral care—almost everything except "administration." The clergy leader may agree and happily avoid responsibility for management—at least in theory. In practice, clergy want their way on certain things, and congregations expect them to play a bigger role in management than they realize. Management decisions must be made, and the person on the scene best suited to make them, often, is the clergy leader. The larger and more complex the congregation, the more time and energy administration takes. Clergy, for all their sense of special calling, often feel a manager's accountability for how the institution runs without the usual authority a manager would have to run the institution.

Clergy and congregations are not alone in this dilemma. Top leaders of many modern institutions have primary expertise in a profession rather than management per se. Hospital CEOs are often doctors, college presidents are usually scholars, and museum directors often begin as artists or art historians rather than as managers. Business leaders, too, increasingly think of themselves as engineers, economists, or marketers who happen to be working as managers. I once heard Dr. Roy W. Menninger, a psychiatrist who succeeded his father and uncle as head of the Menninger Clinic, say that at first he treated the clinic and its managers like patients. When department heads came to him with management issues, he gave them sympathy, analysis, support, and understanding, but they seemed dissatisfied. Later, he became a more effective leader when he realized that in his administrative role people didn't come to him for healing; they came wanting him to make decisions.

Professionals can make good staff leaders because they understand and care about the core work of the institution, be it medicine, education, art, technology, engineering, finance, or building a community of faith. But leadership alone is not enough. Organizations also need someone to make decisions and coordinate the work. Clergy who become institutional leaders need to learn some managerial skills, like project and financial management and supervision. They need to develop managerial traits, like decisiveness, clear boundaries, and a willingness to confront and disappoint people. They also need to cultivate their sense of calling. Other staff can complement a clergy leader's deficits in managerial skill, but it's hard to work around a leader who has lost the heart to lead.

Talking with clergy, I sometimes point out that management, according to a common definition, means "getting results through the efforts of others." Thinking of it that way, some clergy (and board members, too) see that a clergyperson may bring more strengths to staff leadership than they first thought and that his or her deficits may not be so serious, given the availability of others who know things the staff leader does not. The challenge, especially for clergy who have moved from small congregations to large ones (or who have found themselves in larger congregations without moving) is to cultivate a style of management that feels like ministry. The board can support this transition by selecting a staff structure that enables the staff leader to achieve religiously appropriate results with the support of others who contribute needed managerial skills.[1]

One Head of Staff

An effective plan for many congregations with a median attendance between 150 and 400 is to make the clergy leader head of staff and hire an administrator to take charge of building maintenance, budgeting, and finance. Any other building and administrative staff (custodians, secretaries, bookkeepers) report to the administrator. The administrator manages the technical and managerial aspects of the staff's work, such as staff goal-setting and evaluation, building maintenance and use, and financial matters. The clergy leader supervises the administrator plus any program staff: music director, education director, volunteer coordinator, and so on. In this way the staff can be unified under the religious professional while ensuring that administrative matters are well taken care of. Obviously, a great deal depends on finding the right person to play the administrator role.

In larger congregations, staff leadership takes more of the senior clergy leader's time, while the other demands of the position do not go away. In larger congregations, the demand on clergy leaders for visionary leadership, fund-raising, and public visibility require stepping back from day-to-day staff leadership. Unfortunately, many congregations simply add to the number of direct supervisory "reports" the clergy leader has.

A better option is to engage a senior associate pastor or rabbi to assume leadership of the program staff, so that the senior clergy leader has just two direct reports: the administrator and the senior associate. For clergy who enjoy staff leadership, this may be an adequate arrangement even in very large congregations.

The Executive Number 2

More frequently, though, in congregations that can afford it, the best arrangement is for the senior clergy leader to have only one direct report: an executive number 2. The number 2—under the title executive minister or rabbi, church administrator, or executive director—supervises other staff, convenes staff meetings, coordinates reporting to the board, and takes responsibility for ministry performance overall. The number-2 position requires strong management skills, a strong understanding of the congregation's religious mission, and a relationship of total trust with the clergy leader. In business, analogous roles are often designated chief executive officer and chief operating officer. In colleges and universities, the president and provost often have a similar relationship, as do the president and executive director of some secular nonprofits. In the US Navy, a ship's master (captain) decides strategy and relates to the larger command structure, while the executive officer (XO) runs the ship.

One search committee, looking for a number 2, described the hoped-for applicant this way: "If you are a minister, people say to you, 'You could have been in business.' If you're a businessperson, people say, 'You should have gone to seminary.'" They found their candidate—a master of divinity who had an MBA as well.

It should go without saying once again—but unfortunately, I've found, does not—that the number 2 must have the clergy leader's complete trust at all times. This means that the process for hiring and firing must ensure that the senior clergy leader has the initiative and is never required to work with someone who is not compatible.

Two-Headed Staffs

A variant approach, quite common in synagogues, is essentially to have two heads of staff—the senior rabbi and executive director—both reporting to the board directly. Synagogues often have large fee-for-service operations (membership dues, school tuition, life-cycle ceremonies, bookstores, and banquet halls) and, compared to churches, relatively small participation in Shabbat services and other general membership activities. As a consequence, Jewish congregations feel more businesslike than most churches, and the "religious" work of rabbis, cantors, and educators feels more separable from that of the executive director. Also, for historical reasons, many rabbis have favored a more academic or judicial understanding of their role and often introduce themselves as "the rabbi at Beth Israel" rather than "the rabbi *of* Beth Israel." Having as little role in the administration of the synagogue as possible fits the traditional nonexecutive idea of a rabbi. This approach works well in many synagogues—and also a few churches.

I do wonder whether such two-headed structures will work as well in the future as they did in the past. The notion that the business and religious aspects of a congregation can run in parallel depends, it seems to me, on the assumption that our current notions about what to do and how to do it are still pretty much correct. Already, congregations are beginning to see that they have catching up to do with rapid cultural change. In the future, a congregation may have to decide whether it will be a business with some religious staff or a congregation with some business staff.

Collective Forms of Leadership

Congregations have tried a number of alternatives to the clergy-head-of-staff structure, with varying success. One of the most common is cominstry, which works very well in many cases and disastrously in others. If the cominsters trust each other and take 100 percent responsibility for the internal working of their team, then cominstry is as likely to work as well as solo ministry, or better. The attitude of other leaders makes a difference—congregants who try to "help" cominsters fix problems in their relationship can be especially unhelpful. Married cominstry teams benefit in this respect from a social taboo against meddling in the internal workings of a couple. All cominsters, whether they are married or not—indeed, all staff teams—benefit from an understanding that the staff will address staff performance issues on its own or with assistance from outside the congregation.

Another alternative to a solo head of staff is to make the board executive committee the head of staff. This approach has many shortcomings. This blurs the boundary between board and staff; the more involved in staff decision-making leaders of the board become, the more they tend to pull the rest of the board with them into management concerns. Also, volunteers cannot normally match paid staff in their awareness of day-to-day management issues, so they depend on staff to bring them up to speed. If the purpose of giving management authority to the executive committee is to ensure that staff members follow the board's wishes, then it is better for the board to define its wishes clearly enough that it can write them into policies. The executive committee can then review the staff's decisions, not to approve or disapprove them but to spot issues that need board attention.

Another group approach to management is to entrust ministry decision-making to a "ministry leadership team." This group of three to five is not a subset of the board but part of the ministry staff structure, leading the staff as a collective. The team may include only paid staff members, or it may include one or more lay members. In effect, this team is the innermost concentric circle of the staff. It might meet weekly; the whole staff, monthly; and a larger group, including volunteer ministry team leaders, once a quarter. A ministry leadership team meeting does many of the things good board meetings avoid—problem-solving, arbitration, and case-by-case decision-making.

For any collective or team leadership structure, it is important to address some sticky questions: What, exactly, does it mean to say, "The team decides"? Do team members vote? What happens in case of a tie? What happens when there is a need to fill a vacancy? Who deals with questions about team members' performance? What does it mean to hold a team accountable? These are not easy questions to answer—in fact, their difficulty is one reason boards so often choose a single head of staff.

Collective leadership tends to bias decision-making toward the status quo because that is the fallback option when a team cannot agree. If the congregation means to continue following the basic strategies it followed in the past, then collective leadership arrangements may be fine. Congregations that see the need for major change—those whose community environment is changing, whose perspectives about faith are changing, or whose younger generations define congregational success in new ways—may want to consider shifting to an individual staff leader partnered with a board that thinks collectively about goals.

MAKING POLICY, STEP BY STEP

You'll find a more or less complete set of example policies in appendix B. Those policies are not for your congregation—indeed, they are for no one's congregation. But some concrete examples might help you imagine the policies you might write on each topic. As I comment on each type of policy in the remainder of this chapter, I will follow the same numbering system used in appendix B to make it easier to flip back and forth.

I will address these comments mostly to the topics rather than the Appendix B samples, as a way of emphasizing that my goal is to help you to discover policy solutions of your own.

Prologue to the Board Policy Book

Many people don't know exactly what a board policy is or how it is related to bylaws, minutes, staff policies, procedure manuals, or Holy Writ. A prologue helps to orient the reader, locating the policies in their larger context.

The best place to store policies is on your website, and the prologue can also indicate where on the web to find a current version of the policies.

I. Board Governance

1.1. Role of the Board

Your state or provincial laws establish the basic functions of the board of a nonprofit organization. Your bylaws may add other information. No need to repeat any of that here. This policy says how *this* board means to fulfill its duties within the role given it by law and bylaws. The annual and not-so-annual work products described in chapter 8 provide one starting point for this policy.

1.2. Board Officers

Bylaws generally create board officers and define their basic powers. The board does not need to repeat what its boss (the congregation or higher church authority) has said already. What board policies do need to do is to assign responsibility for preparing the agenda for board meetings, leading the open-question outreach to the congregation, and communicating to the congregation about the board's work. If the bylaws are ambiguous about the treasurer's role, then the policies should clarify that, as a member of the board, the treasurer is primarily involved with oversight, not management. If the treasurer must manage money for some reason, then the policies say who will oversee the treasurer.

1.3. Board Committees

Board committees are discussed in chapter 4. Because so many congregations are accustomed to using committees as an all-purpose organizational tool, it is important to make it clear exactly what committees the board intends to have and for what purposes.

A board whose purpose is to "run the church" needs lots of committees to manage programs (sometimes on their own, sometimes in parallel with staff). It also needs committees to help manage ancillary or support functions, like finance, building maintenance, and communications.

A board whose purpose is to govern needs fewer committees. The board's function is more focused, and it retains only those committees that relate directly to its primary roles of oversight, strategy, and discernment.

A committee is the creature of its parent and should do only its parent's work. The test of whether a committee should remain a board committee or become a ministry team is to see where the products of its work go. If a committee takes assignments from the board and its reports help the board to do appropriate board work, then it is a board committee. If its work produces or supports a program or activity, especially if it works primarily with a staff member, then it is better called a ministry team.

Standing Committees

The exact list of standing board committees depends on the exact scope of the board's work as defined by its delegation policies. The board that "runs the church" has delegated nothing—it may give assignments, but it has not delegated true responsibility, hence its need for an elaborate system of committees. A board that has delegated management to others so that it can govern needs to be careful not to delegate its governance authority as well. The board needs to do its own part of the discernment and strategy work; it cannot give away responsibility for oversight—though it can and should seek help with it.

Standing committees are appropriate only for those areas of policy where the board needs expert counsel regularly. A typical list of standing committees might be limited to those listed in chapter 4: finance, personnel, governance, and nominating. Most board committees are temporary or ad hoc, appointed in light of the board's immediate needs. Some ad hoc committees, such as an audit committee, may be appointed annually.

The creation of a standing committee is a lasting action of the board and therefore should be recorded in the policy book. Creating an ad hoc committee or task force or appointing someone to a committee is an ordinary action of the board, recorded in the minutes, not the policy book.

1.4. Expectations of Board Members

A smaller board, especially, needs all hands on deck. It derives much of its superior effectiveness from the fact that it asks more of every member. This section deals with the board's expectations of its members and its procedures for dealing with misconduct by board members.

1.4.1. Board Covenant

Today, even more than in Henry Robert's time, it is a mistake to assume that everyone who sits at a board table brings the same expectations about behavior, decision-making, problem-solving, or courtesy. Assumptions differ so sharply that each board needs to develop its own covenant of shared behavioral expectations and review it regularly. New members of the board need to be brought into the covenant and invited to help reshape it. A helpful resource for creating such covenants in groups of any size is *Behavioral Covenants in Congregations: A Handbook for Honoring Differences* by Gil Rendle.[2] I do not recommend that the GTF draft a covenant for the board because that work is better done by the board itself. The work is important, however, and the GTF may well need to urge the board to get around to it.

Boards can be surprisingly resistant to firm expectations. Some members seem almost to prefer complaining about others to stating clearly what the board expects. Sometimes people say, "We have enough trouble getting people to agree to serve without making this even more difficult." This concern sounds reasonable, but experience shows that people are more attracted to highly disciplined groups than to lax ones. This is especially true of people who can make the greatest contribution. The board member who likes to cruise into every other meeting unprepared may enjoy that freedom, but he or she makes the board experience much more frustrating for everyone else. Expectations can be firm and clear without needing to be rigid or unreasonable.

Basic Duties.   In creating a board covenant, a good place to begin is with a frank discussion about the basic duties of board membership: attendance at meetings, diligent preparation, and thorough understanding of the congregation's overall situation. Some members may have accepted nomination despite known schedule conflicts. These need to be resolved or explicitly excused, or else those members need to leave the board if it is to arrive at manageable baseline expectations.

Some boards have an automatic resignation policy, either in the bylaws or in their covenants. If a board member misses more than a set number of meetings, then he or she is deemed to have resigned and is so notified. Other boards give warning notices and phone calls before asking members to come back or please resign—but why? How does treating people like children help them to be more responsible? Adults can be expected to understand the consequences of their own decisions, especially if they have agreed to them.

Nothing helps people to arrive on time more than starting whether they have arrived or not. Likewise, the best way to encourage members to read the packet is to assume that everyone has read it and proceed. Of course, the packet needs to be of reasonable length and focused on important issues, and it must be published to board members in a timely way. E-mail fortunately makes the packet easy to publish but unfortunately also makes it easy to be careless about dumping reams of reading onto a board without vetting it for relevance. The board's covenants about its work routines need to include limits on how much the board expects of members.

Shared Study and Spiritual Practice. In working with boards to create covenants, I urge them to explore topics that make them uncomfortable. Often one such topic is the board's spiritual practice. Boards will adopt a wide variety of spiritual or study practices appropriate to their traditions (for one example, see "Shared Study and Spiritual Practice" in chapter 6). It is important that it be in conversation periodically about what practices it deems appropriate and that it ask each member to commit to a shared routine that touches the transcendent meanings of the board's work. The benefits are difficult to predict precisely, but boards that engage regularly in spiritual practice grow in their ability to speak frankly in love and to stay focused on the congregation's mission.

Financial Support. Even more challenging, on many boards, than covenanting to engage in spiritual practice is defining expectations about members' financial support of the congregation. Many nonprofit boards espouse the Three G Rule: "Give, Get, or Get Off." Board members are expected to contribute generously and to acquire large gifts from others—or to resign. In congregations that care about welcoming people of diverse economic circumstances, this formula is problematic.

Because they care about inclusiveness (and because they dislike confrontation), boards often err in the opposite direction and say nothing at all about what they expect board members to contribute. This omission can lead to the bizarre but not uncommon result that a board in whose name the congregation asks for generous support includes a member who can afford as much as others can but who gives little or nothing. By the power of negative example, this kind of behavior by leaders has its effect on the congregation's overall giving even if it is, in theory, secret.

It is tricky but possible to define expectations for board members' giving that are both clear and inclusive. Simply announcing to board members the total of their own giving can make a difference. Paying attention to this total gives the message that board members' giving is important. In addition, it can be helpful for the board to set a goal for its own giving from year to year.

Another approach is to define an overall standard (a percentage of income or even a dollar amount) and then acknowledge that no one standard will be reasonable for everyone, so some generous members will give less, but fortunately others can and will give more. One way of stating the expectation is to say that each board member is expected to consider giving at the requested standard and will have a conversation with one other board member about how he or she arrived at a decision.

There will always be board members who, for various reasons, cannot give as much as others do. Rather than letting this limitation inhibit those who can give more from celebrating and encouraging each other, the board covenant should recognize that everyone can afford to be generous—though the dollar value of a "generous" gift will vary from one person to another. It can go on to articulate an expectation that board members will be generous toward the congregation and mindful that their example influences others. Balancing firm expectations with openness and inclusion is hard work, but if the board can do this work internally, then it sets the stage for the congregation to be more effective in its wider efforts at fund-raising.

Decision-Making and Conflict Management. A final topic a board covenant needs to address is how the board will make decisions and manage conflict. These topics go together: Decision-making is difficult only when people disagree. Some boards assume that voting is an adequate system for resolving conflicts, but it's not. Voting may be a fairer way to make decisions than arm-wrestling, but it is no less an exercise in power. The majority has the legal right to compel the congregation to accept its views. By prevailing in a vote, the majority tacitly invokes the power of the state—the courts and even the police—to enforce its will. Surely, this is not ideal from a religious point of view!

It may surprise some people to know that General Robert was a great believer in consensus. In his own civic work, he went to great lengths to avoid divided votes, which he regarded, especially in a small board, as a mark of failure. Many arcane motions—to commit, refer, postpone, and place before a committee of the whole—essentially are ways to buy time for more discussion as an alternative to rushing to a vote. Robert gave what he called "substantial minorities"—more than one-third—the right to require a slower, more deliberate process in order to stop the majority from barging ahead. Robert also understood that *requiring* unanimity can lead to tyranny by the minority. It is as unfair for the few to prevent the many from deciding as it would be for the many to prevent the few from trying to change the majority's minds.

A covenant might well provide a process to identify decisions that need special attention and would benefit from a more gradual process of discernment. Such decisions merit one or more "premeeting meetings"—meetings with a "discussion that is only a discussion." Such meetings lower the temperature considerably and increase the chance of finding a compromise or a third way that will allow the group to stand united in the end. A board might also covenant to seek assistance from the denomination or an outside facilitator if conflict overwhelms the board's ability to deal with it alone.

1.4.2. Conflicts of Interest

Many congregations accept practices that in other contexts we would question. When the driveway needs retopping, why deal with someone we don't know when good old Tom of Tom's Blacktop sits right here at the board table? We know he'll give us a good price (don't we?). In any case, if we suddenly quit using him, he'd be upset.

No doubt he would, but we are living in a changed world, where in some ways the corporate and legal standard of good stewardship exceeds the common practice in religious institutions. If anything, the reverse should be the case. The scriptures are full of stories and admonitions about how to handle the fiduciary role, from Jesus's parables about good, bad, and indifferent stewards back to Cain's wrong answer to God's question about Abel. We are our brother's keeper, and in congregations, our brothers and sisters have entrusted resources to manage—not for our own benefit but for a higher purpose.

Because intertwined relationships are typical of congregations, it is not realistic to avoid all conflicts of interest, but the board can protect its members from criticism and embarrassment by having a clear policy for handling them. There are three levels of response to conflicts of interest: disclosure, recusal, and resignation. Mild conflicts of interest (for instance, when a board member's cousin holds stock in an office-supply chain) can be managed simply by disclosing them. If the remaining board members agree that the conflict is minor, then the affected member can continue to participate in the decision. More serious conflicts—for instance, where a member's daughter is a candidate for a scholarship—require recusal: The member leaves the room and does not discuss or vote on that item. More serious conflicts of interest—for instance, if a board member is a contractor who wants to bid on a new building—involve such a pervasive division of loyalty that resignation is required. The choice of the level of response that fits a specific case is best made by board members who are not affected by the conflict.

It is a good idea to make disclosure of ongoing potential conflicts of interest an annual routine. This is a good occasion to note that conflicts of interest are inevitable. This acknowledgment makes it easier for members to disclose conflicts that arise later, when the board takes up an issue that affects them.

The most obvious conflicts come up when, as in the case of Tom, the blacktop man, the board considers transferring the congregation's money to a board member. Such conflicts also happen when a board member applies for a paid position on the congregation's staff or offers a computer for the office at a "reduced" price.

Clear conflicts arise when a board action benefits the spouse or child of a board member. When family of board members serve in paid staff roles, potential conflicts come up whenever the board acts on salaries or budgets.

When a board member serves on two nonprofit boards that deal with one another, yet another type of conflict can arise. Probably the most common case of this is where a congregation rents space to a nonprofit school or social agency and one person serves on both boards. Here the conflict is between two charitable missions—which may be compatible but not identical. You don't have to be selfish to have a conflict of interest!

This policy treats conflicts of interest as a normal and expected fact of life and provides a process for addressing them routinely and when they come up.

1.4.3. Discipline and Removal of Board Members

The board only needs a policy for how to remove board members if it has the power to do so. If the bylaws or foundation documents do not provide for the removal of board members, then amending them should be a priority. Your state or province nonprofit corporation act may provide a process, but it may not be the process you prefer.

Assuming that the board has the power to remove board members, this policy spells out the procedure it will use in doing so. For obvious reasons, the best time to adopt a policy or bylaw on this subject is when no wants to remove a board member. Then if the need occurs, the board can act without needing to create a process under pressure.

1.5. Auxiliary Organizations

Men's, women's, and youth groups in churches and synagogues have a long and distinguished history of service. They raise money, build relationships, recruit for religious leadership, and have pushed their congregations to update their thinking about everything from women's suffrage to gay marriage. A congregation that wants freedom of thought and expression will encourage freedom of association among subgroups of all kinds.

However, an auxiliary that uses the congregation's nonprofit and tax status is not actually independent but is an integral part of the congregation. Its money is congregation money; its actions are actions the congregation is responsible for. One way of treating such an auxiliary is as a "ministry team" under the direction of the staff. Another is to acknowledge its quasi autonomy and adopt board policies to enable the board to exercise fiduciary oversight of its activity.

1.6. Delegation to Entities Other than the Staff

In exceptional cases, a board might create a committee and delegate to it authority to manage something on its own. A congregation with a large endowment fund might have an investment committee with the power to direct investment of the funds in order to avoid entrusting both the conservation and the spending of endowment money to the same person. This board-to-committee relationship does not run through the head of staff, which is why the policy is located here, under "Board Governance."

The board might also delegate authority directly to the board of a major subsidiary enterprise. A church that owns a large retirement home, for instance, might create a committee that is, in effect, a retirement home board that appoints its own executive director and reports directly to the church board. This might make sense, especially if the need for coordination between the staffs of the church and the retirement home is minimal. The drawback for the board is that it then has to supervise the retirement-home committee, which will certainly distract it from its own core work.

At some point, when a project of the church becomes a major institution in its own right, it can be of mutual benefit for them to separate entirely. The institution may find that it can secure public and foundation support more easily if it not part of a congregation, and the congregation may be better off not having to devote time to managing a relationship that confers no benefit on either party. For these reasons, separation can be the best choice even when the missions of the church and institution are closely aligned.[3]

2. Delegation to the Staff

This set of policies delegates management authority to the congregation's staff, identifies the head of staff, and gives any other direction the board chooses to give about the structure and functioning of the staff.

2.1. Global Delegation to the Head of Staff

The board's global delegation policy (discussed earlier) ensures that, when unanticipated questions come up, there will always be a way to decide them short of bringing them automatically to the board. In place of a "zero-based" system of delegation, the global delegation policy delegates everything about management to the head of staff. Other policies then limit and constrain the delegated power to whatever extent the board thinks necessary. Section 3, "Guidance and Limitations for the Staff," contains most of these constraints.

2.2–2.4. Structure of the Staff

Board policy defines the structure of the top-level staff, making it clear who is responsible for staff performance, and provides the primary communication link between the staff and board. This is the place to state who the head of staff is and what that role entails. This topic is important enough that I addressed it at length in the first section of this chapter.

3. Guidance and Limitations

Having given all its management authority to the head of staff, the board now has a chance to limit that authority and say how it wants it to be used. Guidance and limitations is the most complex set of policies. I suggest dividing them into four categories.

3.1. Personnel Decisions

The only thing worse than getting fired is to get fired by an organization with an unclear process for getting it done. In addition to the normal pain of job loss, the employee experiences false hope, personal criticism in group situations, and pointless politics. By addressing personnel decisions in advance, the board performs a kindness to its staff.

3.2. Care for Paid Staff

Boards are often reluctant to delegate decisions about personnel and money. Their concerns are understandable, but it is not practical for a board to make all such decisions directly. The most effective way for the board to ensure that important decisions are made as it would wish is to create policies that guide and circumscribe the actions of the staff.

3.3. Care for Members and Guests

The board's duty of care requires that it ensure the personal safety of all who come under the congregation's umbrella. As with other operational matters, the most effective way for the board to fulfill this duty is to state clearly what it expects of the ministry leadership. Individual board members who have skills or talents to offer can doff their board hats temporarily and join the staff as volunteers.

3.4. Care for Material Resources

Whether the person who manages the congregation's finances is paid or unpaid, he or she is part of the staff, acting with power delegated by the board. Because of the potential for misconduct, the board needs to create a thorough framework of guidance and accountability in the area of finance. Well-written financial policies protect the congregation's funds from misuse or misappropriation and protect financial managers from false accusations of misconduct.

4. Board Oversight

The board's duty of care requires it to ensure that the congregation's human and material resources are used for the benefit of its mission. The board fulfills this duty both negatively, by preventing theft and loss of resources, and positively, by requiring that the ministry be active, forward looking, and appropriately bold. To fulfill this responsibility, the board needs to say what it wants (through policies on discernment and strategy) and whom it will empower to lead (through policies on delegation). Oversight policies complete this picture by establishing a plan for monitoring and evaluating that work so staff and lay program leaders are accountable and so that the congregation learns from its experience.

A board that spends too much time checking up on its staff might just as well not delegate in the first place; by second-guessing the decisions of its staff, it trains staff members to be overcautious. Policies on oversight set performance and reporting standards for all who work in the congregation's name and establish annual routines for planned evaluation by the board of staff performance.

Completing the necessary elements of sound delegation, the board needs a plan for monitoring staff performance and for evaluating the performance of staff members who report directly to the board.

There is a balance to be struck between due diligence and oversolicitude. A board that spends too much time looking over the shoulders of its staff might as well not have delegated authority in the first place.

In the area of oversight, the buck stops with the board. It can share and delegate pieces of the work—an auditor, for instance, will physically examine the books—but the board is ultimately responsible and cannot shrug off this demand. In some cases, individual board members can even be held liable for failure to oversee the institution adequately. Each board member therefore needs at least a basic understanding of the congregation's finances and property and of the measures taken to ensure that no one who participates in congregational activities is placed at risk.

4.1. Mission Focus

Often when boards think about their oversight responsibility, they remember their duty to protect the property and manage the money but forget that oversight has a positive aspect as well. Making sure that the congregation acts to fulfill its mission is a part of the board's oversight role. A balanced budget is no virtue if no lives are changed. A budgetary surplus, in this light, may actually reflect a failure of board oversight if it means that people have entrusted it with money that it didn't use for the intended purpose.

4.2. Monitoring

From the board's standpoint, monitoring is passive. Monitoring policies call for the staff to provide regular reports focused on progress toward achieving the annual vision of ministry and compliance with board policy.

Monitoring needs to be focused if it is to mean anything: Flooding board members with irrelevant paper or tedious oral reports actually reduces their awareness of the congregation's ministry. Staff reports do not answer the question, What are you doing? and they do not invite the staff to impress the board with how busy they are. Instead the focus is on compliance with the board's policies—including the annual vision of congregational work, which sets positive goals, and the policies on guidance and limitation, which modify and limit the authority granted to the staff.

4.3. Evaluation

The board does not need to adopt policies about the evaluation of staff members other than those who report directly to the board. Where that person is a clergy leader, it is important to provide a more widely inclusive review process—in the example, I suggest once every three years—to recognize that the total job of a minister or rabbi includes much more than simply being CEO.

Policy-writing is an acquired taste. Those who can develop skill at writing policies that others can read and understand perform a valuable—if not always adequately appreciated—service for the congregation. So in case no one else remembers, I say, Thank you! You have made life easier for many who will never know it!

ⅠⅠ

LAY AND CLERGY PARTNERSHIP

The relationship of lay and clergy leaders has a colorful American history. From the earliest struggles between colonial ministers and magistrates to recent headlines about abusive clergy and their stunned parishioners, high drama has rarely ceased. American congregations have rarely tolerated clergy leadership without resisting it to some extent, and most of the time, clergy have felt they should get at least a little more respect. Clergy and their lay employers—or to put it differently, lay members and their clergy leaders—experience highs and lows found only among people who care deeply about the purposes for which they partner.

For the first Europeans in most parts of colonial North America, clergy power was a worry but not actually a problem—at least for a while. Lay settlers came first and set up congregations on their own, with laymen firmly in control. The Separatist colony at Plymouth Plantation, for example, had a church immediately but waited four years for the first ordained minister, John Lyford, to arrive in 1624. Soon afterward, Governor William Bradford, who had served as the lay preacher before Lyford's arrival, caught him writing hostile letters about the colony to its enemies in England. The governor hauled Lyford into court and gave him six months to get out of Plymouth. Lyford responded with an eloquent confession, "melting into tears" before the company. But before he actually left, his wife Sarah sealed the reputation of the first Pilgrim pastor by denouncing him for a long history of sexual misconduct toward parishioners, servants, and herself.[1] To any clergy leader who has followed such a predecessor, it will come as no surprise that, for a long time afterward, the Plymouth church was slow to trust its pastors.

While the abuse of clergy power was a recurrent worry for lay leaders, the burden of *lay* power was a daily fact of life for clergy. Anglican priests who eventually arrived in the southern colonies found lay vestries well established and ready to defend their local parishes—which local landowners had come to regard as their collective property—against ecclesiastical control. Even in Puritan Massachusetts, contrary to the stereotype of tyrannical "theocracy," magistrates, town officials, and deacons struggled to contain the power of ministers from the 1600s on. North American clergy, since their first arrival, have complained of being hemmed in, censored, and kept poor by wary laity—not everywhere and always but often enough to have produced an occupational resentment still expressed wherever clergy gather.[2]

Despite their many challenges, lay and clergy partners often work together happily, disagree without explosion, and feel strong in their roles without needing to diminish one another. Some clergy seem to create positive relationships wherever they go, and some congregations form strong partnerships with clergyperson after clergyperson. We should pay attention to the organizational practices of clergy and congregations that consistently form healthy partnerships. A major purpose of this book is to lift up some of the ways of organizing that seem to produce harmony between lay and clergy leaders and enable them to produce mission-focused practical results as well.

To be sure, the partnership of lay and clergy is not quite the same as the relationship of "governance and ministry." Governing boards in most traditions include clergy, who have considerable influence even if they do not vote. Lay staff and volunteers do most of the work of ministry, even when the clergy lead. Still, whenever leaders debate governance arrangements, age-old tensions between clergy and lay leaders flare up. Oftentimes, resistance to a clear division between governance and ministry arises from lay worries about whether clergy can be trusted with the management of practical affairs and from clergy worries about how well laypeople understand or can appreciate their spiritual work.

Each lay-clergy partnership has its particulars and can be healthy only when the people on both sides of the relationship have come to trust each other. In this final chapter, we must look at the psychology and sociology of partnership along with the explicit terms of the arrangement. No amount of tinkering with policies and bylaws can create a partnership of accountability and trust all by itself. To do that, we need to look a little deeper into the sources of mistrust between lay and ordained leaders and consider how they can be overcome.

CLERGY: FLAWED CARRIERS OF A SACRED MESSAGE

This book began by pointing to the paradox of "organized religion." Religion calls us to become better than we are, while institutions try to get us to behave predictably. Sometimes we succeed so fully in our organizing that we almost squeeze the life-transforming power out of faith by making it routine. We almost squeeze it out but hardly ever quite. Burning somewhere deep in even the most sanitary sanctuary is a smoky flame, a blunt reminder that it all began when somebody was changed. Housing the disruptive power of faith within the routinizing structures of an institution without snuffing it out is hard, not because we lack some magic formula, but because it really is hard.

The challenge of lay-clergy partnership stems from a related paradox. In a culture that highly values personal autonomy, clergy represent the claims of an ultimate Other. Those claims are understood in different ways by different faith communities, but every tradition asks the individual to transcend personal and family interests, attend to wider sympathies, and consider meeting higher expectations. Clergy, whether we like it or not, represent the claims and also the promises of that Other. As a consequence, our presence never is entirely comfortable, and our failings provoke strong reactions.

Anyone who doubts this should pay attention when a clergy leader resigns from a position. Along with rational, adult responses—like congratulations, sadness, and concealed delight—come surprising bursts of anger, often from the very people who most benefited from that pastor's service. These strange reactions have a simple explanation: In our childish inner hearts, a clergyperson's job is to reflect God's promise of eternal love. When my pastor tells me there is something he or she would rather do than be my pastor, how can I not feel at least a bit betrayed?

We clergy often feel betrayed as well—when, for instance, friendships that flourish in the course of ministry wither soon after the pastoral dimension is withdrawn; or when, standing on the pedestal of admiration, we suddenly discover what an easy target we've become. When we leave, we have a repertoire of strange behavior of our own: There's the swaggering departure, with unsubtle mentions of the bigger, better, higher-paying congregation that seduced us into leaving. There's the dramatic exodus, replete with stagy sympathy for all the grief the congregation must be feeling now that we are leaving. Or its opposite: the quick and furtive exit, "running through the thistles," as if we thought by leaving fast enough we could spare everyone the need for feeling anything at all.[3]

To the extent we take our role as messengers at all seriously, we clergy know that our performance will fall short of the legitimate expectations of lay leaders, whose applause or silence indicate how we are doing. A few clergy—many of them famous, one way or another—are by personality insensitive to feedback, sure they're doing fine no matter what. More of us, in my experience, brush off praise and internalize complaints and criticism, blaming ourselves for what we know is our inevitable failure to perform to an unreachable standard. At our best, we manage to exhibit charming, if not quite convincing, modesty. At worst, we suffer from depression and its many side effects.

Health requires that all of us back off from time to time and get perspective on the paradoxical mismatch between unbounded hope and human capability. In the process, we may learn to see in that paradox not only tragedy, but comedy as well. A leadership transition is a good time for learning how to see ourselves, not as incarnations of two sides of a paradox, but as players wearing masks. A time of transition, if we make good use of it, offers an opportunity to get perspective.

And so a clergy parting is a teaching moment of the highest kind, a chance for both clergy and lay leaders to learn (again!) to differentiate our wishful thinking from reality, the human messenger from the content of the message, not-God from God. The learning is not always pretty, but what lesson could be more important? A partnership whose purpose is to prod the partners out of our most cherished forms of self-absorption *should* be a challenge. Only after our presumptions have been punctured can we forgive each other for not being what we thought we were entitled to expect. Only after we are disillusioned can we partner honestly and well.

THE ROAD TO HEALTHY PARTNERSHIP

What makes for a healthy partnership? No doubt compatibility, shared values, and emotional intelligence play some role; it's hard to dance with a partner who steps on your toes all the time. The ability to differentiate oneself—to be aware of one's own feelings, opinions, and reactions while staying connected to others—is a key strength for clergy and lay leaders alike.[4] Open, relaxed, flexible relationships, lubricated by some social time, often seem to help. Many people say the right mix of personal and relational qualities in the leadership team is the key to a successful partnership—which is, it seems to me, 100 percent half right. The other half—the half we are especially concerned with in this book—is the structure of the partnership itself, consisting of agreements about power and role and process.

Unfortunately, experience offers no one recipe for structuring lay-clergy partnership. Almost any organizational structure you can imagine works well in some congregation somewhere, thanks to the social skills and dedication of its leaders. However, such exceptions are no proof that structure doesn't matter. Structure and other formal understandings matter most when social skills are less than perfect and when dedication is combined with ordinary human traits, like selfishness, ambition, vanity, and pride—that is, all the time.

By healthy partnerships, I don't mean ones in which the partners necessarily are comfortable or happy all the time. I mean *effective* partnerships that yield consistent positive results for people other than the partners. Effective partners disagree on many things but share commitment to a mission and work hard to realize it. They speak to one another frankly about what is going well and what needs fixing. Over time, they learn what to expect of one another, and they grow in trust. The negotiation and trust-building process begins during the selection process.

Long before the future partners even talk to one another, their respective histories exert strong influence on them. A congregation has a history with clergy, even if it never has employed one before. And a clergyperson, even a new graduate, has a history with congregations. And so each partner brings sensitivities and expectations into the relationship based on past experiences. Their histories influence the selection process, obviously. Less obviously, as years pass, initial motivations continue to influence our choices.

Partnership Beginnings

For a congregation, the most influential bit of history often is the memory of its previous clergy leader—or perhaps a longer-tenured predecessor. Occasionally, experience with a former clergy leader was so good (or so traumatic) that its influence extends for generations. Sometimes the true "predecessor" is a series of short-tenured clergy or a period of lay leadership, like the one in Plymouth Colony before John Lyford. Every congregation has some history with (or without) clergy, and that history has an influence on the selection process and the way the partnership develops.

Especially if the predecessor's ministry was long, the congregation probably accepted certain compromises. For example, someone usually wants
changes to the worship service that a given clergy leader is unable or unwill-
ing to make. Or the congregation lives with a clergy leader's failings on account of strengths in other areas. When that leader leaves, the compromises
go away as well. What was settled is now open for discussion; postponed
wishes become urgent needs. As a result, in filling out the profile for the
next clergy leader, too many congregations pay too much attention to the
things it found most troublesome about the predecessor rather than the
things it found most helpful.

In this respect, a congregation in the search process is like a healthy person with an itch: It is unconscious of the health but very conscious of the
itch. When the clergy search is used to scratch the itch, the result can be
a flip-flop: the top priority is to find someone strong where the predecessor is perceived to have been weak. The areas where the predecessor was
considered strong are simply taken for granted.

The trouble with this pattern is that congregations are more likely to
rely on clergy strengths than weaknesses. Giving too little weight to the
strengths the congregation is accustomed to sets up some of the challenges
the partnership will face. For example, if the predecessor was seen as a
strong intellectual preacher with a chilly personality, then the congregation
may well yearn for a warmer pastor. If the search produces a compassionate but inarticulate successor, then the congregation will be pleased—for
a while. At some point, members will become impatient with "stickles and
goo" from the pulpit, however happy they may be may be with all the visits.
The subject matter of the third-year crisis often can be predicted from the
congregation's areas of dissatisfaction with the predecessor.

In a variation on this theme, some congregations so revere their clergy
that the top priority is to find a clone (younger but just as mature). In this
case, it is the weaknesses, rather than the strengths, of the past clergyperson that are overlooked in the search. Especially after a long tenure, it is
a mistake to underestimate people's impatience with the former pastor's
perceived weaknesses, even if it is taboo to mention that he had any. People
will forgive the sainted Dr. Smith's familiar sexist language, for example,
but let the new young pastor say the same words, and he (or she!) may learn
the power of pent-up frustration.

The lessons in these observations start with the search process and continue well into the partnership. For the search committee (or the bishop),
one lesson is to see the difference between what a congregation wishes for
and what it needs. A great deal of what members say about the future stems

from feelings about the past. If the search committee can work through those feelings to a vantage point where it can glimpse the future, then it can make a wiser choice. It is important to sort through committee members' feelings about the past clergy leader until the committee as a whole achieves a balanced view and can see the predecessor's strong and weak points with a cool eye.

What is true of congregations holds also for clergy: Whatever was most disappointing about the past exerts too strong an influence at the beginning of a partnership. From the clergy leader's point of view, the takeaways from the previous discussion add up to a complicated syllogism:

1. You probably were chosen partly because your areas of strength appeared to match your predecessor's weaknesses.
2. It follows that you may be weakest and least interested in the areas of ministry where your predecessor was considered strongest.
3. Therefore the congregation's real needs probably are greatest in at least some areas you'd rather minimize.
4. To succeed, you need to work hardest in the some of the areas you like least. Especially in the first few years, you're likely to receive high praise for doing what will do you the most harm in the long run—namely, being different from your predecessor.

On the other hand, if you are lucky (or unlucky) enough to follow the sainted Dr. Jones, the clergy leader of whom no one can speak ill, then you need to do all you can to inherit Dr. Jones's laurels while preparing for the day someone discovers you are not a clone, nor even Dr. Jones's firstborn. Strong and consistent backing from the lips of Jones himself helps, as does real ability at doing what Dr. Jones did best. Most of all, it is essential that no one hear a word of criticism from you about Jones. This is a good rule in any case but especially where he or she is frequently confused with God!

The past exercises a strong influence on all of our choices. The point is not to somehow achieve perfection in the search process but to remember, as the partnership unfolds, to occasionally look back at our own past conflicts, triumphs, and disappointments; to pay attention to our feelings and reactions as you enter; and to renegotiate from time to time. Years after the partnership begins, it can be useful to look back at the dynamics of the search process—not to criticize the searchers but to draw fresh insights about how past wishes contribute to the normal turning points in a lay-clergy partnership.

History, Meet the Future

The importance of the partners' histories extends long beyond the selection process. Issues stemming from the past normally come to a head in the third year or so of a new clergy leader's tenure. As folklore has it, the first year may be a "honeymoon," followed by a year of polite cooperation. Then, in the third or fourth year, the gloves come off. The scenario plays out in many ways. What is almost universal is that some of the initial understandings—both tacit and explicit—do not hold. The real needs and expectations of both partners come out—often in the form of criticism and complaints—and adjustments must be made.

The result is not always a fight, though every congregation has some people who enjoy a fight and some who get caught up in anxiety of any kind. Still others think that the best way they can help in times of crisis is to seize authority themselves—I call this the Alexander Haig syndrome, at least with people old enough to know who I am talking about. (Younger people: Google "I am in charge.") Overreaction tends to step up the conflict level, putting people into "fight or flight" mode, which is not helpful. In moments of potential crisis, leaders need to *under*react—by responding to anxiety with less anxiety, to confident assertions with curiosity about facts. By giving less emotional intensity than they get, anyone can help step down the conflict level.

Knowing that the third-year crisis is normal in the shakedown of a new relationship (and that it doesn't always come exactly in the third year) helps quite a bit. A sense of humor and perspective about the "honeymoon" stage helps, as well. Mature people—those who have said hello and goodbye before—can often make a special contribution. They know that the excitement of a new relationship pays off as it ripens into something deeper and more lasting. And they know ripening generally includes an element of disillusionment.

Successful completion of the third-year crisis marks an important milestone in lay-clergy partnership. Having recognized the fact that both partners entered with deep yearnings that the other cannot satisfy completely, the partners are ready to consider other purposes their partnership might serve.

While the core leadership has worked through the initial crisis well to a point of greater realism and maturity, the same is never true of every member of the congregation. In choosing members for the governing board, it makes sense to exclude the harshest critics of the clergy leader. Less obviously, it's also wise to look beyond the strongest boosters. Moderate board members accept adjustments and compromise more easily and can also help the clergy leader to let go of his or her initial stances. As the partnership matures, some members will want to be on the board in order to undo this work and to revive old grievances and disappointments. Working with the nominating committee, the board must gently but effectively insist that board members be ready to work with the clergy leader.

An important venue for this work is the annual planning and goal-setting process described in chapter 8. In the early years, the planning process is an opportunity to renegotiate the mutual expectations of the board and clergy leader. Later on, it becomes a setting for vocational discernment—for the partners to ask, What are we here to do and for whom? By acknowledging that every year has different goals and that some questions are truly "open"—in that no one has correct or easy answers to them—the planning process is a forum for the board and clergy leader to reflect on how their roles and emphases may need to change from year to year.

ADDRESSING MISBEHAVIOR

No matter how well leaders build relationships, write policies, set goals, and communicate about performance, everyone will not be happy. And some people will express their unhappiness by acting out. And so responding to misconduct is an essential element of healthy partnership.

The world is full of people who, for reasons of their own, behave badly. Sometimes the reasons are quite innocent: confusion, mental illness, grief, or posttraumatic stress. Other reasons are more sinister: bigotry, greed, the lust for power, or the desire to get revenge for real or imagined injuries. Some writers about congregational conflict pay great attention to "dysfunctional" behavior, "clergy killers," and "antagonists." In my opinion, this attention is misplaced. People inclined to misbehave are distributed more or less at random through the population and can be found in every congregation. Where congregations differ is not in whether they have troublesome people or even in how often people misbehave but in how others respond to misbehavior when it comes.

Many years ago in the church where I grew up, on a Sunday when our minister was out of the pulpit, I saw a man approach my father after service. I didn't recognize the man; apparently, he was returning after a long absence and recognized my father as a fellow old-timer. After a moment's small talk, his nose wrinkled in disgust. He said, "Is that Jew still preaching here?" The question hung in the air a moment. Several people heard it, and I imagine some were struggling to frame a soft answer to defuse the situation. Not my dad. He said firmly, "There is no room in this church for that kind of talk." After another awkward silence, the man turned on his heel and left. As far as I know, he didn't come back.

I would not recommend my father's bluntness to everyone. Other responses might have marked the boundaries of acceptable behavior just as well while offering more room for the man to clean up his act and stay. But every congregation needs people—many people, not just one—who know the boundaries of acceptable behavior and feel authorized to give them voice. Such people act like antibodies in the congregational immune system, helping to sustain health and homeostasis in a world of threats. Governance can encourage healthy over unhealthy responses to misconduct and provide a means for setting limits for those who misbehave, up to and including exclusion from the congregation.

Strong Immunity

The first step in dealing with a threat—for a congregation as well as the immune system—is to identify it accurately. Objective policies, written with no specific person or situation in mind, achieve this goal much better than a board can by deciding cases. Because a congregation is a tangled web of personal relationships, a board that first addresses misconduct in the context of a case inevitably is making moral judgments about the goodness or badness of someone who may be a friend, relative, generous donor, or active volunteer. Boards have a hard time being objective in these circumstances and are prone to over- or underreacting on the basis of personal feelings. A healthy governance structure, like a healthy immune system, identifies and deals with a threats accurately, not anxiously or in a hurry.

But note: The immune system is not a scheme for *exterminating* threats; it is the body's way of *coexisting* with them. Some parts of the immune system, like white blood cells, do kill germs, in something like the way my father drove away the visitor. But the immune system is a system, not an uncoordinated gang of vigilantes. White blood cells are a last resort. Most of our immunity comes from everyday, whole-body functions, like firm boundaries, unimpeded circulation, body heat, and the expulsion of ingested hazardous materials. Healthy immune function is more a matter of daily routine than of emergency preparedness—though an occasional threat does keep the system toned. Without external challenges to practice on, the immune system can be compromised, so that it underreacts to big threats or overreacts to small ones. Instead of blaming or resenting individuals who misbehave in congregations, we might be grateful for the chance they give us to strengthen our capacity for kind but firm response.

Like all analogies, this one has its limits. Misbehaving congregants and clergy are not germs, and a congregation—St. Paul notwithstanding—is not quite a body. But like bodies, congregations depend on wise individual responses and also on good organizational design. Neither good people nor good governance is enough by itself. By adopting clear policies on acceptable and unacceptable behavior and by grounding them in the congregation's ethical values, the board and clergy establish a framework that encourages individuals to confront misbehavior informally and creates a process for dealing with it formally if need be.

The toughest cases come when the board has to deal with the behavior of a well-established member, leader, member of the board or staff, or—most challenging of all—a clergy leader. Some threats to the body or the congregation cannot be addressed without some cost or damage to the whole. Saddest of all, misconduct by a person you know well often seems innocent, in the sense of being easy to excuse. A common example is the longtime treasurer to whom everyone is understandably grateful but who fails to practice proper controls on the handling of cash, discourages a thorough audit, or protects friends who seek reimbursement for questionable or ill-documented spending. Or a clergyperson in a marriage "everybody" knows has been unhappy for a long time who takes up with a congregant whom other people love as well.

Elements of Health

No easy answers can be found in circumstances like these. Often none exist that are not costly both to individuals and to the congregation. Still, some teams of leaders handle situations of misconduct better than others. I believe the factors that make the most difference are (in order of importance) the following:

- A clear sense of mission and a shared conviction that the mission, not its leaders or its members, "own" the congregation, so that the best choice is the one that serves the mission best, not the cheapest, easiest, or least embarrassing.
- Forethought and written policies about how problems will be handled. If the bylaws provide no method of removing a board or congregation member, for example, and a member needs to be removed, then the

board has two fights on its hands: one about the wisdom of removing someone and the other about who can do it.

- A willingness to reach out for help. Denominational leaders, professional consultants, and neighboring clergy often have experience and skills in dealing with misconduct situations. It can be helpful to encourage accused persons to seek counsel also and to appoint an advocate for any injured parties as well. Local leaders need to take responsibility, but they don't need to take it on alone.

Behavior problems are endemic to congregations, in part because people have more freedom there than they have in many other parts of their lives and also because they may have higher expectations. It is important to remember that a flow of minor conflicts, complaints, and criticisms is part of the normal "noise level" of a congregation's life. The most helpful leadership response is often a bit less intense than the event that triggered it. By underreacting, leaders serve as step-down transformers who dampen, rather than amplify, the noise. But a healthy leadership team, like a sound immune system, recognizes a real threat when it sees one and has a plan for dealing with it, even if the person who is behaving badly is one of their own.

BOUNDARIES AND PARTNERSHIP

Building a healthy partnership—negotiating roles and goals, addressing misbehavior, setting and achieving goals—is hard work that requires an atmosphere of trust. Leaders can help by vigorously gauging their reactions, toning down both praise and criticism. Gauging one's own reactions does not mean staying always emotionally "cool." It does mean trying to express only your own feelings, judgments, and positions. It means listening passionately while others express feelings without getting caught up in the intensity of others or confused about whose feelings are whose. Firm boundaries and self-differentiation—knowing who I am and how I feel while keeping lines of communication open—are essential for a healthy partnership.

Firm boundaries fall at the center of a spectrum, with rigid boundaries at one end and fuzzy boundaries at the other. Rigid boundaries are marked by secrecy and unilateral decision-making; fuzzy ones by frequent, anxious checking in and checking on and checking back. Firm boundaries are just right: Each partner takes responsibility for his or her own actions and for keeping channels of communication open.

Firm personal boundaries are not easy to establish or maintain, especially when the boundaries of authority are ill-defined. When I consult with boards, sometimes I mark two columns on a piece of newsprint and ask, "Which decisions does the pastor (or rabbi) make? Which decisions does the board make?" The first response I hear is often an objection: "We share leadership," they say. So I draw another column for decisions shared between the two. Some groups doggedly insist on putting almost everything into the "shared" category.

In real life, thousands of decisions need to be made each week; it is impossible to "share" them all. And so the person on the scene when a decision has to be made—often the clergy leader—faces a dilemma. He or she can decide and ask forgiveness afterward. Or he or she can decide and wait to see if anyone complains, knowing that when authority has not been clearly given, complaints come with an extra sting: "Who said you could do that?"

A third way—the coward's way—is not to decide at all and instead to wait and ask permission at the next board or committee meeting. The wait-and-ask approach, followed consistently, can turn what could have been an energetic, mission-driven congregation into a ponderous bureaucracy whose first principle appears to be that nothing gets decided until everybody's fingerprints are on it. In practice, the "shared" column often is a "fuzzy" column. Lacking clear authority, the person on the spot has to guess what he or she can get away with.

Rigid Boundaries

Some clergy and lay leaders like to divide authority up into watertight compartments, so they don't have to engage in give-and-take. Clergy who take their authority over worship as a license to persist doggedly in the style they happen to prefer, volunteers who take advantage of the congregation's gratitude to treat positions of trust as if they were personal property, staff who refuse to be evaluated, and boards that insist on inappropriately punitive or quantitative systems of evaluation are all erecting rigid boundaries around themselves. Such rigid, unilateral approaches rarely achieve the hoped-for outcomes.

Rigid boundaries are an early warning sign of conflict. A simple way to think about the conflict level in a congregation is to map the relationships among the leaders. When the boundary between two leaders becomes rigid, they stop talking with each other except "officially" at meetings and stop checking in with one another informally. They may need encouragement to listen to each other—starting with noncontroversial topics—as a way of softening their boundary.

One reason people erect rigid boundaries is to protect themselves by blocking the flow of potentially painful information. When you've staked out a contentious position, you have reason to expect that others will reciprocate. Unfortunately, setting up a rigid boundary cuts the phone line. Without the chance to receive information or feedback from others, rigid boundaries makes it impossible to learn, adjust, or even to persuade others.

Forty years ago, it was quite common to hear clergy and lay leaders defend rigid boundaries on principle. In those days, claiming you knew your job and didn't need advice about it was much more acceptable. Today most leaders espouse mutual goal-setting and evaluation as "best practices"—even when their actual practice is never to find time for them. In the meantime, the reverse mistake—defending fuzzy boundaries—has become more common.

Fuzzy Boundaries

In too many congregations, leaders actually believe that partnership works best when boundaries of authority are fuzzy. Terms like *shared leadership* have become popular in recent decades, for reasons some of which are understandable and sound. Traditional modes of congregational life, where men dominated women, clergy dominated laity, and wealthy people dominated everybody, have fallen out of sync with the egalitarian principles not only of congregations but also of society at large.

In industry, for instance, top-down styles of management have lost favor (at least in theory) to an emphasis on teams and group decision-making. In a team-oriented company, team members have a voice in shaping their own work. There's nothing fuzzy about that, especially when, in business, participative management takes place against a background of nearly absolute executive authority. A collaborative approach helps managers to make decisions that reflect the insights of a wider circle, including workers, engineers, and customers—without blurring ultimate accountability. When a person who works in such a setting joins a congregation, he or she expects to have a voice there, too.

But the authority of clergy leaders to manage—much less to innovate or make big changes—has in many relatively liberal congregations almost vanished in favor of vague notions of shared leadership. As a result, congregations that once suffered from a lack of lay participation now suffer from lack of anyone who can decide on a direction, align resources, and take action. In that context, empowering volunteers at every level to participate in making every decision only makes a fuzzy allocation of authority worse.

The result is sometimes painfully ironic. In congregations, one of the best fruits of the egalitarian trend, starting in the 1970s and 1980s, has been an increased willingness to ordain women. But as women started to accept positions of authority, they sometimes found that the authority had largely vanished out of the positions. Old stereotypes about women's "natural" abilities—their supposed lack of leadership potential, courage, and math skills, for example—reinforced similar stereotypes about the clergy. Lay leaders, who have long been a bit skeptical about the manliness of clergymen, sometimes step in to take paternal care of clergy—male and female—to protect us from our own gentle, nurturing, naïve selves. Like a couple in a 1950s television marriage, clergy and lay leaders in too many congregations collude in limiting their own and one another's growth by idealizing and exaggerating supposed differences of personality and skill.

Congregations have become more democratic and egalitarian, which is good. In the process, however, many have become too anxiously preoccupied with hearing everyone and too committed to offending no one, which is not good. As a result they never seem to choose a goal, much less empower anyone to stir things up—with serious consequences for their partnerships with clergy. Boards and clergy leaders need to make a choice. Is the purpose of the congregation to keep people happy, or is it to achieve a larger mission? Only with the mission in the driver's seat will lay and clergy leaders work together to identify the short- and long-term results the mission calls for and then put the clergy leader in the hot seat, where it is more comfortable to act than not to act. Then, and only then, will clergy and lay leaders, knowing that change always brings about resistance, have each other's back.

Firm Boundaries

The way to move beyond old, unjust ways of allocating power is not to pretend there is no power to allocate nor to allocate it so unclearly that no one feels responsible for taking action. A congregation that truly cares about participation needs a board that leads an open process of discerning mission and selecting strategies. And it needs empowered ministry leaders who accept responsibility for achieving well-defined results. Joined in a common purpose, the partners compensate for one another's shortcomings without needing to invade each other's space. And over time, trust grows.

Leaders can stay self-differentiated more easily when the boundaries of authority are firm—firm about which decisions the board makes and which it delegates; firm about who leads the staff and with what authority; and firm, for every category of decisions, about who leads the process, who must be consulted, who finally decides, and who takes charge of implementing the decision. When everybody knows which buck stops where, no one needs to hide information or defend turf. People actually can move closer to each other when they don't have to worry about losing power if they enter into give-and-take. This principle applies to partnerships of all kinds, including partnerships of lay and clergy leaders. When it is clear where each buck stops and who will bear each cross, daily interactions can be more relaxed and flexible than when roles need to be negotiated every day.

The partnership of lay and clergy leaders is in some ways like an employment contract or a marriage or a president's relationship with Congress—but such comparisons are only metaphors; their usefulness must be evaluated in the light of what is special about congregations. In communities of faith, lay and clergy leaders partner to produce changed human beings. The paradox of "organized religion" arises from the mismatch of our lofty purposes with our sometimes comically stiff-jointed institutions. Organized religion is a paradox worth puzzling over, a polarity worth managing, and an oxymoron worthy of a laugh. Congregations can infuriate, amuse, and outrage us—and they also can protect the vulnerable, inspire the cynical, and heal the sin-sick soul. If, as leaders, we can learn to walk together on the boundary between excessive order and creative anarchy, then we may help to change lives for the better. Sometimes, in the process, our own lives may be transformed as well.

APPENDIX A:
WRITING TIPS FOR POLICY WONKS

Writing policy is different from writing poetry or prose. The first virtue of a well-written policy (or bylaw provision) is that it be clear and unambiguous, even when quoted out of context. Each numbered section should be as complete and independent as the board can make it. Sometimes elegance has to be sacrificed in favor of precision; more often the best wording is both beautiful and clear. Minimizing commas seems to "smooth out" sentences and make them run downhill more smoothly: Subject—verb—object. Subject—verb—object. There is no Pulitzer for policy; perhaps there should be.

JOHN CARVER'S MIXING BOWLS

For writing policy, John Carver, an author and consultant for nonprofit boards, has suggested a helpful metaphor.[1] Policies, he says, are like a set of nested mixing bowls: They come in graduated sizes, like those shown in figure A.1. Carver makes the point that, if you want to control a set of mixing bowls, then you take hold of the outer bowl, which gives you power to put the whole set where you want it. The inner bowls still have limited freedom of movement: Within the outer boundary, they can still slosh back and forth. If you want to control the bowls more closely, then you can push your thumbs in toward the center to pin down one or more of the inner bowls.

Figure A.1. John Carver's Mixing Bowls.

A board can do something similar with policies, controlling the largest policy issues directly and allowing others to control the smaller ones. The "largest" policies in a given area announce the most general principle or goal the board wishes to achieve. In the area of personal safety, for instance, the largest principle might be that all who participate in congregational activities must be kept safe. A second-level policy might say the staff must pay special attention to protecting children and young people who participate in congregational programs from abuse or harm. The third-biggest mixing bowl might include specific practices: performing criminal-offender record information (CORI) checks on staff and volunteers who work with young people, requiring two adults at all activities, and so on. The board would definitely want to make the largest policy and probably the second. But instead of pinning down third- or fourth-level policies, the board might choose instead to require the staff to make all further decisions in a way that carries out the board's intent as stated in the larger policies.

Similarly, in the area of financial management, a top-level policy would say, in effect, "Thou shalt not steal." Midsize policies might require financial managers to be covered by an honesty bond. The most specific policies would say how many signatures a check must have, how cash is counted, and who must authorize checks to be written. The board will certainly want to make the policies at the top level and probably the second. At some point it will choose to trust those to whom it delegates financial management authority to deal with smaller matters.

A good policy-making practice is to write and adopt your policies in order, starting with the largest. After writing each level of policy, the board (or governance task force) asks itself, Have we said enough that we are ready to stop? Are we prepared to accept anything our leaders do so long as it adheres to the policies we have set so far? Or do we want to be more specific? When boards follow this procedure, they usually stop sooner than they think they will. Stating the board's most general purpose so explicitly may seem a little silly (what board would want to encourage theft?) but saves a lot of time in the long run by providing a safe way for others to fill in the gaps away from the board table.

A convenient way of representing policies of different sizes is to print them as an outline. The largest policies are at the top, with related smaller policies below them and indented. Board policies must be consistent with the bylaws and other foundational documents, which function as the largest mixing bowl of all. For this reason, bylaws should include only the congregation's "largest" concerns, leaving the rest to the discretion of the membership and board.

POINT OF VIEW

Fiction writers talk a lot about who should be talking in their novels. For example, is it be better for the story to be told by

- *An all-knowing narrator*: "It is a truth universally acknowledged that a single man in possession of a good fortune must be in want of a wife."
- *A narrator, from the viewpoint of a character*: "My wife felt certain everyone would feel, as she did, that a rich, single man should have a wife."
- *A character*: "I've always said, and everyone agrees with me, that 'A single man with a good fortune should get married.'"

Fortunately for policy writers, our options are more limited. The narrator, in board policy, always is the board. Keeping this fact firmly in mind helps to avoid some of the most frequent errors found in policy books, such as the following:

- *Passive voice*: "Children shall be protected" rather than "The senior minister must ensure that the staff protects children."
- *The board, talking to itself*: "The board shall conduct its business with courtesy" instead of "The board expects its members to treat one another with courtesy."

- *The board, trying to govern the ungovernable*: "When the pastor is absent, the presbytery shall provide a moderator pro tempore" instead of "If the pastor expects to be unable to chair a meeting, then he or she must ask the presbytery to appoint a substitute."

You can minimize such errors by remembering that with policy the "person" speaking always is the board. The same consideration applies to bylaws, where the congregation, rather than the board, is speaking.

Sometimes it is tempting to repeat or restate what the bylaws say already for the sake of having a complete rulebook "all in one place." I advise against such repetition because it can create confusion to have two versions of the same rule, especially when one of them is changed. It is better to refer to related bylaws in the text of a policy and then to keep a copy of the bylaws handy.

SHALL WE "SHALL"?

Most policy manuals—like many government regulations, the US Constitution, and the Ten Commandments—say *shall* a lot. I used to assume there was some good reason for this antiquity, which has not been part of ordinary American speech for at least a century and a half. As it turns out, many experts on legal drafting recommend abandoning the word *shall* altogether because its habitual use has occasioned quite a bit of ambiguity and needless litigation.[2] In place of *shall*, use *will* when the board is promising to do something, *must* when it means to impose a duty, and *may* when it is offering an option. To describe procedures, use the plain old present tense. The sample policies in appendix B avoid the use of *shall*.

APPENDIX B:

BOARD POLICIES FOR
BOURNE STREET CHURCH

The policies in this chapter belong to Bourne Street Church, an imaginary Protestant congregation where some two hundred adults and fifty children (also imaginary) show up on an average Sunday. In addition to a full-time senior minister, Bourne Street employs a second minister, a church administrator, and some other program and administrative staff, most of them part time. The church has a small endowment fund and owns a separately incorporated retirement home. In the course of writing these policies, Bourne Street considered many options. The process was not easy, but Bourne Street's leaders are proud to have their own policies instead of something copied out of a book.

Chapter 10 has further discussion of most policy issues and uses the same numbering as Bourne Street's policies, so if you're looking for an explanation of one of these policies (or an example of something discussed in chapter 10), then you should be able to find it by the numbers.

WHERE POLICY FITS IN

In the hierarchy of governing documents, as shown in figure B.1, civil law is on top, including laws about nonprofit organizations and their tax exemptions. Next are the foundational documents, including canon law and denominational rulebooks, neither of which exist for Bourne Street. It does have bylaws and articles of incorporation, both of which comply with all applicable state and federal laws. Bourne Street's policy writers try to keep in mind that policies may never contradict the bylaws. If the bylaws already say something, then in order to keep things clear, the board tries never to repeat it in its policies. This practice also helps prevent the policies and bylaws from getting out of sync. Staff policies rank below board policies and have to conform to them, just as board policies have to conform to the bylaws.

The Bourne Street policies name the senior minister as head of staff (see policy 2.1 below and the discussion of delegation in chapter 10). This means that the board holds the senior minister accountable for the performance of the entire staff. From the board's point of view, the senior minister speaks for the staff, and the board speaks to the staff primarily by speaking to the senior minister. This means that the policies can talk about "the staff" generically or "the senior minister" specifically, and either way, the senior minister is responsible for seeing to it that the staff complies with what the policy calls for.

Policy 2.1 gives "global" authority to the senior minister. This means that, when a question comes up that board policies do not address, the senior minister has the authority to act, and in fact, the board *expects* him or her to act rather than waiting for permission. Staff members make a lot of decisions every day, and the senior minister is not even aware of most of them. But as head of staff, the board holds the senior minister responsible for everything the staff does.

In any given area, the board adopts the "biggest policies" (see John Carver's mixing bowls in appendix A, figure A.1) and leaves the rest to the

Figure B.1.　Hierarchy of Governing Documents

staff, which may adopt policies of its own. Board policies and staff policies are made available to anyone who wants to see them as separate documents on the website.

A final category of authoritative documents consists of contracts, gift restrictions, and other agreements entered into by the church. Bourne Street leaders take care, when entering into such agreements, to make sure they conform to the bylaws and board policies. Otherwise, the other parties to those agreements might expect the congregation to do things that would violate its own rules—a situation that would be embarrassing at best. At worst, it could require help from a lawyer to untangle.

CENTERS OF AUTHORITY

Most board policies speak either to board members and officers (describing the board's own operation) or to the staff (delegating authority, giving guidance, and setting limitations). The Bourne Street board has also chosen to address certain other groups. The women's and youth organizations (1.5.1, 1.5.2) are acknowledged as quasi-autonomous auxiliaries within the church. The retirement home (1.5.3), founded by the church twenty years ago, now operates as a separately incorporated subsidiary of the church, with its own management and board.

Finally, the policies place the endowment fund (1.6) outside the management purview of the staff and empower an investment team to manage the invested funds. Policies 1.5–1.6 establish a direct, board-to-board relationship with these four groups.

Many congregations will choose not to create separate centers of authority this way. For one thing, doing so complicates the work of both the board and the staff. The Bourne Street board has to spend quite a bit of time managing its five "direct reports" (the senior minister, the boards of the women's and youth groups, the endowment fund investment committee, and the board of the retirement home), which is much more complicated than entrusting everything to a single head of staff. Bourne Street Church thinks this is worth it; you may not.

It is a good idea to have your policies (and bylaws) reviewed by an attorney experienced with the law of nonprofit organizations in your state or province. Before you do, I encourage you draft them in your own words. By training, lawyers tend to focus on minimizing clients' risks, a concern that sometimes bloats their language quite a bit when they draft something from scratch. If you get your intent on paper first, then it may save you money and help balance your attorney's occupational concern for safety with your congregation's need for readability and the right style to support mission-focused ministry.

BOARD POLICY BOOK

Overview

Using the authority the Church has given it through the bylaws, the Board has adopted the following policies. The Board records all of its actions in its minutes; for ease of reference, it also records in this policy book any action intended to authorize others to make decisions or to control multiple decisions over time.

1. Board Governance

1.1. Role of the Board

The Board will govern primarily by discerning mission; planning for the future; partnering with the Senior Minister and staff; and holding leaders of the Church, including its own members, accountable for their performance.

1.1.1. Annual Board Work Products

In concert with the Senior Minister, staff, and congregation, the Board will produce and adopt:

- An annual short list of **Open Questions** about the Church's future, as the basis for ongoing planning conversation in the Board, with the Senior Minister and staff and with the congregation at large.
- An annual **Vision of Ministry**, consisting of a short list of top-priority areas where the Church will advance its work in the coming year, as a starting point for budgeting and staff planning.
- An annual **Ministry Evaluation** of the Church's success or difficulties in achieving the prior year's Vision of Ministry.
- An annual, mutual **Performance Evaluation** of the Senior Minister's and Board's effectiveness in their respective roles.

1.1.2. Less Frequent Board Work Products

- In concert with the Senior Minister, staff, and congregation, the Board will produce and adopt:
- A **Triennial Evaluation** of the Senior Minister's performance in his or her wider pastoral role.
- A **Strategic Plan**, to be updated every five to ten years, consisting of a short list of the most important results the Board intends to achieve through the Church's ministry and the strategic choices (regarding program, membership, capital and operating budgets, and staffing) the Board has made about how to achieve those results.
- A **Mission Statement**, to be updated as needed, that articulates the Church's purpose and related statements (vision, values, and a tagline) to communicate the reasons for Church's work.

1.2. Board Officers

In addition to the duties defined by the bylaws, the officers have the following responsibilities:

1.2.1.

The **Board Chair** prepares the Board's agenda, facilitates or arranges for facilitation of Board meetings, and works in partnership with the Senior Minister to ensure productive partnership between the Board and staff.

1.2.2.

The **Vice Chair** assists and substitutes for the Board Chair upon request. The Vice Chair is responsible for leading the Board's planning work, including planning conversations with members and supporters of the Church.

1.2.3.

The **Secretary** ensures the safety and accuracy of Board records, including the minutes and these policies. In cooperation with the staff, the Secretary sees that minutes and Board policies are promptly posted on the Church website.

1.2.4.

The **Treasurer** supports fulfillment of the Board's financial oversight responsibilities by working with the staff to ensure that appropriate financial reports are made available to Board members on a timely basis. The Treasurer serves on the Finance Committee and is responsible for directing the annual financial audit or review and therefore plays no direct role in financial management.

1.3. Board Committees

Committees exist to help the Board to govern and not for administration or program management or to make decisions in the Board's behalf. (To manage programs, finances, and operations, the Church uses Ministry Teams responsible to the staff.) The standing Board committees are:

1.3.1. Finance Committee

Assists the Board in its oversight of the congregation's finances, ensures that routine financial reports are clear and helpful, and coordinates the annual audit. From time to time, holds educational sessions to ensure that Board members have adequate understanding of the congregation's financial status and goals. The committee has no management authority and does not participate in day-to-day financial decision-making.

1.3.2. Personnel Committee

Assists the Board in developing personnel policies, ensuring compliance with applicable laws, and carrying out the staff-grievance process as defined by these policies. The Committee has no staff management authority and does not participate in supervision or personnel decision-making. When it is necessary to hold a hearing on a staff grievance, the board will appoint an ad hoc committee in each case.

1.3.3. Governance Committee

Helps the Board to focus on its chosen role, to recruit and train Board members, and to lead the annual Board self-evaluation process.

1.3.4. Nominating Committee

In addition to the duties prescribed by the bylaws, consults annually with the Board and Governance Committee to ascertain future leadership needs in the light of members who are rotating off the Board.

1.4. Expectations of Board Members

1.4.1. Board Covenant

We, the members of the Board, enter into this covenant of mutual expectations for Board service. New members of the Board will be asked to join us in these commitments, and the Board will review and update this covenant at least annually. As Board members, we will:

- **Prepare** for Board meetings. We will read the Board packet sent prior to each meeting and accept responsibility to seek and provide information necessary for the Board to make well-informed decisions.

- **Attend** Board meetings. When possible, we will attend all duly called Board meetings. If it is necessary to miss a Board meeting, then we will inform the Board Chair as early as possible. If we do not expect to be able to attend meetings consistently, then we will resign for the good of the Board.

- **Participate** in Board meetings. We will listen carefully to others, giving special attention to ideas and perspectives different from our own. We will feel free to state the obvious and ask questions when we do not understand. We will speak forthrightly in Board meetings and vote according to our understanding of the Church's mission.

- **Share** the work of the Board. We will respond to e-mails and other communications in a timely manner. We will accept assignments and other tasks and complete them as agreed. Each Board member is equally responsible for speaking up to ensure compliance with the bylaws, ethical values, and this covenant.

- **Treat one another with respect and courtesy**. When we have disagreements or conflicts, we will address those directly with the persons concerned, seeking assistance from others as necessary to sustain a positive working atmosphere at the Board table.

- **Use discretion** in communicating about Board discussions. We will treat the views expressed in Board discussion as tentative and refrain from reporting the opinions of others. We will speak respectfully of the Board's authority to make decisions, even when we do not agree. When the Board agrees that certain matters will be kept confidential, we will honor those agreements.

1.4.2. Conflicts of Interest

The Board expects all of its members to carry out their duties with undivided loyalty to the Church and its mission. A conflict of interest exists whenever a Board member has interests or duties that may hinder or appear to hinder the Board member from fulfilling this duty.

1.4.2.1. Definition. Conflicts of interest arise when the Board member:

- Stands to gain or lose financially because of an action of the Church in which he or she has a decision-making role.
- Cannot set aside his or her personal preferences as an individual consumer of the Church's services to act in behalf of the whole Church and its mission.
- Faces any other situation that impairs or reasonably appears to impair his or her independence of judgment.
- Has a close relationship with someone who has a conflict of interest, as defined here. A close relation includes any person, corporation, or other business entity with which the Board member has a close personal, family, or business relationship.

1.4.2.2. Conflict-of-Interest Disclosure. The Board will annually require its members to disclose in writing all existing or foreseeable conflicts of interest. Disclosure forms must be kept by the Secretary and made available to any member of the Board who asks to see them.

1.4.2.3. Conflict-of-Interest Process. When a Board member reports a potential conflict of interest related to a matter before the Board, the Board (minus the affected member) will determine how to handle the situation. Possible responses include:

- Disclosure in Board minutes of the nature of the conflict.
- Leaving the room during all Board discussions and votes related to the conflict of interest.
- Resignation from the Board.

1.4.3. Discipline and Removal of Board Members

In exercising its power under the bylaws to remove an officer or Board member, the Board will follow the following procedures:

1.4.3.1. Removal for Misconduct. The Secretary will notify the member in writing and offer a hearing before the Board. Pending such a hearing, the Board may suspend the member's voting privileges.

1.4.3.2. Removal for Absence from Board Meetings.
If an officer or Board member misses more than three meetings in a twelve-month period, then the Secretary will notify the member in writing that the member may appear at the next meeting to ask the Board to excuse the absences, or the Board will request the member's resignation.

1.5. Auxiliary Organizations

Auxiliaries are chartered by the Board to further the mission and goals of the Church. Their bylaws, including any amendments, must be approved by the Board, and their officers must promptly file all of their official minutes and financial reports with the Church office and make other disclosures or reports as the Board or staff may require in order to ensure compliance with the Church's nonprofit and tax-exemption status.

The current auxiliaries are:

1.5.1.
The Bourne Street Women's Association is an integral part of the Church, functioning as an unincorporated association with its own bylaws and elected leadership.

1.5.2.
The Bourne Street Youth Group is an integral part of the Church, functioning as an unincorporated association with its own bylaws and elected leadership, subject to the direction of the staff regarding program, activities, fund-raising, financial practices, and use of Church facilities.

1.5.3.
Bourne Street Retirement Home, Inc., is a separately incorporated subsidiary of the Church, governed in accordance with its own articles of incorporation and bylaws. The staff of the Retirement Home is responsible to the Church Board through the Retirement Home board and does not report to the Senior Minister.

1.6. Bourne Street Church Endowment Fund ("Endowment")

The Endowment includes all Church funds intended to be held in perpetuity to provide a long-term stream of income to the Church. The Board places funds in the Endowment either by accepting gifts restricted by the donor to Endowment use or by voluntarily placing funds into the Endowment.

1.6.1. Delegation and Guidance to the Investment Team

An Investment Team, appointed by the Board and acting by majority vote, is empowered to direct the investment of all capital funds, subject to the following policies.

1.6.2. Investment Objectives

Capital funds must be invested to produce a maximum rate of total return consistent with the following: prudent management of investments, preservation of principle, potential for long-term asset growth, and socially responsible investment practices.

1.6.3. Permissible Investments

Endowment fund assets may be invested in publicly traded common and preferred stocks, convertible bonds and preferred stocks, bank common funds, mutual funds, and fixed income securities (including corporate bonds and money market instruments). No other investments are permissible.

1.6.4. Shareholder Initiatives

In keeping with our ethical values, the Church is an activist shareholder, lending its support to shareholder initiatives and coalitions of shareholders in support of

- Disclosure of lobbying and political spending.
- Action to address climate change.
- Nondiscrimination based on skin color, age, sex, marital status, sexual orientation, gender identity and expression, disability, national origin or ancestry, economic status, union membership, or political affiliation.

1.6.5. Ethical Investment Screen

Endowment funds may not be invested in:

- Any company that derives more than 10 percent of its revenue from the production or sale of weapons or ammunition.
- Any company that derives more than 10 percent of its revenue from the production or distribution of pornography.
- Any company that derives more than 25 percent of its revenue from tobacco, gambling, or alcoholic drinks.

1.6.6. Endowment Spending

No more than 4.5 percent of a five-year rolling average of the market value of invested funds may be spent or transferred to operating funds in any year. Separate Endowment funds may be pooled for the purpose of calculating this percentage. If the full 4.5 percent is not transferred, then the remainder returns to the Endowment and does not remain available to be transferred in future years.

2. Delegation to the Staff

2.1. Global Delegation to the Head of Staff

The Board hereby delegates all of its authority to manage the work and resources of the Church, except as expressly limited by these policies, to the Senior Minister as Head of Staff.

2.2. Senior Staff Team

The Senior Minister manages the work of the Church in collaboration with a Senior Staff Team. The Senior Staff Team includes the Senior Minister, the Associate Minister, the Church Administrator, the Director of Education, and the Director of Music, all of whom report directly to the Senior Minister. The Board expects the Senior Staff Team, individually and jointly:

- To lead and unify the paid and volunteer staff in directing their efforts toward the fulfillment of the Church's mission and goals.
- To ensure compliance with the bylaws, Board policies, and applicable laws and regulations.
- To uphold a high standard of ethical and professional conduct.
- To accomplish the goals contained in the Annual Vision of Ministry by developing annual goals for its work as a team.

2.3. Church Administrator

The Board hereby entrusts the Church Administrator with management of the financial and operational aspects of the Church and with special responsibility for staff compliance with its policies on Care for Paid Staff (3.2), Care for Members and Guests (3.3), and Care for Material Resources (3.4). The Board expects the Church Administrator to exercise independent professional judgment in reporting to the Board and Senior Minister regarding matters in his or her purview.

2.4. Staff Accountability

All staff members are accountable to the Senior Minister, who is accountable to the Board for their performance.

3. Guidance and Limitations

3.1. Personnel Decisions

The Board expects the Senior Minister to take the lead in the selection, hiring, supervision, and discharge of all paid staff.

3.1.1. Hiring Senior Staff

Before filling Senior Staff positions, the Senior Minister must nominate a Search Committee for appointment by the Board. After receiving the Search Committee's recommendation, the Senior Minister selects and presents a final candidate to the Board for approval.

3.1.2. Hiring Nonsenior Staff

Before filling Nonsenior Staff positions, the Senior Minister must consult with lay leaders and others, including the direct supervisor for the position, before making a selection.

3.1.3. The Church Administrator

Because of its special reliance on the Church Administrator, the Board will play an active role in the selection of candidates for this position by appointing the majority of members for the Search Committee. If the Board formally expresses a loss of confidence in the Church Administrator, the Senior Minister must initiate discipline or termination.

3.1.4. New Positions

New positions are normally created through the budget process. The Senior Minister may create and fill temporary positions, provided that they can be funded within established budgetary limits.

3.1.5. Employment at Will

All paid staff are employees at will, unless the Board approves the terms of a contract that states otherwise.

3.1.6. Discipline and Termination

Prior to discharging a paid staff member, the Senior Minister must ensure that the decision complies with applicable laws, Board policies, contracts, and the personnel manual. The Senior Minister must promptly notify the Board when an employee has been terminated.

3.2. Care for Paid Staff

The Church intends to be a fair, ethical, and attractive employer; to achieve high staff morale and productivity; and to protect members of the staff from all forms of injustice and abuse related to their employment.

3.2.1. Supervision and Evaluation

Each employee will be assigned an immediate supervisor, who will provide an up-to-date job description and complete an annual process of goal-setting and performance review. Individual staff goals and performance reviews are confidential, to be shared only as necessary to support Church decision-making or as required by law.

3.2.2. Compensation and Benefits

As part of the annual budget process, the Board will appoint a Compensation Committee to review compensation and benefits for all paid staff and recommend adjustments for the coming year. In its report to the board, the Compensation Committee must show evidence that it has:

- Surveyed compensation and benefits practices from comparable employers, including similar-sized congregations in our city and denomination, local nonprofit organizations, and the public school system.

- Sought and considered recommendations from the Senior Minister regarding adjustments to staff compensation. These recommendations must be presented to the Board along with the committee report.
- Taken into account the "Care for Paid Staff" goals (3.2 here) in relation to the Church's financial capacity and strategic goals.

3.2.3. Personnel Manual

The staff will maintain an up-to-date Personnel Manual that complies with all applicable legal requirements. The Personnel Manual must provide adequate policies to give practical effect to the following principles:

3.2.3.1. Nondiscrimination. The Church does not discriminate because of race, color, age, sex, marital status, sexual orientation, gender identity and expression, disability, national origin or ancestry, economic status, union membership, or political affiliation. Religious opinion and affiliation may be considered only to the extent that it may be a bona fide occupational requirement or may prevent an employee from being fully supportive of the Church's mission and values.

3.2.3.2. Harassment. The Church is committed to maintaining a work environment that is free of harassment. Harassment of any kind, including sexual harassment, is absolutely prohibited, and allegations of harassment must be reported and acted upon promptly.

3.2.3.3. Grievances. The Church intends to protect the right of staff to raise concerns about working conditions without fear of retaliation. A staff member who alleges that the law or Board policies have been violated to his or her detriment may present his or her grievance to the any Officer of the Church, who must immediately acknowledge the complaint in writing and report it to the Board, which will undertake an investigation and response.

3.2.3.4. Whistleblower Protection. The Church prohibits retaliation against employees or other persons who in good faith report:

- A suspected violation of law, such as harassment, fraud, or misappropriation of Church assets.
- A suspected danger to public health or safety.

• Suspected violations of these policies.

An employee who retaliates against anyone who has made such a report is subject to discipline up to and including termination of employment.

3.3. Care for Members and Guests

The staff must take all reasonable care to prevent harm to members, guests, program participants, and other people affected by the Church.

3.3.1. Health and Safety

The staff must ensure that all Church programs are safe for participants and staff; that facilities are maintained in a safe, sanitary, and secure condition; that required licenses and inspections are kept up to date; and that hazards are corrected promptly.

3.3.1.1. Smoking. The Church prohibits smoking of any kind on Church premises or during off-site programs of the Church.

3.3.1.2. Alcohol. Consumption of alcohol may not be permitted on Church premises or during off-site programs of the Church without specific approval by the Board for each occasion.

3.3.2. Emergency Planning

The staff must create and maintain a written plan for responding to reasonably foreseeable emergencies, including accident, illness, fire, toxic conditions, weather problems, threatening communications, power outages, and natural disasters.

3.3.3. Child Protection

Because of the Church's special responsibility for children and youth in its care, the staff must write and maintain clear procedures for the selection, training, and supervision of anyone who works with persons age eighteen and younger.

3.3.4. Disruptive Behavior

In order to sustain an atmosphere that is truly open to a wide variety of individuals, the Church must firmly and promptly address behavior that threatens the physical or emotional safety of any adult or child or chills the free exchange of opinions and beliefs. When such behavior occurs, the Senior Minister must take immediate action if required and report promptly to the Board, recommending any further disciplinary action, which may include termination of Church employment or membership.

3.3.5. Harassment

Employees, volunteers, and agents of the Church are specifically prohibited from acts of harassment, including sexual harassment, against any member or participant in Church activities or any employee or applicant for employment.

3.3.6. Firearms

The Church prohibits anyone other than on-duty law enforcement officials or off-duty law enforcement officials hired by the Church from carrying a firearm on Church property.

3.3.7. Building Security

The staff must ensure that access to Church buildings is limited to those who have legitimate business there.

3.3.8. Universal Access

The Church intends to make its premises and activities safely and conveniently accessible to persons with disabilities. The staff must ensure that Church facilities, programs, and policies meet or exceed all applicable legal requirements and that the Church engage in continual learning and improvement in this area.

3.4. Care for Material Resources

The staff must take all reasonable care to prevent harm to the Church's financial assets, property, credit, and tax exemptions and develop administrative practices and procedures designed to prevent such harm and must report promptly to the Board on any significant shortcomings in their implementation.

3.4.1. Operating and Capital Budgets

The staff must, by October 31 of each year, present a two-year operating budget and a five-year capital budget for approval by the Board.

3.4.1.1. Proposed budgets must be based on the Annual Vision of Ministry and any strategic plan currently in effect.

3.4.1.2. The Senior Minister must, when presenting a budget, express an opinion whether it is adequate to fulfill the Annual Vision of Ministry.

3.4.2. Spending Authority

The staff controls and is responsible for all spending out of Church accounts, subject to the following limitations:

3.4.2.1. Donor-restricted funds may not be used in violation of donor restrictions or Board-restricted funds in violation of Board-imposed restrictions.

3.4.2.2. Cash operating reserves may not fall below 25 percent of the annual budgeted expenditures without Board approval.

3.4.2.3. Board approval is required to change compensation for any full-time staff position or to change the basis on which benefits are calculated. Normally the staff will propose such changes only in the course of the normal budgeting process.

3.4.2.4. The staff must anticipate and prevent spending in excess of the overall budget. If it foresees any material deviation from budgeted spending, the staff must promptly inform the Board and recommend options for adjusting the budget.

3.4.2.5. The budget will be prepared in outline form, with major budget categories summarizing minor ones. The Senior Minister may approve overspending by up to 15 percent over the budgeted amount in any major budget category, provided overall spending remains within budget and the adjustment is promptly reported to the Board.

3.4.3. Gift Acceptance

The staff controls and is responsible for receiving and acknowledging all gifts to the Church, with the following limitations:

3.4.3.1. All noncash gifts, including securities, real estate, and personal property must be promptly converted into cash upon receipt.

3.4.3.2. The staff may not accept gifts restricted in any way by the donor unless the Board has in advance created a Special Fund to receive gifts with stated restrictions.

3.4.3.3. Lending or borrowing of funds beyond a ninety-day period requires Board approval.

3.4.3.4. Purchase or sale of real estate requires Board approval.

3.4.4. Special Funds

All funds restricted by Board action to be used for special purposes but not permanently restricted to the use of income only are considered special funds. Special funds currently established by the Board and the purposes for which they are restricted include:

3.4.4.1. Memorial Garden Fund. For the maintenance, repair, and expansion of the Memorial Garden.

3.4.4.2. Youth Scholarship Fund. For providing scholarships to persons under eighteen who wish to attend camps and conferences related to the Church.

3.4.4.3. Building Fund. For future capital projects approved by the congregation.

3.4.5. Accounting and Financial Standards

Church accounting and financial controls must conform to accepted best practices for churches of comparable size, including:

3.4.5.1. Cash Management. The staff must maintain written procedures to govern the handling of receipts, access to cash and bank balances, approval of expenditures, payment of invoices and other obligations, and management of invested funds.

3.4.5.2. Separation of Functions. The functions of record-keeping, bank reconciliation, and cash disbursements must be under the control of separate, unrelated persons.

3.4.5.3. Approval Authority. Board Officers, the Senior Minister, and the Church Administrator are authorized to approve cash disbursements. At least one authorized individual must approve all cash disbursements. Two unrelated authorized individuals must approve any disbursement of $5,000 or more that is not part of an existing contract or related to normal payroll expenses.

3.4.5.4. Fund Accounting. The staff must take care to distinguish donor-restricted, temporarily restricted, voluntarily restricted, and unrestricted funds.

3.4.5.5. Reconciliation. Church accounting reports must be reconciled with financial institution statements as often as those statements are issued, and copies of such reconciliations must be provided to the Finance Committee of the Board for review.

3.4.6. Asset Protection

The Senior Minister must take all reasonable care to ensure that Church assets are protected from loss or theft, including:

3.4.6.1. Adequate **insurance** to protect against property losses, liability for injuries to others, corporate liability, personal liability of Board members and staff, and honesty bonds for all personnel with access to material amounts of funds.

3.4.6.2. Maintenance of Church **property and equipment** to keep it in working order, subject to reasonable wear and tear.

3.4.6.3. Reasonable steps to protect the Church's **intangible property**, including intellectual property, electronic data, and paper files from significant damage or loss.

3.4.7. Document Retention

The staff must maintain written procedures to govern the backup, retention, and destruction of the Church's documents, giving definite retention periods for classes of financial, business, pastoral, personnel, and corporate records in both paper and electronic forms.

4. Oversight

4.1. Mission Focus

The Board's duty of care requires it to ensure that the Church's human and material resources are used for the benefit of its mission. The Board fulfills this duty in two ways: by monitoring regular reports provided by the staff and by scheduled evaluation of the Church's progress toward achieving the goals established in the Annual Vision of Ministry.

4.2. Monitoring

The Senior Minister will provide regular written reports from the staff to the Board. Reports must focus on progress of priorities, as set by the Board through the Annual Vision of Ministry, and on compliance with Board policy. Monitoring reports must be e-mailed to Board members in advance of each monthly meeting but will not normally be a subject of Board discussion except when they require Board action or raise issues of compliance with Board policy. Reports must include, at minimum:

4.2.1.

Monthly financial statements that show overall financial performance compared to budget and highlight significant financial or operational issues. These reports will be filed and made available to any Church member who wishes to examine them.

4.2.2.

Quarterly financial statements that show the overall financial position of the Church. These must include a complete balance sheet and funds statement, detailed statement of operations, and a statement of cash flows.

4.2.3. Programmatic Monitoring

On a schedule to be agreed upon annually by the Senior Minister and the Board, the Senior Minister must provide reports to the Board regarding:

- Progress on achieving the Annual Vision of Ministry.
- Compliance with applicable Board policies.

- Each report will focus on selected areas of progress and compliance, so that all in the course of the year the entire Vision of Ministry and all points of policy compliance are covered.

4.3. Evaluation

Everyone responsible for work in behalf of the Church will engage in a continual process of evaluation. The purposes to be accomplished through evaluation are to foster excellence in ministry work by ensuring that all Church leaders:

- Practice open communication and regular feedback.
- Meet performance standards appropriate to their roles.
- Maintain effective working relationships with one another.
- Focus on achieving goals as approved by the Board and staff.

4.3.1. Board and Senior Minister Evaluation

Annually, as part of the creation of the Annual Vision of Ministry, the Head of Staff and Board will together review their respective contributions to the fulfillment of the prior year's Annual Vision of Ministry.

4.3.2. Staff Evaluations

The Senior Minister must ensure that all Church employees develop, with their supervisors, timely annual performance goals supportive of the Annual Vision of Ministry and that their performance is evaluated annually in writing.

4.3.3. Evaluation of Ministry Teams

The Senior Minister must ensure that leaders of teams engaged in ministry develop, with their staff supervisors, goals supportive of the Annual Vision of Ministry and that their performance is evaluated annually in writing.

4.3.4. Senior Minister's Triennial Performance Review

Every three years, the Board and Senior Minister will together appoint an ad hoc Review Committee of three persons held in high esteem by the Church and mutually acceptable to the Board and Senior Minister. Working with the Senior Minister, the Committee will design and facilitate a review of the Senior Minister's performance. The goals of the evaluation are to call the congregation's attention to the mutual, relational nature of ministry and the respective responsibilities of all who contribute to its success and to help the Senior Minister to remain motivated, creative, and flexible. The Committee's report to the Board, together with a written response from the Senior Minister, will be published to the Church along with the Board's plan for addressing any recommendations it may contain.

4.3.5. Annual Financial Audit or Review

At least every three years, the Board will engage a qualified professional to conduct an audit or review of the Church's financial records and report in writing to the Board. In alternate years, the Board will appoint a Volunteer Committee to perform an informal review of some aspect of the Church's financial records.

NOTES

CHAPTER 1: ORGANIZED RELIGION

1. Not all congregations are incorporated; most begin life as unincorporated associations. It is easy to confuse the various aspects of "nonprofit status," which include incorporation, exemption from federal and state income tax, and exemption from various property and sales taxes. All of these are technically separate, though most congregations have them all. The IRS does not distinguish incorporated and unincorporated associations when determining tax exemption.

Until recently, the constitution of Virginia actually prohibited congregations from incorporating. This policy dates from the eighteenth and early nineteenth centuries, when corporate status was a special privilege usually granted by vote of the state legislature. In this context, James Madison and others viewed the granting of corporate status to a church as an establishment of religion, contrary to the spirit of religious freedom. Today incorporation is generally available to qualified applicants; most congregations avail themselves of it to limit the personal liability of members and officers; to qualify for grants; and to simplify owning property, borrowing money, and many other business matters. In 2002, a federal district court held Virginia's policy, along with several other special limitations on churches, unconstitutional. Although the US Supreme Court has not ruled on the question, it seems likely that it would extend the option of incorporating to congregations in the Virginias. See H. Robert Showers, "Incorporation of Churches in Virginia: A New Day and Law," a paper published on the website of the NorthStar Church Network,

www.northstarchurchnetwork.org/uploads/church-inc-article-by-hrs.pdf. The constitution of West Virginia still prohibits incorporation by religious groups, but in
view of the 2002 decision, some such groups have successfully formed corporations.

2. The US Navy, for example, with its long tradition of independent command
at sea, encourages subordinate commanders to report their decisions using the
acronym UNODIR (unless otherwise directed) to indicate that they are *"informing
the boss, not asking permission." The Armed Forces Officer*, US Department of
Defense, revised edition, 2006, www.dtic.mil/doctrine/education/armedforcesof-
ficer.pdf, 86–87.

3. In using the words *power* and *authority* this way, I am walking roughly in
parallel with Max Weber's use of the German terms *Macht* and *legitime Herrschaft*
(legitimate control), which are traditionally translated "power" and "authority." See
Max Weber, *Theory of Social and Economic Organization* (New York: Free Press,
1964), 152–53.

4. For an overview of the size categories pioneered by Arlin J. Rothauge, see
Alice Mann, *The In-Between Church: Navigating Size Transitions in Congregations* (Bethesda, MD: Alban, 1998). Susan Beaumont has helpfully updated and
extended this work in her *Inside the Large Congregation* (Herndon, VA: Alban,
2011).

5. Mark Chaves, *Congregations in America* (Cambridge: Harvard University
Press, 2004), table on p. 19. Chaves finds that the median American congregation
has seventy-five "regularly participating individuals," of whom fifty are adults.
Alice Mann introduced the concept of plateau zones in *The In-Between Church*,
12–18.

6. James Luther Adams, "Guiding Principles for a Free Faith," in *On Being Human Religiously: Selected Essays in Religion and Society*, ed. Max L. Stackhouse
(Boston: Skinner House Books, 1976), 17.

CHAPTER 2: GOVERNANCE AND MINISTRY IN
INTERESTING TIMES

1. James Hudnut-Beumler, *In Pursuit of the Almighty's Dollar: A History of
Money and American Protestantism* (Chapel Hill: University of North Carolina
Press, 2007), 132–41.

2. "Attacks Women Drinkers: Ohio Prohibition Chairman Thinks Woman Suffrage Aids Liquor Traffic," *New York Times*, July 14, 1908, 2.

3. D. Michael Lindsay and George Gallup Jr., *Surveying the Religious Landscape: Trends in U.S. Beliefs* (Harrisburg, PA: Morehouse Group, 2000), 7. In 2013,
about 39 percent of Gallup's respondents said they had attended services in the last
seven days, a level similar to the 1940s. Of course, such self-reports undoubtedly
overstate actual attendance. Frank Newport, "In U.S., Four in 10 Report Attend-

ing Church in Last Week," Gallup, December 24, 2013, http://www.gallup.com/poll/166613/four-report-attending-church-last-week.aspx.

4. Will Herberg, *Protestant Catholic Jew: An Essay in American Religious Sociology* (New York: Doubleday, 1955).

5. "'Nones' on the Rise: One in Five Adults Have No Religious Affiliation," Pew Research Center, October 9, 2012, http://www.pewforum.org/2012/10/09/nones-on-the-rise; Robert C. Fuller, *Spiritual, but Not Religious: Understanding Unchurched America* (New York: Oxford University Press, USA, 2001).

6. Shawn Sprague, "What Can Labor Productivity Tell Us about the U.S. Economy?" *Beyond the Numbers: Productivity* 3, no. 12 (U.S. Bureau of Labor Statistics, May 2014), http://www.bls.gov/opub/btn/volume-3/what-can-labor-productivity-tell-us-about-the-us-economy.htm.

7. "Volunteering and Civic Engagement in the United States," Corporation for National and Community Service, n.d., http://www.volunteeringinamerica.gov/national.

8. Jorge Cauz, "Encyclopædia Britannica's President on Killing Off a 244-Year-Old Product," *Harvard Business Review*, March 2013, https://hbr.org/2013/03/encyclopaedia-britannicas-president-on-killing-off-a-244-year-old-product.

9. John L. Ronsvalle and Sylvia Ronsvalle, *The State of Church Giving through 2011: The Kingdom of God, Church Leaders and Institutions, Global Triage Needs, and the Promises of Jesus* (Urbana, IL: Empty Tomb, 2013), 19.

CHAPTER 3: HOW CONGREGATIONS ORGANIZE

1. R. Stephen Warner, "The Place of the Congregation in the Contemporary American Religious Configuration," in *American Congregations*, ed. James P. Wind and James W. Lewis, vol. 2, *New Perspectives in the Study of Congregations* (Chicago: University of Chicago Press, 1998), 54–99.

2. Lyle E. Schaller, *Looking in the Mirror: Self-Appraisal in the Local Church* (Nashville: Abingdon Press, 1984).

3. American Red Cross, *American Red Cross Governance for the 21st Century: A Report of the Board of Governors* (Washington, DC: American National Red Cross, October 2006), http://www.redcross.org/images/MEDIA_CustomProduct Catalog/m4240145_BOGGovernanceReport.pdf.

4. David McCullough, *1776* (New York: Simon and Schuster, 2005).

5. William M. Easum and Thomas G. Bandy, *Growing Spiritual Redwoods* (Nashville: Abingdon, 1997); Richard Warren, *The Purpose Driven Church: Growth without Compromising Your Message and Mission* (Grand Rapids, MI: Zondervan, 1995).

6. Joy Skjegstad, *Starting a Nonprofit at Your Church* (Herndon, VA: Alban Institute, 2002), includes a good discussion of the pros and cons of establishing a separate board for subsidiary enterprises (pp. 1–17).

CHAPTER 4: A MAP FOR THINKING
ABOUT CONGREGATIONS

1. The phrase *holy conversation* comes from a book that has helped shape my thinking in many ways, as have its authors: Gil Rendle and Alice Mann, *Holy Conversations: Strategic Planning as a Spiritual Practice for Congregations* (Herndon, VA: Alban Institute, 2003).

2. These and many other special terms belong to John Carver's Policy Governance system, presented in his *Boards That Make a Difference: A New Design for Leadership in Nonprofit and Public Organizations*, 3rd ed. (San Francisco: Jossey-Bass, 2006). I appreciate Carver's contributions to thinking about governance and have benefited from the clarity of his thinking. But I have some disagreements with him and some reservations about the use of his model in congregations. In response to frequent questions from Mennonites, Unitarian Universalists, Canadians, Australians, and others who are familiar with the "Carver model," I agree with Carver on the following:

- Boards should focus primarily on long-range, big-picture matters.
- Boards should record their most lasting decisions in written policies.
- Boards should delegate substantial day-to-day management authority, so that decisions can be made away from the board table. In organizations with staff, it makes sense to delegate management authority to the staff leader.
- Boards should exercise effective oversight of those to whom it delegates authority without involving themselves too much in management.

The areas of disagreement are a bit more complicated to explain—which is why I am explaining them here in a footnote, where I won't bother those who don't know Carver's system:

- Carver relies heavily on the distinction between ends and means—what we intend to accomplish versus how we are going to do it. I agree that this is a useful distinction but do not agree that decisions can be clearly classified one way or the other. Like many clear distinctions, this one is a polarity or spectrum, not a set of pigeonholes. This may be especially true in congregations, where "how" we do things is a major part of "what" we want to accomplish.
- Carver seems to me to picture an organization as a machine that can be programmed to follow a set of rational directions. I take a more systemic or organic point of view. The official rules for decision-making account for very little of what happens even in large, well-ordered groups. The special nature of a congregation, with its overlapping constituencies and multiple relationships among people, makes systemic and organic metaphors more useful than mechanical or cybernetic ones.
- Carver states in many places that "chief executive performance is identical to organizational performance." This may be a useful fiction in some orga-

nizations, but in a congregation it is can be quite pernicious, both because "performance" is so difficult to define and measure and because the job of a senior clergy leader is only partly to lead the organization. Clergy contribute a great deal through their personal ministry, and congregations succeed or fail for many reasons, clergy performance being only one of them.

- The separation of board and staff in Carver, while clear, seems to me less than ideal. I have never seen a board that could discern mission or cast vision without leadership from staff leaders. That is why my "map" defines a zone of overlap between the board and staff. While it needs to be clear what bucks stop where, only a shared process can produce the wide support top-level plans require.
- Like me, Carver says the board is a fiduciary for the organization's "true owners." But Carver's "owners" are always human beings. If there are members, they are the owners. But for me, the true owner of a congregation (or any other charitable organization) is its mission. The board's core responsibility is to ensure that the congregation serves its mission; likewise, when members vote, they vote not as owners but as fiduciaries for the mission. I explain in chapter 5 why I say that a congregation's owner is its mission.

I am a grateful reader of John Carver's writings and respect the effort some congregations have made to follow Policy Governance as closely as they can. My approach is similar in some ways, different in others. Perhaps the most important difference is that my "model" is not meant to be a model at all. Congregations are different, and they can and should govern themselves in a variety of ways. I'm always delighted when my readers and consulting clients invent wildly unexpected variations on the basic themes in this book.

CHAPTER 5: THE JOB OF THE BOARD

1. Edward Le Roy Long, *Patterns of Polity: Varieties of Church Governance* (Cleveland, OH: Pilgrim Press, 2001), 64.

2. Specifically, the earnings of a tax-exempt body "may not inure to any private shareholder or individual," and it "must not provide a substantial benefit to private interests." "501(c)(3): Tax Guide for Churches and Religious Organizations (IRS Publication 1828)," Internal Revenue Service, n.d., www.irs.gov/pub/irs-pdf/p1828 .pdf, 4. This is the basic difference between a nonprofit organization and a for-profit business—whose primary purpose is to benefit its owners. The most common examples of private inurement in congregations are excessive clergy compensation, excessive reimbursement of expenses, and allowing use of congregational property without a business purpose. Violations of these rules against "private inurement" and "excess benefit" can trigger substantial penalties against the congregation and its leaders. Richard R. Hammar, *Pastor, Church and Law*, 4th ed., vol. 1, *Church*

Legal Issues for Pastors (Christianity Today International, 2008), 64–73. Congregations and other charities do benefit individuals, of course, but only as members of "charitable classes," such as needy college students, recently released prisoners, or similar objectively defined groups.

3. For the technical-minded: A legal trust creates three roles—a trustor, also known as settler or donor; a trustee; and a beneficiary. More than one person or institution can play each role, and sometimes the same party plays two roles. In a typical trust, the trustor places assets into the trust so that the trustee can control them for the good of the beneficiary. The trust document tells the trustee how trust resources must be managed and the purposes for which they can be disbursed. The trustee is in a fiduciary relation to both trustor and beneficiary; in fact, the duties of trustees have become an influential legal model for the duties of all other fiduciaries. Stockholders, as owners of a business corporation, occupy a position analogous to a trustor who is also the beneficiary; stockholders put up the initial money and have a right to benefit if the enterprise succeeds. The board of directors stands in a fiduciary relationship to stockholders. In a nonprofit corporation, donors are like stockholders in that they put up the initial cash, but because their contribution is a gift, they do not have a right to benefit from it, either by a payout from corporate funds or by retaining control of the organization, so the word *owner* does not fit them very well. Members, too, if a nonprofit has them, are forbidden to benefit personally from its operation. While the board and congregation have the legal power to control the institution, the mission has the moral right both to control the congregation's actions and to benefit from them. What stockholders are to business corporations, mission is to congregations.

4. Peter F. Drucker, *Managing the Non-Profit Organization: Practices and Principles* (New York: HarperCollins, 1990), xiv.

5. The IRS maintains a useful collection of resources about the legal requirements for tax-exempt organizations at www.stayexempt.irs.gov. A sample conflict-of-interest policy is contained in the instructions for IRS Form 1023, "Application for Recognition of Exemption under Section 501(c)(3) of the Internal Revenue Code," June 2006, www.irs.gov/pub/irs-pdf/i1023.pdf, 25–26.

CHAPTER 6: PRODUCTIVE BOARD MEETINGS

1. Henry M. Robert, *Pocket Manual of Rules of Order for Deliberative Assemblies* (printed by author, 1876), http://www.gutenberg.org/files/9097/9097-8.txt; Henry M. Robert, *Robert's Rules of Order: Revised for Deliberative Assemblies* (Chicago: Scott, Foresman, 1915), http://www.bartleby.com/176; Henry M. Robert, Sarah Corbin Robert, Henry M. Robert III, William J. Evans, Daniel H. Honemann, and Thomas J. Balch, *Robert's Rules of Order: Newly Revised*, 11th ed., with the assistance of Daniel E. Seabold and Shmuel Gerber (Boston: Da Capo, 2011).

2. These and other provisions about boards can be found in section 49 of the 2011 edition. The original and 1915 versions mention boards mostly to describe their relationship to their parent bodies and to exclude them from some of the more formal procedures.

3. US Army Corps of Engineers, "Historical Vignette 038: An Army Engineer Brought Order to Church Meetings," November 2001, http://www.usace.army.mil/About/History/HistoricalVignettes/GeneralHistory/038ChurchMeetings.aspx.

4. "The great lesson for democracies to learn is for the majority to give to the minority a full, free opportunity to present their side of the case, and then for the minority, having failed to win a majority to their views, gracefully to submit and to recognize the action as that of the entire organization, and cheerfully to assist in carrying it out, until they can secure its repeal." Robert et al., *Robert's Rules*, xliv, quoting Henry M. Robert, *Parliamentary Law: Method of Transacting Business in Deliberative Assemblies* (New York: The Century Co., 1923).

5. Notably Alice Sturgis, *The Standard Code of Parliamentary Procedure*, 4th ed. (New York: McGraw-Hill, 1993). For practical purposes, the most useful brief parliamentary guide is the "authorized" *Robert's Rules of Order: Newly Revised in Brief*, 2nd ed. (Boston: Da Capo, 2011).

6. A wealth of resources has emerged in recent years for students of facilitation, including Sam Kaner, *Facilitator's Guide to Participatory Decision-Making*, 3rd ed. (San Francisco: Jossey-Bass, 2014); and Lawrence E. Susskind and Jeffrey L. Cruikshank, *Breaking Robert's Rules: The New Way to Run Your Meeting, Build Consensus, and Get Results* (New York: Oxford University Press, 2006).

7. "Calling the question" is a corrupt form of the *Robert's* motion to "Put the Previous Question," which is not debatable and requires a two-thirds vote because it has the effect of limiting the normal right of members to debate. In a large meeting, the chairperson's proper response, because hardly anyone knows what the "previous question" means, is to rephrase the motion: "The member has moved to cut off debate and vote immediately. Is there a second? Because there are members who wish to speak, cutting off debate requires a two-thirds vote. Will those in favor of cutting off debate and voting now say *aye*. Those opposed, *no*." In a board of a dozen or fewer members, the chairperson's proper response (under *Robert's* § 49) is to rule the motion out of order because it is inappropriate for a small body.

8. "NASD and NYSE Rulemaking: Relating to Corporate Governance," U.S. Securities and Exchange Commission, Order Approving Proposed Rule Changes Relating to Corporate Governance, November 4, 2003, http://www.sec.gov/rules/sro/34-48745.htm.

9. The provisions of Sarbanes-Oxley that do apply to nonprofits are the ones requiring written policies on whistleblower protection and destruction of old documents. "The Sarbanes-Oxley Act and Implications for Nonprofit Organizations," BoardSource and Independent Sector, https://www.independentsector.org/uploads/Accountability_Documents/sarbanes_oxley_implications.pdf, 9–10.

10. "Executive Sessions: How to Use Them Regularly and Wisely," Board-Source, 2008, http://www.boardsource.org.

11. *The New Yorker*, May 5, 1975.

12. Outi Flynn, *Meet Smarter: A Guide to Better Nonprofit Board Meetings* (Washington, D.C.: Boardsource, 2004), 17–18.

13. "A common error is to move that a report 'be received.' . . . In fact this motion is meaningless, since the report has already been received. . . . If a motion 'to accept' . . . is adopted and is given its proper interpretation, it implies that the assembly has endorsed the complete report." Robert et al., *Robert's Rules*, §51, 508.

CHAPTER 7: SIZE MAKES A DIFFERENCE

1. Ferdinand Tönnies, *Gemeinschaft und Gesellschaft* (Leipzig, Germany: Fues's Verlag, 1887), translated by Charles Price Loomis as *Community and Society* (East Lansing: Michigan State University Press, 1957).

2. Alice Mann, David Trietsch, and Dan Hotchkiss, "Beginnings of a Theory of Synagogue Size," in *Size Transitions in Congregations*, ed. Beth Gaede (Bethesda, MD: Alban, 2001), 75–83, previously published as "Searching for the Key: Developing a Theory of Synagogue Size," *Congregations* 27 (January–February 2001).

3. Alban size theory had its beginnings with Arlin J. Rothauge, *Sizing Up a Congregation for New Member Ministry* (Episcopal Church Center, 1983), as elaborated by Alice Mann, *The In-Between Church: Navigating Size Transitions in Congregations* (Bethesda, MD: Alban, 1998).

4. Susan Beaumont, *Inside the Large Congregation* (Herndon, VA: Alban Institute, 2011).

5. Mann, *In-Between Church*, 12–13. I have adjusted the size boundaries slightly based on my own observations.

6. Alice Mann, *Raising the Roof: The Pastoral-to-Program Size Transition* (Bethesda, MD: Alban, 2001), offers an extended discussion and many practical aids for congregations seeking to grow through the transition from the pastoral to multi-celled size category, also known as "program size."

7. Gary L. McIntosh, *Taking Your Church to the Next Level: What Got You Here Won't Get You There* (Grand Rapids, MI: Baker Books, 2009), 122–29, provides a useful summary of the history of size-category thinking in evangelical Protestant circles.

8. Edwin H. Friedman, *Generation to Generation : Family Process in Church and Synagogue*, Guilford Family Therapy Series (New York: Guilford Press, 1985); Peter L. Steinke, *How Your Church Family Works: Understanding Congregations as Emotional Systems* (Herndon, VA: Alban, 2006).

CHAPTER 8: LIFE AFTER GOVERNANCE CHANGE

1. Gil Rendle and Alice Mann, *Holy Conversations: Strategic Planning as a Spiritual Practice for Congregations* (Herndon, VA: Alban Institute, 2003), xiv.

2. The "balcony" and "container" images and many other concepts in this chapter come from Ronald A. Heifetz, *Leadership without Easy Answers* (Cambridge, MA: Belknap Press of Harvard University Press, 1994), and Ronald A. Heifetz and Marty Linsky, *Leadership on the Line: Staying Alive through the Dangers of Leading* (Boston: Harvard Business School Press, 2002).

3. John Carver, *Boards That Make a Difference: A New Design for Leadership in Nonprofit and Public Organizations*, 3rd ed. (San Francisco: Jossey-Bass, 2006), 72.

4. Jill M. Hudson, *When Better Isn't Enough: Evaluation Tools for the 21st-Century Church* (Herndon, VA: Alban Institute, 2004).

5. Gilbert R. Rendle and Susan Beaumont, *When Moses Meets Aaron: Staffing and Supervision in Large Congregations* (Herndon, VA: Alban, 2007).

CHAPTER 9: EXPLORING GOVERNANCE CHANGE

1. I believe this useful aphorism is original with Lee G. Bolman and Terrence E. Deal, most recently in *Reframing Organizations: Artistry, Choice and Leadership*, 5th ed. (San Francisco: Jossey-Bass, 2013), 7.

2. Edward Le Roy Long, *Patterns of Polity: Varieties of Church Governance* (Cleveland, OH: Pilgrim Press, 2001).

3. *Robert's* is quite clear that "Bylaws cannot normally be suspended" unless they provide explicitly for their own suspension. Henry M. Robert, Sarah Corbin Robert, Henry M. Robert III, William J. Evans, Daniel H. Honemann, and Thomas J. Balch, *Robert's Rules of Order: Newly Revised*, 11th ed., with Daniel E. Seabold and Shmuel Gerber (Boston: Da Capo, 2011), § 8, p. 88. A "suspension" of any part of the bylaws, whether permanent or temporary, must be accomplished through the normal bylaws-amendment process.

CHAPTER 10: POLICY CHOICES

1. Readers looking for a guide to congregational administration might wish to consult Gilbert R. Rendle and Susan Beaumont, *When Moses Meets Aaron: Staffing and Supervision in Large Congregations* (Herndon, VA: Alban Institute, 2007); and John W. Wimberly Jr., *The Business of the Church: The Uncomfortable Truth That Faithful Ministry Requires Effective Management* (Herndon, VA: Alban Institute, 2010).

2. Gilbert R. Rendle, *Behavioral Covenants in Congregations: A Handbook for Honoring Differences* (Herndon, VA: Alban Institute, 1999).

3. Joy Skjegstad, *Starting a Nonprofit at Your Church* (Herndon, VA: Alban Institute, 2002), 54–65.

CHAPTER 11: LAY AND CLERGY PARTNERSHIP

1. The sad tale of John and Sarah Lyford is told in William Bradford, *History of Plymouth Plantation*, book 2 (New York: Little Brown, 1856), 117–33.

2. "The conditions of religious life in the colonies would, despite all the ministerial self-assertion, tilt the balance of power in the direction of the laity." E. Brooks Holifield, *God's Ambassadors: A History of the Christian Clergy in America* (Grand Rapids, MI: Eerdmans, 2007), 57.

3. Roy M. Oswald, *Running through the Thistles: Terminating a Ministerial Relationship with a Parish* (Herndon, VA: Alban Institute, 1978). Every clergyperson should read this classic statement on the emotional aspect of departure.

4. Building on the work of family therapist Murray Bowen's concept of "differentiation," Rabbi Edwin H. Friedman emphasized the salutary influence of a leader's "nonanxious presence" in an anxious system in *Generation to Generation : Family Process in Church and Synagogue* (New York: Guilford Press, 1985). Friedman's student Peter L. Steinke has elaborated on Bowen and Friedman's ideas for a new generation of clergy in *Healthy Congregations: A Systems Approach*, 2nd ed. (Herndon, VA: Alban Institute, 2006); and *Congregational Leadership in Anxious Times: Being Calm and Courageous No Matter What* (Lanham, MD: Rowman & Littlefield, 2014).

APPENDIX A: WRITING TIPS FOR POLICY WONKS

1. I have adapted Carver's ideas freely, for reasons explained in chapter 4, note 2. Carver's full model can be found in John Carver, *Boards That Make a Difference: A New Design for Leadership in Nonprofit and Public Organizations*, 3rd ed. (San Francisco: Jossey-Bass, 2006), 21–49; and John Carver and Miriam Mayhew Carver, *Reinventing Your Board: A Step-by-Step Guide to Implementing Policy Governance*, rev. ed. (San Francisco: John Wiley and Sons, 2006), 17–37.

2. Bryan A. Garner, "Shall We Abandon Shall?" *ABA Journal*, August 1, 2012, http://www.abajournal.com/magazine/article/shall_we_abandon_shall. See also Plain Language Action and Information Network, *Federal Plain Language Guidelines*, rev. 1, May 2011, www.plainlanguage.gov/howto/guidelines/FederalPLGuidelines/FederalPLGuidelines.pdf.

BIBLIOGRAPHY

I blog regularly at congregationalconsulting.org. A listing of my articles and books can be found at danhotchkiss.com/publications.

BOARD STRUCTURE AND POLICIES

BoardSource. *The Handbook of Nonprofit Governance*. San Francisco: Jossey-Bass, 2010.

Carver, John. *Boards That Make a Difference: A New Design for Leadership in Nonprofit and Public Organizations*. 3rd ed. San Francisco: Jossey-Bass, 2006.

Carver, John, and Miriam Mayhew Carver. *Reinventing Your Board: A Step-by-Step Guide to Implementing Policy Governance*. Rev. ed. San Francisco: John Wiley and Sons, 2006.

Chait, Richard, William P. Ryan, and Barbara E. Taylor. *Governance as Leadership: Reframing the Work of Nonprofit Boards*. Hoboken, NJ: John Wiley and Sons, 2004.

Lawrence, Barbara, and Outi Flynn. *The Nonprofit Policy Sampler*. 3rd ed. Washington, DC: BoardSource, 2014.

Leventhal, Robert. *Byachad: Synagogue Board Development*. Herndon, VA: Alban Institute, 2007.

Light, Mark. *The Strategic Board: The Step-by-Step Guide to High-Impact Governance*. Wiley Nonprofit Law, Finance, and Management Series. New York: Wiley, 2001.

Olsen, Charles M. *Transforming Church Boards into Communities of Spiritual Leaders*. Washington, DC: Alban Institute, 1995.

Rendle, Gilbert R. *Behavioral Covenants in Congregations: A Handbook for Honoring Differences*. Herndon, VA: Alban Institute, 1999.

Skjegstad, Joy. *Starting a Nonprofit at Your Church*. Herndon, VA: Alban Institute, 2002.

CONGREGATION SIZE

Beaumont, Susan. *Inside the Large Congregation*. Herndon, VA: Alban Institute, 2011.

Gaede, Beth Ann, ed. *Size Transitions in Congregations*. Herndon, VA: Alban Institute, 2001.

Mann, Alice. *The In-Between Church: Navigating Size Transitions in Congregations*. Herndon, VA: Alban Institute, 1998.

——. *Raising the Roof: The Pastoral-to-Program Size Transition*. Herndon, VA: Alban Institute, 2001.

McIntosh, Gary L. *Taking Your Church to the Next Level: What Got You Here Won't Get You There*. Grand Rapids, MI: Baker Books, 2009.

CONGREGATIONAL LEADERSHIP

Friedman, Edwin H. *Generation to Generation: Family Process in Church and Synagogue*. The Guilford Family Therapy Series. New York: Guilford Press, 1985.

Heifetz, Ronald A. *Leadership without Easy Answers*. Cambridge, MA: Belknap Press of Harvard University Press, 1994.

Heifetz, Ronald A., and Marty Linsky. *The Practice of Adaptive Leadership: Tools and Tactics for Changing Your Organization and the World*. Cambridge, MA: Belknap Press of Harvard University Press, 2009.

Steinke, Peter L. *Healthy Congregations: A Systems Approach*. 2nd ed. Herndon, VA: Alban Institute, 2006.

——. *How Your Church Family Works: Understanding Congregations as Emotional Systems*. Herndon, VA: Alban Institute, 2006.

HISTORY AND SOCIOLOGY OF BOARD GOVERNANCE

Anheier, Helmut. *Nonprofit Organizations: Theory, Management, Policy*. London: Routledge, 2005.

Chaves, Mark. *Congregations in America*. Cambridge, MA: Harvard University Press, 2004.

Long, Edward Le Roy. *Patterns of Polity: Varieties of Church Governance*. Cleveland, OH: Pilgrim Press, 2001.

LAW OF NONPROFIT AND RELIGIOUS ORGANIZATIONS

Fremont-Smith, Marion R. *Governing Nonprofit Organizations: Federal and State Law and Regulation*. Cambridge, MA: Belknap Press of Harvard University Press, 2004.

Hammar, Richard. *Pastor, Church and Law*. 4th ed. 4 vols. Carol Stream, IL: Christian Ministry Resources, 2007.

MEETING FACILITATION

Flynn, Outi. *Meeting and Exceeding Expectations: A Guide to Successful Nonprofit Board Meetings*. 2nd ed. Washington, DC: BoardSource, 2009.

Kaner, Sam. *Facilitator's Guide to Participatory Decision-Making*. 3rd ed. San Francisco: Jossey-Bass, 2014.

McCandless, Keith, and Henri Lipmanowicz. *The Surprising Power of Liberating Structures: Simple Rules to Unleash a Culture of Innovation*. Seattle: Liberating Structures Press, 2014.

Mead, Loren B., and Billie T. Alban. *Creating the Future Together: Methods to Inspire Your Whole Faith Community*. Herndon, VA: Alban Institute, 2008.

Robert, Henry M., III, William J. Evans, Daniel H. Honemann, and Thomas J. Balch. *Robert's Rules of Order: Newly Revised in Brief*. With the assistance of Daniel E. Seabold and Shmuel Gerber. 2nd ed. Boston: Da Capo Press, 2011.

Robert, Henry M., Sarah Corbin Robert, Henry M. Robert III, William J. Evans, Daniel H. Honemann, and Thomas J. Balch. *Robert's Rules of Order: Newly Revised*. With the assistance of Daniel E. Seabold and Shmuel Gerber. 11th ed. Boston: Da Capo, 2011.

Susskind, Lawrence E., and Jeffrey L. Cruikshank. *Breaking Robert's Rules: The New Way to Run Your Meeting, Build Consensus, and Get Results*. New York: Oxford University Press, 2006.

PLANNING AND EVALUATION

Drummond, Sarah B. *Holy Clarity: The Practice of Planning and Evaluation*. Herndon, VA: Alban Institute, 2009.

Hudson, Jill M. *When Better Isn't Enough: Evaluation Tools for the 21st-Century Church*. Herndon, VA: Alban Institute, 2004.

Rendle, Gil, and Alice Mann. *Holy Conversations: Strategic Planning as a Spiritual Practice for Congregations*. Herndon, VA: Alban Institute, 2003.

STAFF AND TEAM DEVELOPMENT

Blanchard, Ken, Patricia Zigarmi, and Drea Zigarmi. *Leadership and the One Minute Manager: Increasing Effectiveness through Situational Leadership II*. Updated ed. New York: William Morrow, 2013.

Blanchard, Kenneth H., and Spencer Johnson. *The One Minute Manager*. Rev. ed. New York: HarperCollins Business, 1982.

Drucker, Peter F. *Managing the Non-Profit Organization: Practices and Principles*. New York: HarperCollins, 1990.

Rendle, Gilbert R., and Susan Beaumont. *When Moses Meets Aaron: Staffing and Supervision in Large Congregations*. Herndon, VA: Alban Institute, 2007.

Wimberly, John W., Jr. *The Business of the Church: The Uncomfortable Truth That Faithful Ministry Requires Effective Management*. Herndon, VA: Alban Institute, 2010.

———. *Mobilizing Congregations: How Teams Can Motivate Members and Get Things Done*. Lanham, MD: Alban Books, Rowman & Littlefield, 2015.

INDEX

ABOUT THE AUTHOR

Rev. Dan Hotchkiss writes, consults, and speaks widely for congregations and other nonprofits. His specialties include board governance, strategic and financial planning, clergy transition, and fund-raising. As a senior consultant for the Alban Institute for fourteen years, and now as an independent consultant, Dan has directly helped hundreds of congregations and related organizations in more than thirty denominational groups. Through his coaching, teaching, and writing, Dan touches the lives of an even wider range of leaders. He is also the author of *Ministry and Money: A Guide for Clergy and Their Friends.* His website is www.danhotchkiss.com.